Brand Elevation is a must-read for both the managers of mass brands that used to dominate, and teams at start-ups that set out to disrupt the market. That's because brands that want to be relevant and sustain growth need to elevate themselves beyond aspects of price and performance and accrue meaning with customers, employees and other stakeholders that goes beyond the material. This book provides practical guidance on how to do just that.
Russ Klein, CEO at the American Marketing Association

I always believed that a brand is what makes a product worth more than the product itself. And what makes it worth a whole lot more is creating an Ueber-Brand. It takes creativity, courage and cash to make that happen – and the principles outlined in this excellent book.
Ivan Pollard, Global CMO at General Mills

Brand Elevation makes an incredibly complex marketing innovation clear to anyone: it provides the fundamentals to break down what gives a brand meaning and how to give inanimate objects animate characteristics.
Scott Galloway, Professor at NYU Stern School of Business, author of *The Four* and Founder of L2 and Section4

I don't usually read business books; I choose to read other things in my very rare spare time. But I certainly endorse you as experts and inspiring and insightful leaders in this space!
Alexandra Keith, CEO at Procter & Gamble Beauty Care

With an established brand like Kiehl's, our challenge is building on that brand magic, and ensuring it's manifested in an authentic way – never losing sight of our DNA and core values. This book provides insightful guidance and inspiration not only on how to create a loved brand, but how to maintain one.
Leonardo Chavez, Global Brand President at Kiehl's Since 1851

In this second book on 'Ueber-Branding', JP and Wolfgang provide a step-by-step approach on how to build brands that instil strong desires in customers. They show how to Dream, Do and Dare to go beyond the material, thus creating meaningful and experiential brands.

Bernd Schmitt, Professor at Columbia Business School and author of *Experiential Marketing*

JP and Wolfgang provide an astute, practical and ethical guide to branding and marketing for companies willing to self-examine the best purpose of their enterprise and cultivate long-term relationships with their customers on the basis of shared values and identity.

Vincent Stanley, Director of Philosophy at Patagonia, co-author of *The Responsible Company: What we've learned from Patagonia's first 40 years*, and poet

Standing out in a burgeoning panoply of branding literature is no mean feat. Schaefer and Kuehlwein have done it again with *Brand Elevation* – a practitioner's road map to curating brand desire and equity. Rich with vignettes, insights, and applications.

Deryck J van Rensburg, Dean at Pepperdine Graziadio Business School and former President of Global Ventures, The Coca-Cola Company

This book explains perfectly how much the classical approach to marketing has changed and how small new brands – Ueber-Brands with a real story to tell – become so relevant. A must read for everyone who wants to understand this recent development!

Felix Ahlers, CEO at FRoSTA AG

A highly relevant book for every business executive and marketing student, offering in-depth analyses, a hands-on how-to programme, and rich case studies all in one. A unique and outstanding reference to deliver superior brand performance.

Glyn Atwal, Associate Professor at Burgundy School of Business and co-author of *Luxury Brands in China and India*

In the post-pandemic era, more and more spending goes to either products sold on price by mass retailers like Amazon or to brands, like Tesla, Fenty or Nike, selling prestige, purpose or values – at a premium price. JP and Wolfgang offer exceptional insights on how the 'Ueber-brands' of tomorrow will offer increasingly demanding consumers the opposite of bland: an exceptional emotional bond that is priceless.

Erwan Rambourg, Managing Director Consumer & Retail Research at HSBC and author of *The Bling Dynasty* **and** *Future Luxe: What's ahead for the business of luxury*

A must-read for any marketer wanting to elevate a brand – and that is almost every one of us.

Erich Joachimsthaler, Founder and CEO of Vivaldi Group, co-author of *Brand Leadership* **with David Aaker, and author of** *Hidden in Plain Sight*

The first book by JP and Wolf extracted core principles that drive the success of modern Prestige brands. In fact, it showed that any brand can become peerless and priceless if it accrues meaning to people beyond the material. This book follows up with step-by-step instructions on how brand builders can go about elevating their brands and taking them 'Ueber' – above and beyond the crowd of competitors.

Frédéric Fekkai, Executive Chairman and Founder at Frédéric Fekkai & Co and Bastide

With *Brand Elevation* you will raise your branding game by learning about brands that have a higher purpose, that people aspire to have, that connect with stories, that reinvent the category, that energize with ongoing innovation, and overdeliver on the promise in so many ways.

David Aaker, Professor Emeritus at the University of California, Berkeley, Haas School of Business, author of many seminal books on brand strategy and marketing, and Vice-Chairman of Prophet

Honoured to appear in a book that so brilliantly champions how brands can positively reflect, express and guide who we are and how we see the world. – Peas & Love.

Ben Branson, Founder of Seedlip, and Co-founder of Æcorn, Home Grown Club and Birch

A well-curated, practical guide for brand builders who understand the value of values. Wolf and JP's thought-provoking Dream, Do, Dare framework will help you define and operationalize your brand purpose in a way that elevates profit as well.

Virginie Helias, Chief Sustainability Officer at Procter & Gamble

Brand Elevation

Lessons in Ueber-Branding

Wolfgang Schaefer and JP Kuehlwein

KoganPage

Publisher's note

Every possible effort has been made to ensure that the information contained in this book is accurate at the time of going to press, and the publisher and authors cannot accept responsibility for any errors or omissions, however caused. No responsibility for loss or damage occasioned to any person acting, or refraining from action, as a result of the material in this publication can be accepted by the editor, the publisher or the authors.

First published in Great Britain and the United States in 2021 by Kogan Page Limited

2nd Floor, 45 Gee Street	122 W 27th St, 10th Floor	4737/23 Ansari Road
London	New York, NY 10001	Daryaganj
EC1V 3RS	USA	New Delhi 110002
United Kingdom		India

www.koganpage.com

Kogan Page books are printed on paper from sustainable forests.

ISBNs

Hardback	978 1 78966 468 3
Paperback	978 1 78966 466 9
eBook	978 1 78966 467 6

British Library Cataloguing-in-Publication Data

A CIP record for this book is available from the British Library.

Library of Congress Cataloging-in-Publication Data

Names: Schaefer, Wolfgang, author. | Kuehlwein, J. P., author.
Title: Brand elevation : lessons in ueber-branding / Wolfgang Schaefer and
    JP Kuehlwein.
Description: London, United Kingdom ; New York, NY : Kogan Page, 2021. |
    Includes bibliographical references and index. |
Identifiers: LCCN 2020043309 (print) | LCCN 2020043310 (ebook) | ISBN
    9781789664669 (paperback) | ISBN 9781789664683 (hardback) | ISBN
    9781789664676 (ebook)
Subjects: LCSH: Branding (Marketing) | Brand name products.
Classification: LCC HF5415.1255 .S39 2021 (print) | LCC HF5415.1255
    (ebook) | DDC 658.8/27–dc23

Typeset by Integra Software Services, Pondicherry
Print production managed by Jellyfish
Printed and bound by CPI Group (UK) Ltd, Croydon CR0 4YY

CONTENTS

PREFACE

Welcome to the age of brand elevation

'Can we become an Ueber-Brand™ too? How do we do it? Is there a method beyond the principles? Where do we start? What are the musts? Where are the limits?'

Those were the kind of questions that reached us again and again after publishing *Rethinking Prestige Branding: Secrets of the Ueber-Brands*, through our blog, podcast or after talks at events. And they led to many inspiring connections and consultations with interesting brands of all kinds and backgrounds. Sometimes even more than we could respond to or take on, which started us thinking about this book.

We had laid out the theory of Ueber-Branding because we had learned in our daily work and by talking to other practitioners and experts how the world of brands and the way to build prestige was rapidly changing. Traditional approaches to brand building were being updated and upgraded with a focus on mission and mythical narratives, a more truthful, inside out approach to branding and much more culturally tuned go-to-market programmes. A new crop of Ueber-Brands, as we termed them, had begun thriving across categories and price points. Rising above peers and prices by pushing us as people and societies. Reconnecting the material with meaning, engaging us with new kinds of experiences and showing us how to move forward, in commerce and in culture. Elevating themselves by tapping into our desire to evolve and elevate ourselves and the way we work, live and shop. In short: It seemed we were entering an age of brand elevation – in everything and everywhere, for everyone.

But at the time, we weren't quite sure how far this concept could go and how broadly it could be applied. So, it was pleasing to see our idea of Ueber-Brands and the book becoming a new reference for so many marketers and academics alike. And we certainly did not have a set 'How To' programme yet. Yes, we had developed the theory and defined seven key principles. And it was all rigorously based on lots of research and our own 50+ years of combined experience in building brands across categories and countries. But a purpose-built and generally applicable methodology for how to apply this way of Ueber-Branding, a proven path to follow? Not so much.

It developed quickly, though – it had to. Because we were challenged and charged with real-life cases from big blue-chip companies as well as start-ups, from beauty to appliances, alcohol to food, detergents to service providers. Lots of very varied cases, which not only helped us develop ideas as we worked them. They also ensured that all was pragmatically sound and its success proven as it was emerging and advancing, forming and honing strategies with a built-in sense of reality and tactical power.

And after five years of development and 'test driving', here it is: Our freshly minted model, a six-step programme in three phases to elevate your brand. Made for marketing beginners as much as experienced masters, small brands wanting to grow as much as big ones looking to re-energize themselves. And relevant for all, across industries and sectors, from service providers or institutions to FMCGs or luxury purveyors. At least, this is what we aimed for.

The only ones this Ueber-Brand building programme is not made for are those who think they can keep on looking at brands as mere marketing instruments. Those that are solely profit-driven shareholders, versus widening their perspectives towards all stakeholders. Those that think a mission is mainly something for board rooms or entrance halls and are mostly concerned about value and not values.

This book is divided into three parts:

I. **Recap of the theory**
    A brief review of the seven principles of Ueber-Brands as we laid them out and explained them in our previous book. Not to the same level of depth and detail, but with lots of new cases to demonstrate how the concept is more alive and kicking than ever.

II. **The actual programme**
    Six steps undertaken in three phases and their respective 'to-do' lists, structured to guide you step-by-step through the process of building or evolving your own brand. Hands-on and illustrated through experiences, real-life examples and supporting diagrams.

III. **Lessons from real life**
    Exclusive insights from successful Ueber-Brands. Experience reports and interviews from and with some of the most accomplished practitioners and industry experts. Giving you a heads up on pitfalls and opportunities as you embark on your journey to become an Ueber-Brand.

We hope the following pages will be worth your while, and will help and inspire you. With our first book scoring a rare 8/10 with the experts at getabstract and, more importantly, a 4.8/5 with you at Amazon, a high bar has been set for this follow-up work. We hope to meet your expectations and would be happy to hear from you, as always, at authors@ueber brands.com. Because Ueber-Brands are never-ending stories. And so is learning how to build them.

Cheers!
Wolfgang and JP

Scan the following QR code to access interview recordings, videos, websites, articles and other materials referenced in this book on our Bonus Material page at www.ueberbrands.com. There, you will also find more case studies and resources, our blog, podcast and a link to Ueber-Brand videos on YouTube.

ACKNOWLEDGEMENTS

We would like to particularly thank our brilliant case contributors Tom Szaky (TerraCycle), Laura Burdese (Acqua di Parma), Jim Geikie (Burt's Bees), Samantha Yarwood (Starbucks), Douglas Atkin (Airbnb), Peter Husted Sylvest (Lakrids) and Chris Dale (YouTube) for sharing their deep insights and hands-on experiences in what it takes to build a strong brand and elevate it.

And then there are the very many people who have inspired, enlightened, encouraged and supported us over these past five years as we have been pulling the Brand Elevation method and ultimately this book on it together. Some of you will not even be aware that you helped build, challenge, hone and refine the programme. Others and their brands we are not allowed to mention based on the confidentiality agreements we have signed. Thank you to all of you whether you are listed below or not.

Adrian Molina (Davos Brands/Aviation Gin), Alexandra Mühlbacher (Swarovski), Alyson Cayne (Haven's Kitchen), Andrea Davey (Tiffany & Co), Andrew Hyncik (Zeiss), Anna Borgogni (Kiehl's Since 1851), Anne Veronique Bruel (fresh Inc), Ariel Smullen (Mohawk Fine Paper), Arnaud De Schuytter (Baccarat), Arnaud Plas (Prose), Ben Branson (Seedlip), Professor Bernd Schmitt (Columbia University), Carly Rappoport (Prose), Chris Harrold (Mohawk Fine Paper), Cindy Groenke (MieleX), Claudia Kuhn (P&G), Dr Cordula Kueger (equity), Dave Rapaport (Ben & Jerry's), David Batstone (REBBL), David Bonney (ATHEIST Shoes), David LaRocca (State University of New York), Deb Malone (The Internationalist/Association of National Advertisers), Deniz Yamanel (Maille), Deryck van Rensburg (Pepperdine University), Professor Dominic Pettman (The New School), Dominique Debucquoy-Dodley (Burning Man Project), Erich Joachimsthaler (Vivaldi), Felix Ahlers (FRoSTRA), Francesca Ferrari (Acqua di Parma), Frédéric Fekkai (Bastide, Fekkai), Gabriel Eid (Origins), Gwen Whiting (The Laundress), Heidi Volpe (Patagonia), Herwig Preis (Select World), Ian Ginsberg (CO Bigelow), Jason Chrenka (ExxonMobil), Jason Waterworth (UP Public Relations), Jens Mueller-Oerlinghausen (undconsorten), Jess Morgan (Rapha), Joe Doucet (JDXP), John Goodwin (LEGO), Jonas Tahlin (Absolut Elyx), Judith Azoulay (P&G), Julie Eister (NHA), Julie Marchant-Houle

(Marley Spoon), Karen Snelwar (OXO), Kate Pomeroy (Pernod Ricard), Kelley Brescia (LEGO), Kendra Peavy (S'well), Kennedy Embree (Burt's Bees), Kristin O'Brien (ATHEIST Shoes), Laura Peterson (Ben & Jerry's), Leonardo Chavez (Kiehl's Since 1851), Lev & Alina (fresh Inc), Lia Winograd (Pepper), Maja Lindahl (Lakrids), Markus Langes-Swarovski, Mathilde Delhoume (LVMH), Maud Pansing (E&J Gallo Winery), Michaela Burger (Swarovski), Michael Sabbia (Galderma), Mike Lepre (Bertonni), Oliver Brunschwiler (Freitag), Pascal Dulex (Freitag), Patrick Shank (Ben & Jerry's), Paulo Pereira da Silva (Renova), Peter Rahal (RXBAR), Pieter-Jan Beyls (Beyl), Ramdane Touhami (Buly and Cire Trudon), Reuben Carranza (Luxury Brand Partners), Russ Klein (American Marketing Association), Professor Russ Winer (NYU), Sanaz Lotfi (UP Public Relations), Sarah Maria Carl (Lakrids), Professor Scott Galloway (NYU), Simon Sproule (Aston Martin), Suzanne Hader (John Hardy), Tarané Yuson (Yes Ideas), Tari Reinik (NHA), Tennille Kopiasz (fresh Inc), Thomas Noroxe (Joe & The Juice), Thomas Vince (L'Oréal), Tim Sayler (Audemars Piguet), Trisha Ayyagari (L'Oréal), Valentina Colombo (Acqua di Parma), Veronica Rajadnya (TerraCycle), Vincent Stanley (Patagonia), Virginie Helias (P&G), Yasar Hanli (Miele X), and Wolf's and JP's students at XU University, Potsdam, NYU Stern and Columbia Business School and the fine team at Kogan Page.

We dedicate this book to our families, partners and friends
for always encouraging, supporting and humouring us and
to the memory of Benoit Ams, founder of Smith & Norbu and
a dear friend – Tu nous manques!

PART ONE

Recap: The principles of Ueber-Branding™

The idea of Ueber-Brands™

'Ueber' is German for 'above and beyond', and that is where we have found brands to go as they seek to acquire meaning beyond the material. Our research showed that brands that are considered peerless and priceless go beyond conventional approaches to brand identity development and marketing execution by following seven principles that we review and illustrate below.

These principles are guided by three deep-seated desires people have and value in brands that can satisfy them:

- The desire for meaning that can be found in a higher Mission and a Myth to believe in.
- The desire to be special, but also to belong, which can be achieved by balancing exclusivity with inclusiveness.
- And the desire for truth, which requires brands to make that mythical dream come true but also to put your money where that Mission is and shine from the inside out.

The principles account for key dimensions of a brand: They provide a vision to follow but also guide the brand's actions in the here and now. And they guide the relations the brand has with its customers as well as how to live its promise as an organization. At the heart, though, a Brand Myth needs to escape total rationalization to be able to provide that inexplicable attraction of Ueber-Brands.

FIGURE P1.1 The Ueber-Brand Model – seven principles that can elevate a brand to become meaningful, peerless and priceless

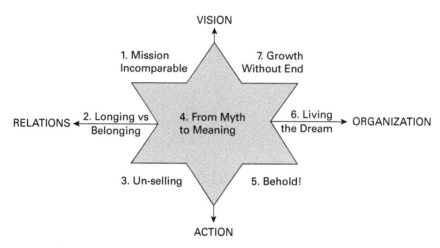

SOURCE The authors (2015)

Principle 1: Mission incomparable

Having a distinct, brand-guiding Mission

Having a higher calling, a reason-to-be that goes further than 'making money', lies at the core of every Ueber-Brand. A higher calling not only guides the organization and elevates the brand. Importantly, it helps fulfil the aspirations of its stakeholders and supports them in their identity construction. To do this, Ueber-Brands need to go beyond good ideas and individual relevance, to offering ideals and societal resonance. Even the leading CEOs at the US Business Roundtable recently changed their guidance for 'the purpose of a corporation' from 'maximizing shareholder value' to 'promoting an economy that serves all Americans' (Business Roundtable, 2019).

To note: When we talk about Ueber-Brands being guided by a Mission, we are not referring to those grand but generic 'save-the-world' declarations that often have no discernible link to the business at hand. What we are talking about are Missions that are rooted in the business but give it a bigger reason for being, beyond profit. Ueber-Brands differentiate themselves through daring visions combined with unique creativity and the guts to pursue them. They enrich the brand experience and offer their fans the chance to feel bigger or better, no longer just buying but buying *into* something. Something that reflects the values, tastes or abilities they seek to signal, for example.

We found two ways for brands to gain this kind of personal and social significance: The first is following a higher calling that gives the brand a socio-ecological or spiritual purpose beyond the economical one. The second is re-defining the category they're in by setting new standards and making us change how we think and feel about and interact with it.

Mission Route 1: Following a higher calling

Vincent Stanley, one of the early employees at Patagonia, a nephew of the founder Yvon Chouinard and its Director of Philosophy, told us of a time in the early nineties when a team finally sat down to formalize the Mission the organization had been following intuitively for two decades. It read 'Build the best product. Cause no unnecessary harm. Use business to inspire and implement solutions to the environmental crisis.' It felt strange to Vincent and others to write it out, but it also felt necessary as the organization and brand were growing rather fast. In 2019, Yvon and his team raised the bar, urged on by what they experienced as an overwhelming escalation of the environmental crisis. The 'Reason For Being' is now preceded by the declaration 'We're in business to save our home planet' (Patagonia, 2019b). This update and upgrade ensures the brand stays ambitious in pursuing its Mission and becomes even more outspoken in opposing what it sees as traumatic threats to nature, supporting local activist groups, for example, who seek to convince Balkan states and the European Union (EU) to stop investments in hydro-plants that are destroying some of the last wild rivers (Rose, 2019). In the United States (US) the brand has joined a law suit against the Federal Government over the downsizing of lands that are protected National Monuments (Patagonia, 2019a).

Young Everlane provides an example of an apparel brand with a more moderate approach to brand activism. Founded in 2010, this digitally native label also seeks sustainable ways for its clothes to be made and consumed. But it does not take to the streets to save the world. Rather, it promises 'Exceptional quality. Ethical factories. Radical transparency.' Its website shares its moral compass with its customers: 'At Everlane, we're not big on trends. We want you to wear our pieces for years, even decades, to come' (Everlane, 2020). Offering fewer choices allows for an in-depth vetting of the supply chain. Everlane asks every supplier to provide sturdy products, to pay its workers living wages and to ensure their safety. It also works with suppliers on minimizing the negative impact on the environment. Documenting this work and the place each garment comes from is as much part of its 'radical transparency' as is opening its books. Each product description on its site comes with an account of how well it is made but also how much it costs to source materials, make it and ship it – and thus how much the company will earn.

FIGURE 1.1 Everlane manifesting its Mission of 'radical transparency', item by item

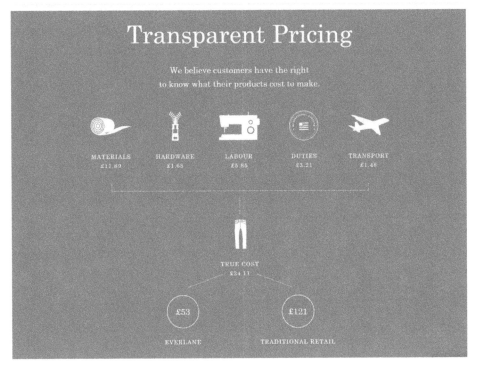

The appeal to customers of seeing a company pursue a philosophy in making its products that goes beyond the material is being recognized across industries and markets, as the example of Indian handbag maker Hidesign shows. The company not only puts its indigenous designs and craftsmanship forward but now also explains its respectful treatment of workers, the environment and its vegetable tanning process (Atwal *et al*, 2020).

It might be tricky to tell an Everlane T-shirt from any other high-quality one. But its commitment to transparency imbues its product with moral values that its young fans started to miss in the 'fast fashion' brands and has inspired some, like H&M, to follow suit. The true sign of an Ueber-Brand: Charting the course and inspiring or forcing others to follow suit.

But beware, you can't just fake living a higher purpose or grab one for your communications, when needed. Particularly in our social media world, it is better to be held in esteem for one's humility than to be humiliated for having hopped on the 'value-signalling' bandwagon without any actions to back it up. Take Audi, which aired a tear-jerking Superbowl ad in support of equal opportunity for women in the workplace – just to face an immediate backlash for the fact that it had not a single female board member in Germany or the US (Peck, 2017). Similarly, financial services firm State Street pulled quite a stunt placing a 'Fearless Girl' statue in front of the 'Charging Bull' on Wall Street – and then had to settle a claim by the US Labor Department of pay discrimination against its female employees (Stevens, 2017). Or, not least, read in our Epilogue about the recent HR troubles of the aforementioned Everlane during the COVID crisis.

Mission Route 2: Reinventing the category

If pursuing a higher calling is felt to be disingenuous or too onerous, an organization can still build a 'missionary' brand by concerning itself primarily with its product and service. What it takes, then, is to make a true step-change in how the category is experienced by people or to disrupt it outright.

Airbnb, Etsy and many other internet platforms come to mind. Spotify, founded in 2006, for example, has transformed how we consume music by enabling us to call-up any song anytime, anywhere. But Spotify also created a structural and cultural shift in the formerly monolithic music industry that is now reflected in its Brand Mission: 'to unlock the potential of human creativity – by giving a million creative artists the opportunity to live off their art and billions of fans the opportunity to enjoy and be inspired by it' (Spotify, 2020).

This gives the way in which Spotify reinvents the category a meaningful perspective people can rally around. Which is something other popular platforms have noticeably failed to accomplish. Just think of Facebook's 'Giv[ing] people the power to build community and bring the world closer together' (Limbachia, 2017) or Uber's 'ignit[ing] opportunity by setting the world in motion' (Uber, 2020), and contrast them with the heated public debates about these platforms' ethics, privacy or pay practices. We will discuss the challenges of wanting to be a fast-growing unicorn and an Ueber-Brand at the same time in Principle 7 and Part Two of this book.

A classic example of category reinvention we talked about in *Rethinking Prestige Branding* is Starbucks and how it changed the idea and experience of coffee in the US (Schaefer and Kuehlwein, 2015). In Part Three of this book, we have added a direct account of how the Starbucks team in Europe was challenged to re-invent and re-energize its quality and service core in response to a different cultural context and the threat of equity dilution as the brand expanded.

One thing is interesting to note: The repeated attempts by Starbucks founder Howard Schultz to embrace a socio-political calling around community building for the brand (Mission Route 1) have fallen mostly flat. For example, racial harmony initiatives like #RaceTogether were met with scepticism, at best. Even well-meaning customers and employees commented that 'talking race' did not accord well with either Starbucks as a place or as a pick-me-up ritual (Mainwaring, 2015). Starbucks has done well pursuing Mission Route 2 and creating that famous 'third place' – between home and office. It might be better off sticking to this and keeping that place special, given how many competitors its success has spawned.

As with many approaches to brand elevation, combining them can make an even stronger impact. Airbnb, for example, has artfully linked the re-invention of the hospitality industry (Mission Route 2) with the idea of community and a Mission of making people feel like they could 'belong anywhere' (Mission Route 1), as the direct account in Part Three will illustrate.

But no matter which approach a brand chooses in offering more than a 'quality product', when expectations are high, it is hard to satisfy everyone. Ueber-Brands often cause controversy in acting on their Mission, but they'll take it in their stride. Where traditional mainstream brands will compromise in order not to alienate any sizable customer segment, Ueber-Brands will prioritize delivering on the promise to their core target over trying to please everyone. In other words, they might 'alienate to attract'.

Here is a simple test to see if you have 'Ueber-Convictions': If everyone can easily agree with you, then your convictions won't set you apart. Only those who dare to be different can claim the privilege to lead us in a new direction and be 'beyond compare'. As David Rappaport, Global Social Mission Officer at Ben & Jerry's, told us on our podcast: 'It is when social justice comes under siege that you look around to see who can really be counted on' – usually, B&Js is one of the first and few (ueberbrands.com, 2019b).

You will recognize an Ueber-Brand for doing what is right in the light of its *raison d'être* – not for doing what is popular or most profitable.

RECAP: MISSION

- Ueber-Brands have a Mission that resonates and that they can live up to.
- They either follow a higher calling and/or re-define the category by setting new standards.
- Either way, they need to show conviction, and evolve constantly while staying true to themselves.

Principle 2: Longing vs belonging

Balancing exclusivity and inclusion

Very different from traditional luxury or prestige brands, Ueber-Brands have developed new go-to-market strategies that balance a need for exclusivity with a sense of inclusivity, which is invariable in our digital age. They do this by setting up a 'Velvet Rope' that separates and yet connects the wider strategic target and what we call the Ueber-Target. The latter becomes an inspirational group of 'insiders', creating a desire of 'longing to belong' among the rest. Note that while the Velvet Rope can, of course, be a true barrier, it more frequently consists of more subtle factors like the time, money or connoisseurship required to get past it.

The 'Ueber-Target': Muses, tastemakers and meaning co-creators

The Ueber-Target plays a key role in creating an Ueber-Brand's aspirational value and the target's desire to make it past the rope and access the brand. They are the groups of people that play the role of muses or disciples to the brand (or both) and that act out what the broader audience might aspire to do, or be. In our previous book we examined the role of the Hells Angels and Harley Davidson, or the 'wingmen' and Red Bull in this respect (Schaefer and Kuehlwein, 2015). It is important to note that the actual purchases by these Ueber-Target groups might only represent a fraction of the brand's revenue, or may even generate a financial loss. Their appeal to the business lies in how they enrich the brand's story and how they inspire significant segments of 'regular people' to acquire that brand and join their world – even if it is just in their dreams. Those segments are often called 'strategic targets' or 'potential users' in marketing speak. In the case of Harley, one of those target segments will be made up of middle-aged, high-income male professionals who might suffer from a midlife crisis. They are unlikely to be 'born wild', roaming the country like modern outlaws... but they can certainly afford to buy into that dream.

Peloton illustrates how to leverage an Ueber-Target community to reach up and disrupt what was largely a commoditized and boring category – home fitness equipment. The cultish brand launched in 2012, and by 2019 had gone public at an eye-popping valuation of over $8 billion. Peloton redefined how a home-workout is experienced, including the appropriate look, place and price for a stationary bike and treadmill – over $2,000 and $4,000, respectively. As the ads suggest, the brand's pieces of high-tech design are meant to be proudly displayed in the living room rather than hidden in the basement.

But what truly differentiates and elevates the Peloton experience is its Ueber-Target, communities of dedicated, often wealthy and/or well-known 'home exercisers' with their own rituals, language, legends and heroes. The Peloton bikes allow their users to virtually join workout sessions happening in one of the brand's studios – for a monthly fee, of course. Your name will pop up next to other subscribers as you compete to get to the top of the rankings, urged on by an instructor. Some of those instructors have become the demi-gods of various Peloton tribes. There is 'Robin Arzon', for example, with more than 200,000 Instagram followers, who is all about 'sweat and swagger', and 'Jess King 'or 'Ally Love' who enjoys being called a superhero (Huddleston, 2019). There is also an Ueber-Target group that could be described as the 'disciples'. They seem to live the tribe's ideal lives – 'super moms' and 'alpha-dads' who are hyper-busy-yet-relaxed-and-in-perfect-shape – and they help to shape the dream and spread the word. They rave about the Peloton convenience and its competitive but convivial community. They strut Peloton garb and might have bought one of the large 3-D Peloton logos to decorate their living room. There are dozens who flaunt a tattoo of that logo on the brand's social site. And, of course, there are several podcasts and other forums hosted by 'Peloton-heads' as well that are popular with the community (Frieswick, 2016). The way we first became aware of all of this was by overhearing a conversation on a train to New York. Two zealots were raving about their position on the 'leaderboard' and were pitying a 'poor soul who still schleps her body to SoulCycle – how lame'. It's priceless to belong to this suave elite of fitness warriors, it seems.

The 'Velvet Rope' principle: Distinction that drives desirability

Why do people stand in line for hours for a chance to buy a 'limited drop' item sold by street-wear brand Supreme in one of its stores? Why do others jump through hoops to try to get their hands on one of those tickets for the annual Burning Man festival, the temporary fantasy world out in the Black Rock desert of Nevada? Well, one of the reasons is precisely because they are difficult to get – tickets usually sell out within 30 minutes (Kane, 2018). You could call this the first-level Velvet Rope of Burning Man.

After getting tickets comes actually getting to the inconveniently remote place and then the challenge of finding one of the scarce cellular signals to share your Instagram snaps to the 'outside world'. But the hardest and more seldom reached stage of this pilgrimage is to join the ranks of the 'real Burners'. For that, one has to convince a festival camp and its tribe that one has the skills and creativity to support their particular interpretation of that year's festival theme, to demonstrate 'radical self-expression', one of the core principles of Burning Man. Only then does one get admitted to the elite group of those who get guaranteed access to tickets the following year... for just $425 and only 48 hours.

All this is part of the intricate multi-layered Velvet Rope that helps define the highest rank of the 'Burner' Ueber-Target. All the 'normal people' get a chance to bid for one time access to this festival of dreams by applying for a 'FOMO (Fear of Missing Out) Ticket' at some $1,400 (Burning Man, 2019b). That might get them 'in' and get the admiration of people outside, but deep inside, they probably also feel a bit like those Harley-riding dentists who wish they truly were the Hells Angels.

The urge to belong is also what helped generate $2.4 billion dollars in sales in 2018 for the online video game brand Fortnite – which can actually be played for free in its most basic version (Hoggines, 2019). Yet, over a gaming season, many players – or rather their parents, given most players are 21 or younger – will pay small fortunes to buy accessories like the latest 'skins' (avatars) or 'emotes' (celebratory dances) to be cool and recognized as a regular player (Gough, 2019).

The Fortnite brand is inspired by and often collaborates with popular gamers, rappers and other pop icons in developing these accessories and rituals for sale. For less than a week, a limited-edition skin by famous mixer-streamer 'Ninja' went on sale in 2019, for example, creating a frenzy to get it before it was gone. But the highest respect in this community is reserved for the most seasoned player who can show off unique skills and vintage accessories that are no longer available. They are the dedicated players or even 'Pros', earning dollars at gaming tournaments rather than spending them. And they are the admired Ueber-Targets that the Fortnight brand seeks to pamper and please just like Burning Man seeks to keep the flame alive among the true Burners.

For the Velvet Rope principle to continue to work over time, people must perceive that it continues to be tricky to get past it. That's why brands like street wear label Supreme keep it hard to shop for some of its gear, applying arbitrary rules like releasing products in quantity-limited 'drops', spacing them out over time and space, limiting how much a single person is allowed to buy, etc. It's the old 'scarcity principle' of luxury re-invented for the 21st century. And it has created an entire parallel market for Supreme goods run by people who pay others to stand in line for hours for them and then re-sell at a significant premium. And remember, we are mostly talking about T-shirts and hoodies with big red logo on them!

To avoid boring their taste-making Ueber-Targets, Ueber-Brands need to throw them off balance from time to time and keep them on their toes. This is where Supreme collaborations like the one with Meissen, the iconic German porcelain maker founded in 1710, come in (Taschjian, 2019). Meissen's collectibles can be found in grandmas' living rooms all over the world. But it's not an obvious fit with the lifestyle of the average Supreme fan. And that is exactly the point. Only the in-the-know crowd is meant to penetrate the meaning of this angel with the pierced 'juicy heart'.

RECAP: LONGING VS BELONGING

- Ueber-Brands balance proximity with distance – physically, financially, intellectually, emotionally.
- They first seek for disciples – the Ueber-Target – then reach out more broadly through them.
- A fine balance is created between inclusion and exclusivity to keep people longing.
- The Ueber-Target is kept on their toes, so they can be proud to be the ones 'in the know'.

Principle 3: Un-selling

Mastering the art of seduction

Selling, while definitely needed, is decidedly un-sexy. How can a brand pitch to its constituencies without looking like it is selling to them? It's a conundrum for brands that want to elevate themselves. The solution is to 'un-sell' – to seduce, rather than sell.

Ueber-Brands avoid blatant sales attacks. Instead, they communicate in artfully crafted codes only understandable to those who are 'in the know'. Or they approach us in silence, at a soft pace, with lots of expensive and thus respect-inducing space around them to underscore how they are different from the mass-brands, hustling and screaming for attention.

A good example is the newspaper print ads by The Row, a New York high-end fashion label by actor-designer twin sisters Mary Kate and Ashley Olsen. You have to know all of that or you will be confused, at best. It's a blank, full page except for 'THE ROW' written in a skinny, modern and modestly sized font in the middle of it and an address and phone number in small print at the bottom – presumably of its showroom. That's it.

Ueber-Brands also turn the classic 'celebrity endorser' advertising approach on its head. Rather than the celebrity more or less blatantly recommending you buy a product, Ueber-Brands will show the celebrity as having fallen under the spell of the brand. Peloton seems almost casual, for example, about re-tweeting professions by Ellen de Generes, Richard Branson, Usain Bolt or Michael Phelps that they are addicted users. In Nespresso ads celebrities – George Clooney in particular – are passed over by other people wanting to get a cup of coffee before he does.

Being cultural icons and arming themselves with social media technology, celebrities are now able to shape their own brand, spawn more brands and be their own medium to promote them. This is how the aforementioned Clooney co-founded tequila brand Casamigos and sold it for $700 million less than five years later. The acquirer, Diageo, understands that the brand value lies in founder George and less in the liquid. They promised another $300 million, if he stayed on long enough (Whitten, 2017). Not to be outdone by the boys, Rihanna and Kylie Jenner have even become beauty billionaires, the latter not the least by selling a good chunk of her business to Coty in 2020 (Strugatz, 2019; Friedman and Testa, 2019).

A marvellous piece of un-selling by celebrity-owners comes to us from Marvel superhero actors Hugh Jackman and Ryan Reynolds. In 2019, they succeeded in turning advertisement into a pop-culture moment and good business at the same time. The two had built up a reputation on social media of being extremely envious of each other and locked in a personal feud. Hence the big draw when they posted a YouTube clip in which they announced a truce and, as a proof of goodwill, produced an ad for each other's brand – Ryan for Jackman's Laughing Man Coffee and Hugh for Reynolds' Aviation Gin... Suffice it to say that one of them cheated, and that the video amassed millions of views, which both brand owners had as much to smile about as their viewers.

FIGURE 3.1   Actor Ryan Reynolds goes beyond the traditional celebrity endorser role, being Aviation Gin's brand owner together with Diageo and creating the brand's messages and media platforms

SOURCE Reproduced with permission of Davos Brands – Aviation American Gin (2020)

Show pride and provoke, rather than get pally and smile

We may dislike arrogant people, but secretly admire their strong convictions and pride – at least at times. And psychologists confirm our hunch that arrogant people often have a leg up on their nicer peers in the career or in the mating game (Johnson, 2010).

High-end brands have played with our hidden envy in their communications for a long time to get paid more, as well. Look their ads up in the medium of your choice and chances are you get a broody stare back or can observe behaviours bordering on the arrogant; certainly compared to all those happy people in the ads of popular brands. That's likely one reason why it is hard to find a picture of the two Olsen sisters smiling since they have founded their fashion label – just google it for yourself.

Other Ueber-Brands like to provoke by having an 'attitude' or a controversial opinion. Nike has been known for praising those who push themselves harder, rather than praising the shoes. In 2018 Nike chose a particularly provocative way to give meaning to its 'Just Do It' tagline. It chose Colin Kaepernick as a spokesperson. The NFL quarterback had caused heated debates in the US and lost his job over kneeling during the playing of the national anthem to protest racial injustice and police brutality. 'Believe in something. Even if it means sacrificing everything' the headline quoting him in Nike's multi-media campaign read, showing a close-up of Kaepernick with his recognizable hairdo.

A few people were so upset that they burned their Nike shoes on social media and asked for a boycott of the brand. But black urban youth and many black athletes – a Nike Ueber-Target – openly applauded the gutsy move. And, importantly, the larger crowd of liberal-leaning, higher income people that make up Nike's strategic target showed their support and thanked the brand with a $6 billion boost in sales (Abad-Santos, 2018).

A NOTE OF CAUTION ABOUT SOCIO-CULTURAL PROVOCATION

A film shot by the Dior fragrance brand Sauvage in 2019 featuring Johnny Depp gave rise to an unintended social controversy. The film includes a few scenes showing a tribesman dancing. Quickly, voices could be heard criticizing Dior for being demeaning to Native Indians by associating them with a product name that sounds like 'savage'. The debate continued, even after the French brand affirmed that the name should be translated as 'wild', that it had worked with a Native group on the script and film to ensure the intended positive interpretation.

This example illustrates the increasing frequency of backlashes at anything that someone might interpret as inappropriate. With everyone having a smartphone at their fingertips, public critique is only an anonymous comment away. Add a hashtag and enough people who 'repost' and a 'movement' is born. Many of these movements and associated discussions have done much good for society. Others, though, are rather hollow exercises in mass 'virtue signalling' without much consequence for those who jump on the bandwagon. Brands can benefit in these signalling games, as the Nike x Kaepernick example showed. But brands need to be cautious, make sure they actually live the values they endorse and be ready to engage when social conversations about them go awry. Particularly when they choose to provoke and play with social media fire. Just ask Dolce & Gabbana how things went in China when it showed Chinese models struggling with Italian foods in rather suggestive ways. You can watch the Dolce & Gabbana public apology video on YouTube (Dolce & Gabbana, 2018). Scan the QR code at the front of the book for a direct link.

Avert the overt: Mystify, make it an art

Everyone talks about 'de-mystifying marketing' – a February 2020 Google search yields a 10,000 to 1 ratio versus 'mystifying marketing'. Ueber-Brands have recognized, however, that avoiding the obvious draws attention and makes mundane transactions feel more meaningful – or even mysterious.

In the absence of much 'performance' to advertise, categories like liquors or perfumes have relied on mystery to make them interesting, forever. Why would a vodka – Tito's – come from Texas, and what does it have to do with dogs? What wild thing is Johnny Depp doing out there in the desert wearing Sauvage by Dior? And what is Brad Pitt doing in a Chanel No 5 ad?

Beauty company L'Officine Universelle Buly has created an entire mythical universe. Founder Ramdane Touhami told us that he thinks of shopping in his boutiques as a 'hyper-real' dream. Inspired by how Umberto Eco wrote about experiencing Disneyland as the better-than-the-dream dream (Eco, 1986), Touhami says Buly is 'the romantic image people might have of vintage Paris' crossed with mystical beauty potions of yore or from far away. The experience is housed in a curious cross between Renaissance and Modern styles. You have to go and see the shelves bending to become part of the ceiling to feel the magic. You can listen to our interview with Ramdane and see pictures of the stores on ueberbrands.com (ueberbrands.com, 2018b). Scan the QR code at the front of the book for a direct link.

FIGURE 3.2   At Buly's boutiques shelves bend to become part of the ceiling, creating an artful, mysterious universe for the beauty brand

SOURCE JP Kuehlwein (2018)

The manifestations of Buly are so off commercial norms that some refer to it as 'art'. And that is intended, of course. It is certainly no coincidence that the brand was inspired by a Balzac novel, that the first store was opened in the former foundry Rodin used or that the store's Café Tortoni is recreating the Belle Epoque place where artists and writers used to meet. The association with art 'de-commercializes', gives customers a sense of experiencing culture and with that lifts the profile and pricing power of the brand.

Luxury superpower LVMH certainly believes in this power of art. It has bought into Buly via its investment arm (LVMH Luxury Ventures, 2019) and the group's brands constantly involve artists in their work.

The digital Ueber-Brand Netflix seems to have discovered the power of the physical world to provide brand meaning, as well. Netflix already demonstrated how producing outstanding movies can elevate a 'streaming service' to become a cultural player. It crossed the 50 Oscar nomination mark in 2019, the same year in which it acquired the 'Paris' theatre in New York, saving one of the few remaining arthouse treasures from permanent closure while creating what can become a powerful off-line manifestation of its cultural import (Haas, 2019).

Brand as medium... and platform

We have seen celebrities becoming brands and their own medium in advertising them. Some of the hottest internet start-ups have done the same. Beauty brand Glossier was born from comments and feedback left on Into-The-Gloss, a blog about beauty routines started by Emily Weiss, then a styling assistant at Vogue. It has become a product-media empire valued at over $1 billion in its 2019 Series D founding round (Gross, 2019).

Brands across categories and origins recognize the bond-building power of being their own carrier of message and meaning (see Part Two, Step 6). Airbnb started to issue a travel magazine. Cooperative retailer REI has a journal, podcast and cinema online film channel to move further from selling to inspiring and guiding.

The LEGO Brand Group went beyond the bricks a long time ago in promoting creativity through play. There are online games, the brand's movies (five by now), the Legoland theme parks... But maybe most significant in securing that parents and society see the LEGO brand as an

FIGURE 3.3 LEGO Education has become a valuable platform for experiential learning for key stakeholders of the brand – children, parents, educators

SOURCE Reproduced with permission of LEGO Education (2020)

invaluable partner for child development is the 'Education' platform the brand has built. Parents can send their children to LEGOLAND Discovery Centers where staff 'will prepare today's children for tomorrow's world… offering a wonderful balance of learning and fun' (Legoland Discovery Center, 2019).

At the LEGO Academies, teachers can get trained on how to 'integrate our classroom solutions into the existing STEM curriculum and daily lesson planning', as the website says (Lego Education, 2019). And there is the LEGO Foundation, which researches and disseminates learning-through-playing techniques to education authorities and NGOs around the globe.

RECAP: UN-SELLING

- Ueber-Brands master the art of seduction.
- They are bold and inspiring but leverage codes or art rather than a loud sales pitch.
- They walk rather than just doing the talking and…
- seek to become a medium or even the platform on which Ueber-Targets interact.

Principle 4: From Myth to meaning

Giving the brand soul

If a brand's Mission provides rational, tangible *raison d'être*, its Myth adds the emotional, intangible dimension. We put Myth-making at the centre of the Ueber-Branding principles because going deep – beyond the here and now – is the best way to go up. Up through crafting a narrative that prompts fascination, inspiration or even becomes a revelation. Also, Myths are about believing. And shared beliefs have the power to make people feel part of something bigger, of the chosen few – whether they are customers, employees or suppliers.

Humans not only process and retain a vividly told story much better, they also have a tendency to share it and act on it much more than if they were only given facts and figures. That is why Economics Professor and Nobel Laureate Robert Shiller gave the subtitle *How stories go viral and drive major economic events* to his 2019 book *Narrative Economics*. He observes that listening to popular myths might yield more accurate predictions than the kind of econometric modelling he won a Nobel Prize for (Shiller, 2019).

This does not come as a surprise to anthropologists, who know that humanity has literally grown up on stories. They have found stories to be common to every known culture and to provide patterns of information in which we find meaning. And in that they are central to our existence. As neurologist, psychiatrist and holocaust survivor Victor Frankl wrote in his book *Man's Search for Meaning*: 'Those who have a "why" to live, can bear with almost any "how"' (Frankl, 1962).

That said, people in modern societies are bombarded with more messages across more media than at any other time, causing mass attention deficit disorder and an increasing disorientation. This means that stories that want to cut through and provide meaning need to be well told – they need to be Ueber-Stories.

Are myths still relevant and powerful today? You bet they endure! Just consider the extreme popularity of *Star Wars* or *The Avengers* but also of the Silicon Valley myth with its founder-heroes, its out-of-a-garage origins, VC mentors and odyssey towards the land of 'Unicorns'. This modern-day myth is inspiring a whole generation of leaders, directing billions of dollars in real-world investments, shifting talent flows, and skewing economic and political power around the world.

Myths provide a perspective on life or an ideal we can live by, and they do so by going beyond logic and adding elements of mystery or magic. They might involve legendary figures like a Steve Jobs, a Coco Chanel or a Jack Daniels. They certainly will tell and teach about fateful actions and their life-changing consequences. In our last book we analysed how the skilfully revived myth of 'the little car that could' has yielded deep emotional attachment and solid commercial success for the modern Mini brand.

Like all industries, the world of cars is full of myths that wait to be leveraged. Take the story of Ferrucio Lamborghini being told by a certain Enzo Ferrari that he better stick to making tractors rather than giving him advice on how to build a better race car – it's called a Founding Myth. Or watch the film *Ford vs Ferrari* to learn about a piece of Ford's legend being made at the 1966 24-hour Le Mans race (Mangold, 2019)… just to be lost again. Might this film be the beginning of a Ford Brand Myth revival?

Note that Brand Myths do not need to be built on a long history. Many Ueber-Brands are more forward-looking than past-oriented – just think of Tesla. But Myths should include elements of lived truth combined with that higher calling to provide credibility and meaning.

HOW CONSUMPTION, STORIES, OUR 'SELVES' AND SELFIES RELATE

Humanistic psychologist Carl Rogers posited that everyone's personality is composed of a 'real self' and an 'ideal self', the latter being the dream person we aspire to become as we 'actualize ourselves' (Stevens, 1973). Think of it as our 'Ueber-Self'. Professor and consumer researcher Russell Belk showed how possessions serve us as 'extensions of our selves' (Belk, 1988).

Put these pieces together and you can see how products, their Myths and perceived cultural meaning are collected and 're-purposed' by people to become part of their identity making and appear in their social media streams.

A stylized selfie can be a relatively fast and efficient way to project the ideal self to the world (until we become addicted and feel compelled to post dozens a day, that is). A quick shot, filter, crop and post on Instagram, Snap-Chat or TikTok can do the trick. Sometimes a brand might even enable us to dip into what psychologist Jane Bybee calls our 'fantasy self' – our daydreams of wealth, power, celebrity or magic – social media props included (Bybee, 1997).

Just imagine if we had to invent, construct and communicate all aspects of the 'self' we want to project on our own. No wonder that most jump willingly on the building-blocks brands have to offer – particularly those labelled as 'lifestyle' or 'luxury' brands and which we call Ueber-Brands in this book.

FIGURE 4.1   The self-states: The 'Ueber-Self' is situated on the ideal or fantasy side of the spectrum

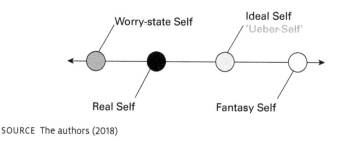

SOURCE The authors (2018)

There are few people more qualified to talk about the function of myth than literature professor and comparative mythologist Joseph Campbell. In his famous interviews with Bill Moyers, Campbell states that 'Mythology pitches the mind beyond that rim [...], to what can be known but not told' (Moyers, 1991). We detailed the four functions of Myths, and how to create lasting ones in our previous book and pick up on that in Part Two. Let's just recap here the two distinctive paths Myths might send us on. The first we call the 'metaphysical–cosmological' route and the second the 'sociological–pedagogical' route:

The metaphysical–cosmological route: Reaching beyond with Myths

The first route is to connect us – and the brand – with that which is beyond our grasp and control – the big powers like weather or water and the big unknown like the heavens and their stars. This might be the harder Myth to create, but if successful, a Myth that reaches beyond can exert magical appeal, however, and also powerfully complemented the world of business, science and reason.

Just think of Elon Musk and his enterprises from Tesla to Solar City and SpaceX. These are technology companies, but they venture out to the edges of the known universe with them – literally and figuratively. One of Elon's pet projects – Nuralink – is looking to 'Unify the brain with AI' and link biology and technology in search of superior intelligence, for example (Rosso, 2019). Another was to shoot his Tesla roadster into orbit to reach Mars...

The MIT Technology Review calls Elon Musk a prime example of the 'Great Man Myth, [...] the one-man embodiment of the future'. Musk fuels the Myth with pronouncements that go far beyond his already ambitious 'plan to change the way the World uses energy' (Schaffer, 2015) to 'spreading humanity to other planets' (Mosher, 2018). He declared that he will be the first person to live on Mars and will lead a million people to follow him to 'ensure that humanity has a future' (Andersen, 2014). It turns out that sending his car into space is just one of the stages of his odyssey.

Musk seems to be 'out there' beyond where the mere mortals can imagine. And his Myth is a guiding light for his fans and his customers, who feel some of his visionary boldness rubbing off on them as they glide over the highway in their Teslas.

The sociological–pedagogical route: Guiding with Myths

This route is more down-to-earth and practical in its guidance. It's about taking a stance and setting an example for others to follow, personifying values and behaviours to live by. In *Rethinking Prestige Branding*, we showed how the mythical stories about Coco Chanel and women's liberation have imbued that brand's products to become icons of emancipation. In Part Three of this book you will read about TerraCycle and its founder Tom Szaky. One of the personal stories he likes to share is how his family was fleeing the Eastern Block and the radiation caused by the Chernobyl nuclear disaster and how he fell in love with the capitalist system. It provides a human backdrop to his company's Mission: 'Eliminate the idea of waste', but do it through the way we consume and with the companies that produce packaged goods, rather than against them. The fact that Tom looks a bit like a prophet with his long, scruffy hair and beard only helps.

Another bearded figure who plays a central role in a Brand Myth is Burt Cohen of Burt's Bees. This time, the Guiding Myth is one of finding inspiration, healing and happiness in nature – more specifically in the systemic and symbiotic manner bees live, work and organize themselves. The transformative experience takes place in rural Maine and was triggered by discovering the wondrous being of the bees. As Bee Wilson's book *The Hive* shows, Burt was not the first to impute a quasi-sacred status to the bee by virtue of its chastity, industriousness, stinging defence but abundant sweet secretions. Bees, she says, have historically been called 'the gift of the Gods to man' (Wilson, 2004). What the Burt's Bees Myth does is to take the inspirational guidance into our times and expresses it through beauty products and regimens. Read the direct account of how Burt's Bees linked purpose with profit in Part Three and a sidebar on the Burt Myth below.

A GUIDING MYTH: BURT AND HIS BEES

Ingram Berg ('Burt') Shavitz was raised in New York City in relative comfort. A skilled photographer, he roamed the city in the 1960s and 70s as a photojournalist documenting that turbulent era. It was an ideal occupation for a perceptive introvert. He decided, however, to leave the city in search of a different lifestyle. In rural Maine he met a beekeeping guru and developed an interest in the intricate social structure of bee colonies. By chance, he found a swarm on a fence post, and took it as a sign that he should live with bees. He figured that, if he lived modestly, he could make ends meet by just selling their honey. He settled into a converted turkey coop, grew a wild beard, and lived a reclusive life. He became known locally as 'Burt the bee man', and for stencilling 'Burt's bees' on his hives so they would not get stolen.

This is in the 1980s, when Roxanne Quimby meets Burt and is taken by his quirky mix of eager genius and relaxed recluse. She is also the one who recognizes the potential behind both, the products as well as the meaning that Burt and his bees could produce for people left behind in the cities, yearning for a life that is more in tune with nature. To help deliver the message, a woodcut illustration of Burt's iconic hatted head went on every product. Burt himself was all too happy to tell his story to the visiting press but otherwise just to hang out by his coop and close to his bees and not to worry much about the business side of things.

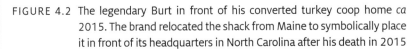

FIGURE 4.2 The legendary Burt in front of his converted turkey coop home *ca* 2015. The brand relocated the shack from Maine to symbolically place it in front of its headquarters in North Carolina after his death in 2015

SOURCE Reproduced with permission of Burt's Bees (2020)

Later the Myth gained a contemporary sustainability dimension as Burt helped raise awareness for Colony Collapse Disorder, which is decimating the world's bee population. In 2013 a feature-length biopic on Burt was released at the Toronto Film Festival, drawing in a new generation and becoming a primary vehicle for discovering the brand's origin.

Burt passed away in July 2015, at age 80. The company purchased his iconic turkey coop home and relocated it to its head office in North Carolina. There it stands as a physical symbol of Burt's values of simplicity and essentialism and of the romanticized idea of a life lived in harmony with nature (Shapiro, 2013).

Cadillac illustrates how deep seated and universal a brand's legend can become – and how difficult and risky to stray away from it. General Motors has struggled to re-energize its Cadillac brand since its heyday in the early 1970s. Then a new brand president and his team came up with the idea to make it 'a luxury brand that happens to sell cars' and which would inspire young urbanites to 'Think Greatly' (Motavalli, 2018) and connect the brand with the 'creative set'. But despite a new campaign, plenty of edgy new models and a hip art-and-car-gallery and café in New York, sales continued to stagnate in the home market.

Over in China, the local distributors largely ignored the re-positioning. To them, Cadillac was a very traditional manifestation of the glitzy and glorious part of the post-war American Dream. A conspicuous celebration of success and celebrity. They would put a 1954 Eldorado 'land yacht' next to the latest, equally oversized Cadillac SUVs at tradeshows and make customers dream about Elvis or Marilyn… while admiring the brute exuberance of these cars (Andrews, 2017). This approach worked more magic and moved more cars – in what has become the brand's biggest market (Eisenstein, 2017) than the global messaging did (Greimel, 2017).

Maybe this is because 'Think Greatly' felt more like part of Apple's creative and non-conformist DNA rather than that of the rather classic and conformist Cadillac one? In the meantime, the management team has changed, again. They might want to listen to the legend-tellers as much as the trend forecasters as they write the next chapter in the brand story.

RECAP: MYTH

- Ueber-Brands harness the power of legends and move higher – from story to Myth.
- They understand that believing is a compelling complement to knowing and…
- keep sharing and spinning the story – but not out of control.

Principle 5: Behold the product!

Making your product manifest the Myth

After all this seducing, the expectation that the goods actually 'deliver' is high. That's why Ueber-Brands put immense effort into providing a superior product and service, using a broader than usual definition of what that means. Beyond typical considerations of 'getting the job done' and distinctive aesthetics, Ueber-Brands think of their product as the essential manifestation of the brand's Mission and Myth. Exemplary pieces will feature idiosyncratic design codes and be elevated and celebrated. Occasionally, they will be refreshed but they will never be relinquished. The goal is to make them icons of the brand, if not the culture.

When Ueber-Brands design their product, it is both the detail that counts as well as that total pattern – the 'Gestalt' – which expresses the essence of the brand. Contrary to popular belief, the attention is not directed at 'every detail', though, but rather at those that make the brand different – but that in often exaggerated ways.

Take the insane acceleration and top speeds of a street-version Ferrari, for example. Such performance serves no practical purpose in 90 per cent or more of the usage situations for these cars. In fact, the deafening roar, stiff suspension and low-lying body makes the car rather uncomfortable for its often-mature buyer. But practicality or 'average' is not what defines this thoroughbred of a race car. In a similar way, the 'falcon wing' doors of the Tesla Model X SUV were not necessarily chosen because they are a more cost efficient or intuitive way to open the car. Some reports suggest they might be rather accident prone (Lambert, 2017). Rather, the unusual 'wings' and other unique design choices are there to shout 'I am a technological marvel of the future', and in that they reflect the essence of the brand.

Make it the holy grail

Ueber-Brands relate the distinctive ways in which they might have been conceived, sourced, made, sold, or – increasingly – how they might be used, re-used, refurbished or even disposed of. The goals are to showcase the skill and deep-rooted dedication that goes into creating these marvels, to instil respect and to provide vivid stories and memorable experiences to share.

For example, the co-founder of start-up Allbirds, Tim Brown, talks about taking over a year to perfect its unique merino wool shoe. How they persist in figuring out the use of sustainable materials like castor bean oil, recycled plastic or sugar cane. They ship direct to consumer in a carton that lets you feel that you received something special. It folds open to the sides and alludes to the origin story and Mission through graphics and words printed on the inside.

And product elevation works for business-to-business suppliers, as well. Mohawk is a manufacturer of specialty papers for printers, design studios, offices and the like in upstate New York. They have recognized the graphic designer community as an Ueber-Target and discovered a mix of product education and art to be of powerful appeal to them. Its *Maker Quarterly* is a different kind of catalogue in which the products themselves are being used by photographers, writers, poets and other artists.

Each *Quarterly* is a differently designed and themed tome of what has become a colourful and coveted art book series among aficionados. And with it, the unique Mohawk paper stocks used are elevated and celebrated. The *Quarterly*s get launched at events where artists show and tell about their work and the role the paper plays in it. They also get mailed to select customers and are made available for sale online – while limited supplies last. Listen to our interview with Creative Director Christopher Harrold on ueberbrands.com (ueberbrands.com, 2018a). Scan the QR code at the front of the book for a direct link. You will read about another paper company, Gmund, and their education programmes in Part Three, Step 3.

A test to see if you might be in the presence of an Ueber-Product is to strip off its logo or even hide most of it and see if the target group still recognizes the brand. In other words, does the brand own codes and other soft assets that make it unmistakable?

Those Allbirds shoes are recognizable by their merino wool upper but also the stitched holes and thick laces well before the recessive logo becomes visible. Most Bottega Veneta accessories are recognizable by their iconic 'intrecciato' leather weave than the hidden logo. Porsche's 911 models are

FIGURE 5.1 Making your catalogue Mission and Myth: The artistic, colourful and coveted *Maker Quarterly* by Mohawk

SOURCE Reproduced with permission of Mohawk Fine Papers Inc (2020)

immediately recognized by their silhouette – no matter the year – just like Harley Davidson bikes are by their sound (Harley actually trademarked it in 1994) (Staab, 2016).

The codes are not only unique identifiers. They also help tell the brand's story and further its Myth. Take Acqua Di Parma and its iconic Colonia fragrance, which has been left unchanged since its invention in 1916. This makes generations recognize it as something a loved one wore when they were little. But you don't need to smell it to recognize it: It has been bottled in an iconic Art Deco bottle made from Murano glass with a solid Bakelite stopper lid since the 1930s when it became a favourite of stars around the world. The outer pack is an equally recognizable 'hatbox' which is coloured in a singular golden yellow. That 'Parma Yellow' is the same that graces many noble facades of its home town since the 18th century. The yellow and gold on the label and the round shapes also relate to the 'frutti d'oro', the golden citrus fruit used for the fragrance... You can read more about marketing this icon from the CEO of the brand, Laura Burdese, in Part Three. What is important to note here is that Ueber-Brands don't give you a simple 'reason to believe'. They give you a 'story to believe in' that can also be 'read' by getting to know its products, as elaborated upon in Part Two, Step 2.

On occasion, Ueber-Brands will carefully play with their established codes to attract attention or stay current. Bottega Veneta's designers can be found changing the size or use of that intrecciato weave. But brands must beware not to abuse their codes and create something equivalent to 'logo inflation'.

Make it personal and keep it fresh

Specifically crafting a product for a client your way creates a personal and meaningful bond between brand and client. That's how prestige brands like Hermès or Louis Vuitton established their reputation, after all.

But what works for artisan or artsy products at the top end also works for more mundane products. Nike and Rapha, for example, allow clients to custom-design their own shoes and cycling kits. In fact, technology has given rise to an entire new breed of mass-customizers like Prose, a purveyor of personal hair care products, Curology, which does the same in skin care or Care/of, which ships clients a regimen of nutrients and vitamins that is adjusted 'as your health needs change' (Care/of, 2020).

The CEO and co-founder of Prose, Arnaud Plas, told us that its ever-smarter formulation algorithm analyses the wants and needs clients provide through an online questionnaire and assembles a targeted solution from almost 100 active ingredients. There are a theoretic 50 billion possible outcomes and 'we were surprised how rarely identical formulations are generated the million times, or so, we have done this, so far,' says Plas. A set of personalized shampoo, conditioner and a treatment will set you back about $80–100. It might not be luxury but the price is significant – 5 to 10 times higher compared to the mass brands many customers say they used before.

Those who know something about high-end watches know about Audemars Piguet (AP) and will easily recognize the Royal Oak model. That is because the Swiss watchmaker misses no opportunity to celebrate its icon, be it as a centrepiece at its stores, its spectacular museum and workshop in Le Brassus or at the annual Salon International de la Haute Horlogerie.

AP seeks to keep the icon fresh by launching what seem like ever more outrageously expensive editions at the top. These are the diamond-studded type priced at a million dollars or more. But it is also reaching down with colourful, more modern sports versions at an 'affordable' $20,000 or so. This keeps the Royal Oak icon at the centre of attention, all the while extending its reach and buzz across generations. Read more on balancing extensions down in Principle 7 and listen to our interview with Tim Sayler, Chief Marketing Officer (CMO) of AP, on ueberbrands.com (ueberbrands.com, 2016b). Scan the QR code at the front of the book for a direct link.

FIGURE 5.2 Making it mine and keeping it fresh: Prose custom-formulates its hair care regimens for every client and every order, taking into account the feedback from the last use experience

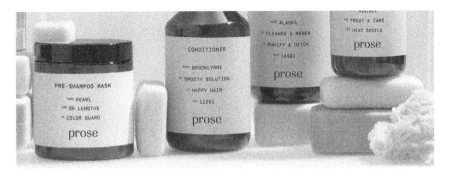

SOURCE Reproduced with permission of Prose (2020)

In 2019 fashion brand Lacoste could be observed trying to bring attention back to its 'original polo shirt'. It released a limited edition featuring endangered species rather than its famous crocodile as a logo. The critical question is whether such initiatives succeed to feed not only the conversation of the moment but actually the essence of the brand in a more enduring way.

RECAP: BEHOLD!

- Ueber-Products express the Brand Myth and have codes that make them unmistakable.

- The most iconic products are celebrated and rejuvenated to never lose their glow.

- Product personalization or customization serve to further strengthen the bond.

Principle 6: Living the dream

Letting the brand radiate from the inside out

Living the dream is about bringing the promise of the Ueber-Brand to life, starting from the inside of the organization and radiating out across all relevant touchpoints.

This is easier said than done, because dreams are hard to create but the appearance of 'trying too hard' will be disenchanting. In the same way, 'good enough' doesn't pass when it comes to execution, so absolute attention to detail is essential. And we are not 'just' talking about the user experience on websites or in stores. We need to start much earlier at the organization structure and company culture and through to sourcing, making and marketing.

Abercrombie & Fitch cast a spell on its young customers through the 1990s and early 2000s by dreaming up a teenager's sexual fantasy world through its ads, dark stores and half-naked guardians at the door, imbibing its apparel with irresistible appeal and its 'Fierce' fragrance smell.

But those initially very successful brand rituals and experiences became a cliché at one point, the brand not evolving with the very fickle youth culture and falling out of fashion and then favour. Sales went on an extended tail-spin. Quite literally turning on the lights and dressing everyone up was a harsh and expensive pivot undertaken in 2018. Twenty months on, it is still not clear if the significant investment into new ads and store designs will pay off (Wu, 2019). The moral: You can't just turn a dream on a dime and change who you are overnight – at least not if you previously succeeded in actually meaning something in people's minds.

UEBER-LEADERSHIP: OPERATORS, ARTISTS AND, POTENTIALLY, PROTECTORS

We often get questions about which kind of 'Renaissance man – or woman' is able to guide and orchestrate all dream making while running an efficient operation and making money. The answer is that it usually is a team. We often find an 'artist' and 'operator team' placed at the top of Ueber-Brands. At Gucci, CEO Marco Bizzarri and Designer Alessandro Michele succeeded the famously successful Tom Ford and Domenico De Sole at the top. At start-ups it is often a group of 'co-founders' like Tim Brown – the creative one – with Joey Zwillinger – the operations wizard – at Allbirds. Many are intuitively looking for a partner to complement their skills.

Sam Altman, President of famous Silicon Valley seed-accelerator YCombinator, and the experts at Foundr Magazine agree that 'two or three [founders] is the target' and that the perfect team needs to carry the DNA of 'a Visionary, a Hacker and a Hustler' (Chan, 2019).

And what if the brand has been acquired and is now part of a larger corporate group or if it has a powerful and active investor? That's when a third role comes into play: The 'protector' shields the Ueber-Brand from a desire to skip anything that might come in the way of scaling or getting big returns, fast – like paying attention to detail. Today, most big corporations seek to avoid the problem by creating internal but semi-autonomous venture groups and incubators (Alsever, 2019). We call it the art of 'ring-fencing' what is essential to the authenticity of a brand.

Freitag is a curious animal, as we discovered in the previous book. The Swiss company transforms old, printed truck-tarps into sturdy bags and accessories. Each of the bags is unique, cut in a way to yield whimsical decorations, yet they are fashioned using a precisely normed pattern. Once you get to know them, the approach seems like a natural reflection of their organization and its culture.

Freitag people are process and documentation freaks. There is a bible that lays down everything from the company Mission to how to dispose of beer bottles, a popular drink on 'F-ridays'. It has a lot of diagrams but is also written in a unique Freitag language involving the use of 'F-words', wherever possible and an idiosyncratic sense of humour. Of course, it's a ring binder for easy page replacement and recycling, in line with the brand DNA. It's title: 'What the F, how and why' (ueberbrands.com, 2016a).

No wonder the organization had a hard time finding fitting leaders when the brother-designer-F-ounders declared they wanted to step back from daily operations. After trying 'the CEO thing', the organization found an organic solution: They established a 'holacracy', 'organizing the company like a city, with functional, self-contained cells that are driven by passion'. We talk some more about this in Part II, Step 4. For a detailed account of Freitag's inner workings, listen to our interview with Oliver Brunschwiler the 'Lead Link' (aka CEO?) at Freitag on the Ueber-Brands podcast on ueberbrands.com (ueberbrands.com, 2016a). Scan the QR code at the front of the book for a direct link.

Note: The point of this example is not to say that holacracy is the organization form of choice for Ueber-Brands. It definitely is not. Rather, the point is to illustrate how deeply the equity of these brands is reflected in the organizational culture and vice versa.

We quoted Ben & Jerry's Dave Rappaport above telling us about a cultural 'moment of truth' for the brand's organization. It came about when social justice seemed increasingly threatened by the actions of the newly installed US Government in 2016. The organization felt compelled to 'stand

FIGURE 6.1   Stand up for your Mission and be counted: Ben & Jerry's in front of the White House to resist and protest about unfair immigration restrictions

SOURCE Reproduced with the kind permission of Ben & Jerry's Homemade, Inc.

up and be counted'. And that even more so, after they saw only a few of the brands willing to join their call to action for fear of a political backlash.

Ben & Jerry's independent Board of Directors – a unique organ that is protected by its company constitution and is responsible for preserving and furthering Ben & Jerry's social mission – decided to start selling a 'Pecan Resist' flavour, provide funds to non-governmental organizations (NGOs) supporting immigrants, write open letters to legislators and protest in the streets – knowing full well that this would attract scorn and boycotts from conservatives. And all that while the premium ice cream category was struggling to find an answer to the exploding popularity of a low-calorie wonder-brand 'Halo Top'. Corporate owner Unilever likely bit its tongue watching its subsidiary Ben & Jerry's 'acting out'. As they probably also did at the beginning of the COVID crisis, when Ben & Jerry's started advocating for the safety of prisoners (see Epilogue).

The world according to you

Crafting an Ueber-Brand world means being considerate of all the things – even those we may not consciously register, but which 'feel' right or wrong – to create your own world. A cosmos that takes your Mission and Myth live into unique, multi-sensorial experiences and re-invents or upgrades the standards of your category in your very own way.

If you are a reader of *The Economist*, you will likely recognize an article by the news magazine in more than one way: By the choice of subject and headline, the authoritative but occasionally derisively mocking style, the very British choice of words, the layout and illustrations, the premium price... and that whether you encounter the 'newspaper' (its language) online, in paper or through its 'Intelligence Unit'.

And then there is the unique practice of not having a 'byline' that states who the authors of the articles are. Some 175 years ago, when the paper was founded, not naming the author was customary in the industry to hide a often very small staff. But, since then, bylines have become an industry standard. In fact, featuring star reporters has become a major selling point – its pictures and Twitter addresses included. *The Economist* ignores the modern practice to preserve a consistent voice of the paper, which it says is 'the product of *The Economist* hive mind' (*The Economist*, 2013). This separates it not only in how it approaches news and opinion but also in who will be motivated to join the organization. There is no place for egocentric journalism in *The Economist*'s world.

If *The Economist* has created 'a bible of global affairs for those who wear aspirations of worldliness on their sleeves' (Peters, 2010), then Rapha has created the club of the debonair road biker, as we showcased in Principle 2. The brand's vision of this singular biker's world is lived out in the Rapha Clubhouses and Cycling Clubs (RCC). 'Nothing is too small or too insignificant,' the CEO founder says while describing the products, communications and clubs (Rapha, 2019). Employees are told to 'Suffer [because] 'good enough' isn't'. And he works only with the best, as is befitting of the brand: Architect Sir Norman Foster, photographer Cait Oppermann, fashion designer Paul Smith.

You might find yourself sipping on a cup of Rapha's signature artisanal coffee at the club bar, while admiring the chic cycling kits (on the racks and on the people), collections of club ride caps or some of the bikes 'parked' by 'Raphia' hung on hooks on the walls. But the brand will make you sense whether you are fully part of its world yet, or not. For one, the coffee is free for the members and some of the most desirable items in the store can only be bought by them. But, more importantly, stories swapped about RCC Prestige Rides, the reputedly 'cool' staff, the tech-talk, etc, will either pull you in or put you off. Outsiders dismiss it all as a 'wealthy metrosexual fiefdom' (Neate, 2017).

RECAP: LIVING IT

- Ueber-Brands radiate from the inside out, led by their Mission, Myth and culture.
- Most are led by both an artist and an operator, and, if part of a large group, seek to protect against pressures to standardize and scale fast.
- They create brand experiences that transcend reality and go beyond the store.

Principle 7: Growth without end
Balancing scaling and brand building

This last principle deals with the art of expanding the business without losing what makes the brand feel special – to 'grow without losing the glow'. Ueber-Brands have developed ways to avoid the deadly feel of ubiquity and yet develop scale – in a more 'stealthy' manner. And at the core of this is ensuring their Ueber-Target remains dedicated, personifying and upholding the brand's cool as it becomes more mainstream.

Be it through foresight and planning or because of the limited means and the organic way in which Ueber-Brands accrue meaning and appeal, the shape of the revenue curve of many of these brands is what mathematicians would describe as 'exponential'. And while that sounds like the explosive take-off that mass marketers are after, that ideal curve would be 'logarithmic' in shape.

The exponentially shaped curve starts rather flat, reflecting that 'incubation time' during which a brand is mostly adopted by its Ueber-Target, people who want the brand exactly because it is new and special. Eventually, a tipping point is reached, the 'niche brand' and its community are 'discovered', the word gets out and adoption takes off on a broader scale. It is at this point, at the latest, that Ueber-Brands put measures in place to avoid 'over-exposure'.

As the number of 'Joiners' rises every year, the Burning Man festival organizers, for example, have kept increasing prices and also put renewed emphasis on the 'Burning Man principles' – creative participation, in particular. Finally, Burning Man has branched out into regional festivals and auxiliary events to capture demand without further inflating the main event (Burning Man, 2019a).

The two charts in Figure 7.1 illustrate the exponential growth in participation. Combine those attendance numbers with the price increases graphed

FIGURE 7.1 Plotting exponential growth: Burning Man participant numbers and tiered ticket prices exponentially increasing and multiplying over time

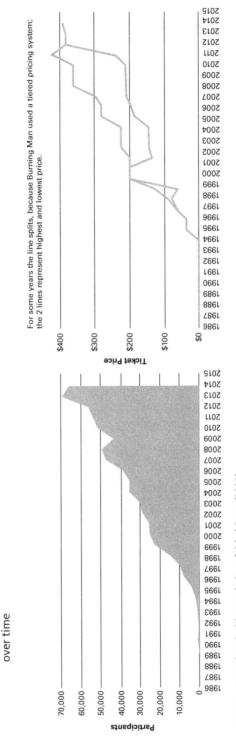

For some years the line splits, because Burning Man used a tiered pricing system; the 2 lines represent highest and lowest price.

Ticket Price

Participants

SOURCE Reproduced with permission of Jishai Evers (2020)

on the right and you arrive at an even steeper increase in revenues. Notice also the tiered pricing at one point to encourage original 'Burners' – the creative Ueber-Target – to keep coming, while 'Joiners' pay a higher price.

Note that the marketing spend has always been very limited, with the pull based on word-of-mouth and all those tweets, pics and videos. And even that has been curtailed through their 'decommodification' principle – see also Part Two, Step 6 (Burning Man, 2019b).

Grow with gravitas: Slowing down to grow stronger

Hermès has an owner-family that keeps an eagle's eye on the brand image not being diluted by one too many bags being sold. And between the appeal of all movements that are 'slow' and the sophistication associated with requiring time for making a product, quantity limitations will only increase the perceived value.

But even scale businesses can signal how they are better than average by going it slow, on occasion. For example, rather than complaining that Everlane did not come out with a much requested denim line earlier, there was much praise for the reason why the company gave at launch: It could not find a factory that could make jeans how they wanted them to be made – 98 per cent water efficient and converting the usually toxic leftover sludge into harmless building materials (Segran, 2018).

IS 'GROWING WITH GRAVITAS' DEAD?

In *Rethinking Prestige Branding* we described Ueber-Brands as taking a graceful pace to grow, focusing first on the Ueber-Target and organic word-of-mouth before increasing marketing spend as revenue rises (Schaefer and Kuehlwein, 2015). Are those times over?

One might think so, when looking at the brand start-up scene circa 2020. Venture capital is injecting billions of dollars into tech but also into luxury, lifestyle, beauty, food and beverages. The model is to invest heavily into e-commerce-based direct-to-consumer distribution and social media-based awareness campaigns that employ 'influencers' – from celebrities down to thousands of 'micro-influencers'. Rapid expansion of the organization, product line and subsequent multi-channel distribution are combined with subsidized pricing to add buyers fast but also millions of dollars in losses.

But many of these so-called 'indie brands' really are 'banked brands', burning through cash faster than one can say 'unicorn valuation' – which seems to be the ultimate business goal. The Mission: A fabulously profitable exit – ideally within five years of founding.

That last part is – hopefully – somewhat of an exaggeration rather than the norm. But it definitely feels this way, when we interact with these shooting stars. Some of them feel like 'Ueber-Brands on steroids'. They have nailed the talk about higher purpose, their beautiful designs and storytelling and bulk up desirability and reach by pumping money into building themselves a fan community. The question is whether this construct and pace can be kept up, if it allows for a true sense of shared meaning to emerge (or whether it feels betrayed) and if it can lead to a sustainable and profitable long-term business.

The once high-flying work-space brand WeWorks provides an example of almost all that could go wrong. Building buzz behind the idea of a work and life community made for the millennial generation, pretending to be a tech platform, scaling ahead of building a solid brand and business model, attracting and burning through billions of dollars... crashing as the dream turns out to be a bubble and bursts (Ovide, 2019).

Everlane, Peloton and Rapha are all heavily venture funded, as well. At Rapha, a VC took over majority ownership in 2017 for a reported $270 million. A large part of the money was said to go towards an accelerated expansion of those Clubhouses–stores (Neate, 2017). We continue to think that key to the long-term success of Rapha and similar premium brands will be whether that money is spent in tune with how fast, how broadly and how authentically the brand legend can be brought to life. It needs to be done without compromising a reasonable path to profit and, most importantly, without turning off the Ueber-Target. If those dedicated 'Raphia' who carry the flame and inspire others smell get-rich-fast motives, that flame might be snuffed out, fast. Read also about Everlane's IPO troubles in our Epilogue.

Some Ueber-Brands might feel they need to cut back, at times, to correct over-extension, stay strong and secure profits in the long run. When Felix Ahlers, a trained chef, became CEO of German frozen food maker FRoSTA, he decided to elevate the brand's Mission and only use fresh, natural ingredients (see also Part Two, Step 3). To deliver the promise, the brand's line-up had to be cut almost by half in the first year and prices had to be increased to mitigate higher ingredient costs. The company paid a high price, too. Its revenues fell by over 40 per cent in 2003 and it made a loss for the first time in decades.

But when we asked Felix whether it was 'worth it', his response was that there was really no alternative if the company was to feel good and be proud of the product it sells – and employees were to eat its own products again! By 2017, revenues had quadrupled and profits were up more than tenfold versus the pre-line-up-pruning period, according to the company's annual reports. Listen to our interview with Felix on the Ueber-Brands podcast on ueberbrands.com (ueberbrands.com, 2019a). Scan the QR code at the front of the book for a direct link.

Rather than shrink itself, the premier design and innovation consulting firm IDEO found a way to re-frame itself internally and to clients to keep its 'boutique' agility and appeal. As the organization was growing and becoming a multi-layered corporate monster, its founder David Kelly agreed with his partners and leadership to form physically and organizationally independent 'studios' that declared their own areas of specialization and let employees choose which studio they wanted to join (Buchanan, 2014).

This is one way to execute what we call 'sideways steps', steps taken to keep growing while avoiding the perception of becoming omnipresent or, in the case of IDEO, becoming too big to remain 'special'. Other such steps can involve expanding internationally rather than selling more at home, or getting into new product categories that fit the identity rather than selling cheaper and/or too much of the same. That's how you get to enjoy a Bulgari bijoux, bag, boutique hotel or bottle of perfume – with the last being its way to bow down and reach POME (price of market entry) customers.

Keep reaching up and out to the Ueber-Target, to balance scale and time pulling you down

Further elevating your brand as it gathers appeal might slow down volume growth but can keep revenues and profits growing. There is also the potentially lucrative option of combining a reach up for equity with a reach down for substantially more revenue.

Tesla, for example, is extending down with its Model 3 and Cybertruck, priced around $40,000 while also introducing the SUV Model X at twice that price and talking about a next Roadster that will cost over $200,000 (Brown, 2019).

Whiskey Johnny Walker has done an outstanding job pursuing the elevation strategy in the opposite direction. It started from the humble Red Label sold for around $25 via the Green, Blue and Black labels ($50–500) to Reserve labels and limited editions that go into the thousands of dollars. The brand never abandoned its low-priced scale business on the way but has steadily traded people up over the last 25 years. Listen to our interview with the marketing leader of Diageo's Reserve Brands at the time on our podcast on ueberbrands.com (ueberbrands.com, 2016c). You can scan the QR code at the front of the book for a direct link.

No matter which growth strategies are pursued, Ueber-Brands must ensure not to lose the involvement and support of their Ueber-Target. They are the energy centre of the brand cult. Without them, the soul, aspiration and perceived authenticity of the brand might get lost – and with it the premium pricing power.

Let's close this section and review of our principles with an example that illustrates both the power of the Ueber-Target core as well as the dangers in straying too far, too fast. Shoes of Prey a digitally native, bespoke shoe start-up was founded in 2009 in Australia. It quickly gained a dedicated followership among women who loved the possibilities of creative expression and the high-quality finish of the shoes.

Based on their 'proven concept', the founders were able to secure some $25 million in funding and found a 'strategic investor' in Nordstrom. The investors saw an opportunity to enter the mainstream by adding lower-priced base models and to scale via advertising and accessing Nordstrom's customer base and stores (Wahba, 2015). But the more general 'fashion shoe buyer' segment found the choices of the bespoke line rather overwhelming and stuck to base models, while the early adopters lost interest. Revenue growth stayed far below what was needed to cover all the spending and the brand was closed down in 2019.

In hindsight, co-founder Michael Fox told reporters that the brand should have proceeded more carefully in radiating out, first catching more of its original fan base in the new market and letting them talk about the brand (TFL, 2019), leveraging the type of tastemakers to whom the opportunity to show off their creativity was truly priceless.

RECAP: GROWTH

- Ueber-Brands go to market in measured steps to always remain a bit out of reach.
- They let reputation precede their presence and balance moves down by reaching further up.
- And, most importantly, they never abandon their Ueber-Target.

PART TWO

How to: Six steps to elevate your brand

Brands, elevated

The new millennium has brought a major shift to the world of brand building. Brands, especially those that we call Ueber-Brands, are no longer seen as mere marketing instruments, they are embraced as guiding the enterprise overall. No longer just attracting consumers, but inspiring and engaging all stakeholders inside and out.

If you look through the various schools of brand models, you'd think this isn't really so revolutionary. And yes, in theory brands were often already given an overarching role. But in practice, particularly among mass brands, they were often focused on one thing only, namely their original function: Marker of product quality. Or, a bit more advanced, as 'added value', wrapping the product in lifestyle. Either way, brands were often all about selling. And this is changing: More and more they're about inspiring and leading.

How did this happen? Well, there are two big drivers that pushed this – and are still furthering it:

1 Technology. Digitization has brought transparency and accessibility. The first forces brands and companies to practise what they preach. The second empowers and commands direct brand–consumer interaction. Together they've made the brand as purely external 'image' or 'label' impossible. The brand must be lived.

2 People. We've all been over-marketed to. The 'hidden persuaders' are obvious to pretty much everyone by now. And, we've become generally more critical of crude commercialism, expecting more reflection and responsibility, while we of course still run for the sale. We want to shop ourselves a better world.

Apart from this, there's been a general trend towards independent 'company brands', where the brand is the sign over the door and thus all-covering anyway. As it's traditionally been with the *grandes maisons* in luxury and fashion: My name. My work. My reputation.

All this led us in 2015 to revisit the way today's Ueber-Brands are built, brands that appear above and beyond their competition, peerless and priceless. And it's the reason we're now sharing the way we translated our theory into action, a very praxis oriented 'How to' process we've successfully used across categories and have often been asked for, now 'due to popular demand'.

There are four things where our process differs markedly from standard theory and which we highlight before getting into all the details.

First: Start with yourself

This is nothing less than turning the traditional model on its head – or feet as we see it: Don't start with market or consumer research in developing your brand and its products, start with your ideas and ideals.

Of course, business realities still matter. But they come into play once you're clear about what you want to dedicate your brand to and why. Then you will use them to validate your concept, adjust, find the right target, ensure profitability, etc.

If you start out by looking outside for consumer needs and market gaps, you'll never be anything but opportunistic. You'll be running after opportunities rather than leading with a sense of Mission. You'll be defined by what is rather than inspiring what could be.

But it is important to ensure that brands today are first and foremost change agents. Their job isn't to make overblown promises their products can't keep. They must give us hope for a slightly brighter, better tomorrow. Help us become who we want to be and live how we want to live.

And for this they must hold meaning rather than being just 'mirages' of marketing. From an individual, psychological perspective, to remind us who we are, as Hannah Arendt already understood in 1958 (Arendt, 1958) and want to be, as Grant McCracken expanded in the 1980s

(McCracken, 1988). From a sociological perspective, to not just echo and mirror us but enable true, resonant dialogues and experiences (Rosa, 2019). And, not the least, from an economic perspective, to re-strengthen our belief in capitalism and democracy to still be the best way going forward (Martin, 2019).

There are many good examples of this throughout the book. And all our guest authors and their respective brands show how this works by sharing their experiences in Part Three.

Second: Don't let data drive your dream but share it

Marc Pritchard, CMO of P&G, was one of the first to kick off a more mature and balanced assessment of our shiny new digital world when he said in 2017, 'The days of digital all are numbered' (Scharrer, 2019). This attitude is gaining ground. One of the latest to prominently announce shifting their focus from performance marketing back to including more traditional brand-building communication was Adidas in the autumn of 2019 (Vizard, 2019). Neither of these two are rejecting the possibilities of online communication, data mining, re-targeting, individualized interaction... What they are doing is recognizing and utilizing these possibilities while being equally aware of their limitations.

There's a difference between tactical communication and strategic brand building. Quantity and quality are often opposing goals. Efficiency is not the same as effectiveness. Individual marketing fulfils other functions than public campaigns. Thus, it can never be either/or, you always need 'as well as'. This realization is settling in now. The big data party isn't over by any means, but it seems we're coming back to our senses.

As with the previous point, we are convinced that it's necessary to re-order and reprioritize things a bit. Ueber-Brands are built on conviction, not calculation. Their point is to give perspectives vs hunt us down; inspire us and not just track our cookies. They work best if they pull more than they push. Data and performance marketing can thus be very helpful in connecting with targets, but they shouldn't take over. They are tools for sharing your dream, but they shouldn't drive it. Because today's algorithms and AI aren't really good at that yet, if they'll ever be (McEwan, 2019).

US philosopher John Searle made the interesting distinction between machines and programs in his famous 'Chinese Room Argument' (Searle, 1980), explaining how the latter can't think because they don't understand.

They follow pre-set formulas and don't interact with meaning. They don't 'make sense', they simply run their program.

Unfortunately, that is still the big problem with AI in today's marketing world, or the world at large. It is artificial, all right, but intelligent, not so much. Besides, inspiring people needs emotional intelligence, empathy and lucidity, head and heart. And that is why Ueber-Brands must use data and their programs with caution, and our model is built accordingly, giving digital communication an integral but not a dominant role.

Third: Elevate the tangible by reaching for the intangible

'The mystery and the protocol, it's not there to keep us apart. It's there to keep us alive,' says Olivia Colman as Queen Elizabeth II in season 3 of *The Crown*. The same holds true for Ueber-Brands. You need proper context and an entourage to elevate yourself. But above all you need mystery and Myth. To transcend the everyday you must rise to a higher level. Just emotionalizing your products and services, your brand and its relations, is not enough. You need to lift people and connect them with what they want to be and what they could be, beyond what they are and what is. It's about aspiration.

This is why we made 'Write Your Myth' the second step in our six steps to create an Ueber-Brand, right after 'Set Your Mission'. Because, for Ueber-Brands, a brand narrative is not just a means to structure and integrate all their communications and interactions. That too. It's primarily a way to shine brighter and lead higher, hold meaning and have cultural significance, inspire their followers and for all of us to move up and on. And for the same reason, not just any story will do, you need one with mythical qualities.

Because myths aren't just 'false stories' as the word is often used colloquially. They talk about our 'collective dreams', as Joseph Campbell put it (Campbell, 1988). They hold us together as societies, they connect groups and inspire movements, and they help us individually to figure out who we are, what we want to be and where we want to go. So that our Ueber-Brand experiences don't end up making us feel, as TS Eliot put it so poignantly, 'We had the experience but missed the meaning' (Eliot, 1952).

Fourth: Don't declare. Do!

Fourth and finally: We are living in an experience economy. People are sick and tired of dull, self-congratulatory brand promotions interrupting their lives, even if they're just watching some tacky 'unboxing' on YouTube. They want brands to add value right when and where they pop up, not just promise it.

Ueber-Brands thus thrive on 'Ideas That Do' as we called them in our first book (Schaefer and Kuehlwein, 2015). The whole content and community craze in marketing has certainly led to some excess – not every shampoo needs to come with a tutorial in female equality. But, in essence, we don't think there's a way back. The 'podcast class', as *The New York Times* called it (Green, 2019), does prefer entertainment and education, advice, support, connections and experiences over unrequested and uninteresting brand declarations or irrelevant messages. And who would blame them!?

Let's face it, it is indeed one of the biggest advantages of the 'digital revolution' that brands have so many more (and often more economic and effective) opportunities to engage with people directly. Let's use them and think twice before we resort to shouting or retargeting someone with the twentieth offer on Venice flights because they booked some three months ago.

Creativity in marketing today no longer means sugar-coating the 'bitter' brand message. We are all challenged to constantly come up with new and surprising ways on where and how our brand can positively impact people's lives and our societies as a whole. This can lead to great partnerships with NGOs, artists, filmmakers, journalists or technology developers, as P&G announced at the 2019 Cannes Lions Festival (Shoot, 2019). Or it can 'just' mean creating more convenient and exciting retail experiences, like Hublot has attempted with its 'video-clientele suite', which allows customers to connect with the store for a real-life consultation online (White, 2018).

But 'doing' is not just the imperative in engaging and interacting with your targets. It's the rule for your whole brand building, which is why we put 'Do' as the second step in our programme, before your brand should start talking and daring. Above and beyond all, you must live your Brand Mission and Myth in all you do, from sourcing to sharing, truthfully inside out. Because declaring without doing is not good. But not doing as declared is even worse.

Six steps – three phases

Dream. Do. Dare. We've framed our brand elevation programme in these simple and inspiring terms to signal right away that this is about action. No overwrought theory, no complex model, no big words – or only occasionally. This is a simple, but not necessarily easy and hopefully inspiring, six-step process in three phases.

Dream

The starting and anchor point of everything else: Your Brand Mission and Myth. Its reason for being and your reason for even considering reading all this and following suit. And the story you want to tell the world.

1 *Set Your Mission.*
   Start by understanding yourself, check how this fits with your world and put it all in a brand strategy.

2 *Write Your Myth.*
   Unite truth and imagination for mythical stories that take your brand and its fans higher.

Do

The biggest challenge in elevating your brand: Being true to your Mission and Myth in everything you do. Internally and externally. Bringing your convictions and your targets' aspirations to life and living them daily.

3 *Realize Your Dream.*
   Create and celebrate your products and services as ideals manifested.

4 *Live Your Dream.*
   Build your organization and design your Brand Presence and experiences to radiate inside out and outside in.

Dare

The way your brand must interact with the world: Courageous and confident, like a born leader. With authority and integrity. Inspired by and inspiring your targets, above all your Ueber-Target. And letting your Myth shine through in all the stories you'll tell and do.

5 *Find Your Ueber-Target.*
   Define your muse as well as your other fans and targets and use them to guide all your decisions.

6 *Ignite All Targets.*
   Integrate all stakeholders and partners to jointly make your Ueber-Brand succeed and create a movement.

The Ueber-Triangle

Yes, logically, all should happen in the above order. Practically, it'll be often in parallel. And in reality, it must be a non-stop feedback loop. So, our model is a circular triangle.

That's impossible? Well, that's the first lesson: Ueber-Brands should never accept 'no' as an answer and should at least strive to square the circle – or round the triangle. They might not always succeed, but maybe they'll at least come up with something inspiring and illuminating in the attempt, like da Vinci did with his Vitruvian man.

And one last, but essential point: Don't even start this whole process without the C-suite not just aware but involved. As explained, this is not 'just' a marketing exercise, this is all based on the principles of Ueber-Brands. They demand a holistic and wholehearted way of brand building. And as much as they thrive on making the impossible possible, even they have to face the reality that this is only doable with leadership support.

FIGURE P2.1 The six steps to elevate your brand are organized in three phases, building on each other and connected in a continuous feedback cycle

SOURCE The authors (2020)

PS: We use the term 'Mission' in the truest and widest sense, meaning to define why you started your business and what this brings to the world; why this is important. Many, us included, also use here words like 'Purpose' or 'True North' or 'Why'. And that's perfectly fine as long as all are clear what is meant.

What is important however is not to muddle things by heaping statements on top of each other – a 'purpose' statement topped by a 'vision' statement defining the business goal, supported by a 'mission' statement outlining your offers. And to avoid that we simply co-opted the term Mission for the single one statement that you need: outlining your purpose and your vision for a better or easier or sweeter... world. The 'other' mission that defines what you do, we call 'building blocks', because these build (on) your Mission, they don't just state it.

And with that said, let's start setting your Mission.

Step 1: Set Your Mission

The first step is always the hardest. This is true for everything in life, and building an Ueber-Brand is no exception.

It sounds easy to define your Mission, but once you've tried it, you know it's not. Not if you're just starting out with your head full of ideas – and neither when you've been in business for a while, supposedly clear about what you do and why. To a large degree, this has something to do with the good old saying about the wood and the trees – you're lacking the productive distance to see the full picture. You're too involved, cognitively but also emotionally.

This is where consultants usually help – or any other third party for that matter. It's easier for them to find the Archimedean point outside 'your world' that provides the lever to move it – or grasp it in this case.

But the difficulty also comes from the mere fact that you're trying to decide something that reaches deep and far. Defining your Mission, or purpose, as many call it, goes to the core of your sense of self, your perceived reason for being as a brand. And it has long-ranging consequences since you're trying to set yourself up for the future, for as long as this may possibly be.

Alas, it's a job full of importance, laden with expectations and fraught with anxieties. And you had best approach it like any other big and challenging journey: Step-by-step, bottom-up. Starting with yourself.

Your self?

There are as many ways to go about understanding yourself, ie your brand, as there are people – or brands. You can turn every stone, meditate for inner illumination or systematically analyse every aspect of your business from sourcing to service and back again. The key here is, however, not so much what you do but how you do it, which is why we've put down a list of attributes, manners you should take to heart as you embark on this trip of navel-gazing.

THE RIGHT RESEARCH ATTITUDE

- Act like an archaeologist or history buff – every tiny bit holds a story.
- Listen, listen, listen – look and learn, eyes and ears wide open.
- Probe – be investigative, dig beyond the obvious.
- No judgement, evaluation or dismissal. It's about collecting not sorting yet.
- Search different places and faces – factory, marketing, ex-CEO, trophy shelf...
- Be sensitive to nuances and details – often, the best is unsaid or between the lines.
- Use hypotheses as guides, not blinders. Always open to course correct.

The goal in this first step is to gather as many insights and ideas as you possibly can about what makes your company and your brand unique. These can be big or small, trivial or essential, functional or cultural, facts or fiction... everything matters, or could matter, more correctly. Because at this point you're not evaluating yet, you're simply collecting. You're taking stock, looking at anything that could possibly lead to the true essence of why your business must exist, why it's not just a business but a collective must, why it has a reason for being beyond making money. And this can come from pretty much anywhere.

Archive dive

One of the things that invariably yields the most interesting and inspiring results here is a deep look into the archives, or whatever comes close to it. Most any brand we've ever worked with started out by either denying the existence of anything like a brand archive or discounted its value. And yet, pretty much all of them were surprised.

For a big hair care brand, for example, the archives amounted to not much more than a box with some old brochures, packaging samples and newsletters. And yet the old pack copy gave us interesting clues about the way it used to look at its product – long forgotten over the course of countless management changes. Or read our interview with Laura Burdese, CEO of Acqua di Parma, in Part Three of this book. Going through its archives and digging up historical titbits not only gave us a better understanding of the brand and its founders' Mission. It gave the entire team a whole new appreciation of the richness, authenticity and significance of its brand.

Stakeholder interviews

This is a must in every change or purpose finding process. For a start, it is crucial to give all stakeholders a sense of ownership. Nothing is worse than developing a purpose that will not be fully embraced by the entire organization, or at least its majority. But, beyond that, it's really the input you need – the thinking, the knowledge, the ideas of as many people and perspectives as possible. Because only then will you be able to form a well-rounded picture of the whole.

In most cases, a 'Mission finding' process is started by the top management or the marketing department. And it's easy to assume that you can see all – and further – from the top. But, of course, nothing is further from the truth. Visions are nice and shiny. The reality, however, is usually down and dirty. And reality is what we're after, because we are still on a search mission, trying to gather and understand what is and what has been; to put our vision on solid ground.

So, never treat this part as a 'must' to get over with as quickly as possible. Together with the archive dive this is probably the most illuminating part of the journey, if done right – no matter if you do it all internally or with external partners. The least you'll get is a better understanding of your organization and the different points of view within it. For outside partners it's practically inevitable to talk to stakeholders beyond their immediate contacts, else they'd never be able to gain a true understanding of your brand and your business.

We once did a 'Mission and Myth' project for a global apparel brand. The interviews with key market leaders were indispensable in identifying not only the brand perception but also the challenges and strengths around the world. But we also chose to talk to the company founder, long retired by then, as well as a production assistant who had been with the company for decades. And those were ultimately the most revealing interviews, the ones that really helped us 'get' the soul of the brand, its core.

We therefore highly recommend never to short shrift this part but get a good cross section of stakeholder interviews:

- long-standing or past employees with a passion for the brand;
- key decision makers across disciplines;
- international team members, especially from key markets;
- the founder(s) or anyone close to them;
- people in sourcing, production, design… those bringing the brand to life every day;
- retailers, store managers… those with first-hand customer experience;
- trade partners and/or suppliers;
- external experts, eg editors or analysts – if important for the brand and its reception.

In terms of a questionnaire or interview guide: Yes, you should have one, to make sure you capture all the important points. Of course, in most cases you could also go back and ask again, but you'll never get answers as honest and inspiring as the first time around. Which gets us to three other important aspects:

- First, do not send out your questionnaire beforehand. You don't want preconceived, 'correct' responses. You want the truth, and that comes out better spontaneously. Should your interview partner want to check something or need to refresh their memory they can always send you the information afterwards.

- Second, assure your interviewee absolute confidentiality. And mean it! People are never as open and truthful when they know their boss is listening. For this reason alone, it is usually advisable to at least do this part of your Mission journey with an outside partner.

- And third, go with the flow during the interview. Create a casual, conversational atmosphere. Yes, probe, but don't grill. Don't put your partner in the hot seat. You want people to be relaxed, to remember things they otherwise might forget or not deem fit for an 'official' report. And if this means you digress or dive into details at one point – that's exactly what you are there for. To remember you cover everything important, you always have your guide to double-check as you go, or at the end.

Reality check

After the past and the people, of course, you also must look at the facts. What is your organization/structure? What are your rules and processes? Where do you source and how? How do you produce and how not? Which people do you recruit, and what are your recruiting criteria? What is your distribution like? Who are your partners – who do you select and why? What are your budgets – what do you spend money on and what not? And so forth.

This all seems so obvious that it's often overlooked. Far too often. But, again, it can be quite eye-opening.

Once, for example, we noticed during a factory visit of a pet-food client that all employees were wearing hair-nets. A fact that everybody had taken for granted and never even mentioned in any discussion. But for us, looking at it with outsider's eyes, it was indicative and inspiring, ultimately leading the way we captured the Mission around the concept of human-grade pet food.

Beliefs and values

Beyond the above three ways to analyse yourself and your company and hunt for your Mission there are numerous others, of course. Many clients like to do workshops for example, which can help, though we prefer single interviews at this point in the process to ensure we really get the different perspectives without peer pressure. Others already include consumers in their self-search, for example through ethnographies or netnographies (see also Step 5 – page 111), which we have often done as well. For Acqua di Parma, for example, we talked to long-standing regulars of its Milan flag-ship and *barbiere*, which proved helpful in understanding the uniqueness of its service. But these were highly qualitative deep dives. More standard consumer research is often not of much value yet, though it is later (see the next chapter).

What's key in these first steps towards setting your Mission is that you take an honest, inquisitive and open look at the realities of your brand and your business. Gather all that has been and currently is – the factual as well as the anecdotal, the cultural or emotional as well as the functional and processual, the visual as well as the hearsay. Record it all and put the most interesting and inspiring points on boards or charts for further use through-out the process.

And then, out of all this, try to deduct five to ten core beliefs or value statements. Not abstract value terms like 'creativity' or 'passion' or, worse, 'authenticity'. This won't help you one bit because these words are too generic and too all-inclusive. What company would not like to think of itself as creative, passionate and authentic?

What you need to move further towards a meaningful Mission Statement is turning all the above gathered facts and fictions into five to ten true sentences that are as specific and unique as they can possibly be. Ideally even controversial or at least provocative, because then you know you're on to something that only you deliver and that your Ueber-Target will cherish. Something that might not be right for everyone, but perfect for those that will take you further and above the average and the mass (see 'Dare', page 50).

And it is very helpful if your organization's personality or personalities shine through in these statements. If this indeed is 'you' speaking and not some polished marketing gobbledygook. For example, we once put down five core beliefs for a premium, fashion-forward hairstyling brand. Two of those read: 'We believe beauty is boring... bad style is ten times better than having no style at all'. Now that's a gutsy statement for a beauty brand selling style. And one where you immediately get a 'feel' for the brand.

Your world?

Naturally, you don't live in a vacuum. And so, all the self-searching must of course be balanced with a thorough look at what's going on around you – if for no other reason than to understand what it says about you and what it means for you.

Most companies are traditionally good at this, since it is the normal starting point which everyone learns in Marketing 101. As we explained going into this part of the book and in our previous one, we are coming from a slightly different angle. Our experience and research have shown again and again that today's Ueber-Brands are less concerned with what others do or want, but more driven by what they believe in and think the world needs. Which is the reason we started this process with *your self*. Yet, even then, you cannot and should not ignore the realities you live in and the people you market to.

There are far too many methodologies to discuss here and most readers will be familiar with many of them from their daily work. So, let's focus on our goal and share some insights on how to look at your 'market and competition' as well as your 'clients, customers and trends' when you're out to 'Set Your Mission'.

Market and competition

Peter Walshe, Global Director at research group Millward Brown, says, 'Difference makes the Difference. The brands in the Top 100 that score most highly on being differentiated from their competitors have grown much more dramatically – by an average of 124%' (Walshe, 2016). That should give you a good compass on how to look at your market and especially your competition. Where and how can my brand make a meaningful difference?

1 COUNTER

If everyone goes right, look left. Analyse the parameters and para-digms of your market and keep a close watch on your competition. Be sure to respect the base contracts and expectations of your cate-gory. But never be content in simply living up to them – or improving them in convenience or price. Ueber-Brands do not follow, but set new, higher standards or provide a whole new look at a given topic. In that sense, don't so much try to hit category benchmarks, but consider setting new ones, don't think about how to beat your com-petition, but open a whole new playing field. Just think of Red Bull going against all soda taste profiles to become a $6 billion brand. Or Camper, crossing dress shoes with casual footwear in 1975, unleash-ing a whole new market and still being at its top 35 years later.

2 CONNECT

Don't just count but connect the dots. Numbers are all about inter-pretation. There's a false sense of security in quantitative data as it pretends to be objective and give control where it doesn't, and, more importantly, in seemingly talking present or future while in fact only reflecting the past and, possibly, projections from it. Al-ways look twice and harder. Listen to your gut – if something feels wrong, it most likely is. Crosstab, crosscheck and connect results and see if they can provide new insights. We have yet to find an algorithm or AI better at truly understanding what's going on, let alone imagining what could be, than our good old human brains and gut reactions. Because you hardly ever get anywhere interest-ing and truthful without empathy and intuition.

3 COMPARE

Think outside the box. No, really. Never forget to look outside your immediate category if you want to find inspiration. In our previous book we talked about 'code-poaching', brands upgrading themselves by adopting codes from other categories. That is one way of 'inspiring' your brand from the outside, though not the best and most sustainable. What we recommend instead is 'imitative innovation'. Take ideas from beyond your business and see how they can lead to a new take on it. Look at adjacent ones or others that are usually ahead due to a higher churn or trend affinity, eg fashion or beauty. Because they might show you the way – up or out.

Clients, consumers and trends

While setting your Mission is indeed an internal job, your customers should be in the room when you talk about it (see following chapter). Not literally, although that can happen as well. At a big consumer goods client of ours, for example, the trade liaison and category manager are always part of any brand equity discussion, often bringing its customer counterparts along.

No, what we mean is you should use your customers past, present and future as a source of inspiration and as a reality check in developing your Mission. Not more, but neither less. Client research should never be driver or judge of your Mission. It's an old adage that people don't really know what they want – and certainly not what they will want.

But what customers and consumers can do is input, provide insights and ideas – even if it's in the form of cut-outs. One client of ours for example, a global appliance manufacturer, has created life-size stand-up personas of all its target segments to accompany staff to every strategy session. Others, however, are perfectly fine with just creating mood boards, having indicative quotes, surprising facts or unexpected trend statements, etc, to provide perspective and inspiration in the Mission Workshop.

One word to end: No matter what you have or commission in terms of customer and trend research, the general rule is qualitative beats quantitative. At this stage you need insights, nuggets that can stimulate your thinking, take you to a deeper understanding. And those you gain usually more from zooming in, getting as close to people and their dreams and contradictions as possible, rather than looking at cold numbers.

So, if you intend to do extra research as part of this process, go for an approach that uses projective-associative techniques to bring out that which words and numbers, our logic, can't reach. Particularly interesting in this context are ethnographic or anthropological studies, which try to uncover the subconscious motivations connected to a certain product or category and its cultural codes (see also Step 5 on page 111).

And if you're assessing and summarizing existing research or reports, please do so in a way that stimulates more than being overly 'correct'. Sharper points lead to sharper thinking. And if all else fails: Get in touch with us and we'll help.

Your brand!

Now it's time to switch gears from a hunter-gatherer mode to one that brings out the creator-visionary in you. And that is usually best done in company, playful company, that is. Because, as Friedrich Schiller already knew, 'We are only fully human when we play.' And this certainly applies to being creative.

Mission Workshop

The cornerstone and first step in developing your Brand Mission is a workshop. Some clients have done workshops all along the way in gathering information about their brand or their consumers, for example, and that's ok. But be careful to not over-workshop people. We prefer there to be one central workshop, and this is the one where all the essential participants come together, share their ideas and 'play-work' together towards an inspiring Mission.

PARTICIPANTS

Just like with the stakeholder interviews, we prefer the workshop participants to be a good cross-section of employees, senior to junior, management to production, longstanding to fresh-faced, C-suite to R&D. And some inspiring extras – internal or external. At a recent workshop for an optics brand, for example, the most inspiring ideas and phrasings came from the HR person and an external writer.

And creative expression, ie phrasing, is an important aspect – if not the most important one. Because the way you put things makes a big difference, and the words you choose can open up totally new areas. That's why we usually advise that people are invited that are known to be imaginative, playful, creative rather than those that hold the important role.

Generally, 12 is the perfect number of participants – small and intimate enough to keep everyone active and heard, but big enough to allow for variety and break-out in sub-groups. But you can go up to 16 or as low as eight. Anything above or below becomes tricky.

FORMAT/DURATION

The ideal is a day and a half. Start the first day in the afternoon with intro, warm up and initial ideation, often based on some homework (see below), getting people to know each other and in the mood. The next morning, start ideating from various aspects and continue, with little coffee breaks and a lunch break (ideally with some fresh air), through the afternoon. Usually after 4 or 5 pm people are dead, and some participants need to catch planes, etc.

GUIDE

There are many ways to run a Mission-finding workshop. It's best to hire a skilled moderator and let them advise you. Having a workshop run by a team member is never as effective. A person who is involved cannot be impartial enough to treat all members and opinions equally, yet knowledgeable and experienced enough to nudge the team and lead through slumps. Plus, you invariably pull organizational dynamics and politics into the workshop. And, this person moderating could not be a true participant.

In our experience, it's best to start off with a little homework given to participants one week in advance. It should be something that goes to the topic while at the same time explaining a bit about the person and setting a light-hearted tone. Examples are: Bring something that represents brand X for you, and something that doesn't (anything goes, except products of the brand). Tell us about your first encounter with brand X – personally and professionally. When were you most proud working for brand X?

This is followed by an initial, 'unguided' ideation session, using the ideas presented as springboards to develop directions or important points for the Brand Mission.

Then we often introduce the learning and insights from the steps above clustered along the four Cs: Competence and character (the brand); category and competition (market); constituents and concerns (customers); culture and currents (trends). This way, you look at the challenge from various angles – which is why we often also let people rotate seats as we go, to even literally change their perspective.

Once you've gone through all four perspectives, you do a first round of evaluation of the ideated statements or words/kernels of ideas, usually by

FIGURE 8.1 A way to search/organize insights for your Mission workshop

CHARACTER & COMPETENCE	CONSTITUENCIES & CONCERNS
All about the company, its history, its DNA, strengths and weaknesses, milestones and turning points.	All about our stakeholders – internal and external. Employees, partners, consumers... public at large.
Where do we come from? Who and how are we?	What do 'they' want, need, dream of? How are their/our realities?
CATEGORIES & COMPETITION	CULTURE & CURRENTS
Business environment, market dynamics and competitve insights.	The world and our moment in it – societally, politically, culturally.
What and who's driving the environment we operate in?	Where are we heading? What are we missing? What are we up against?

SOURCE The authors (2020)

individual 'power dotting', followed by a joint clustering and discussion of the results.

After lunch we often break into sub-groups to pull people out of their digestive slump, with each group working on one of the previously formed directional clusters. Then a shared presentation of results, potentially followed by another round.

The last 30 minutes are for summary and next steps – because it's important for everyone to understand that this is just the beginning of the journey, not the end.

Mission writing

This sounds easy and fun, yet in reality it's the toughest and often longest part, requiring a lot of back-and-forth and definitely external strategy-creative support.

A Mission (Statement) must be big and bold, yet as specific and ownable as possible. It should be simple and easily understood, but also meaningful – for inside experts and the world at large. And it should be original, inspiringly phrased. Or, as Roy Spence, one of the first to write about the idea of brand purpose, put it: 'Aim high, but don't end up in the ether' (Spence, 2009).

Here are four Mission Statements that we like and why. Two we can take (partial) credit for and two we just like, impartially:

- Natura Pet Food: 'We make food for dogs, not dog food'.
  It's clear and simple yet quite a competitive and bold statement. And certainly, one that's meaningful and differentiated – within the industry but also in our societies at large. And, because of all this, it can easily be translated into very concrete, actionable directions and standards across the whole value chain from sourcing through to distribution, even into CSR.

- Vice: 'The definitive guide to an uncertain world' (Vice, 2019).
  A little less specific than the above, but that's no surprise given the span of the Vice brand vs Natura, which is very single-minded. And that's why we include it here: Because it's much more challenging to find a succinct Mission when your brand reaches further than one product category. This is when you easily end up in la-la land, and Vice didn't. Though it may not be immediately obvious what the brand does, the statement sets a fairly clear purpose for all the Vice activities. And, it does so with a distinct voice in an intriguing manner. Makes you curious to explore the brand and our uncertain world.

- Acqua di Parma: 'Celebrating the sophisticated lightness of Italy'.
  This is another example of how to set a clear and compelling Mission for a brand that covers multiple categories and is still expanding. It's clearly rooted in the brand's iconic Colonia yet opening itself towards anything that captures the easy elegance and sunny sophistication so typical of Italian life and style. For more, see the interview with Laura Burdese, CEO of Acqua di Parma, in Part Three of this book.

- Nike: 'If you have a body, you're an athlete. Bring inspiration and innovation to every athlete in the world' (Nike, 2019).
  Last but not least: An example everybody knows – or thinks they know. Because many would cite 'Just Do It' as Nike's Mission. But that's its tagline. And this is an important point: Your Mission Statement can become your communication idea or sign off, but it doesn't have to. In fact, it most often doesn't. Even Apple, the other famous purpose-driven brand, which some see as the origin of the whole purpose/why movement (Sinek, 2009), doesn't use 'Think Different' as its Mission. Originally, under Steve Jobs, it was 'Making tools for the mind that advances humankind'. Now it's a convoluted mess, if you trust some reviews (Lund, 2017).

Either way, the point is, a tagline is usually far too snappy – and that means unspecific – to be a Mission Statement. It's written to sign off and thus work in conjunction with a whole array of communication. In and of itself it's often meaningless – or certainly not specific enough to give actionable direction to a company, as the above examples show. Neither 'Just Do It' nor 'Think Different' would give you any clue what the heck they talk about – without all the brand products, activities, communication you've come to associate with them. And those were driven by the Mission Statement. The tag just sums it up.

Having said all this, we are not in the same camp as those who think Mission Statements are solely for internal use. The opposite. In order to inspire and motivate all stakeholders it should be communicated to and understood by all – internal as well as external. Which is one reason they should be simple and easily understood.

Oh, and the phrasing issue: Many are adamant that a Mission Statement should always start with 'We exist to…' to set yourself on a path of writing an 'existential' reason-for-being statement. We applaud the sentiment, and it may help, but if you don't need those crutches throw 'em out.

From Mission to strategy

Of course, the Mission Statement is just that: The overarching direction or rallying cry. In order to make it actionable, you must translate it into a proper brand strategy, or as Simon Sinek would say: 'Start with Why, but know How. And then What' (Sinek, 2009).

Apart from why, how, what, there are dozens of brand strategy or equity models in all shapes – pyramids, circles, diamonds… even keyholes. Some are more explicit or complex, depending on your view. Others are simpler or simplistic, like the three questions above. At the end, however, they all do talk about two main aspects: What is it that you do and offer? And how do you do it and come across? Those are the things you need to define next – based on your Mission. Of course, there's always also the question of Who you do this for and what kind of relationship you want to build with them. But that we cover in detail in Step 5, 'Find Your Ueber-Target'.

WHAT DO YOU DO AND OFFER?

Again, lots of terms being used here… benefits, discriminator, points of parity and difference, essence… We like 'building blocks' the best. The things you do to fulfil your Mission and build your brand and its equity.

Try to make them no more than five. That forces you to cluster and think bigger, but still allows you to be concrete. And write them in full sentences, just like your Mission and beliefs. No single buzzwords like 'superior cleaning' or *Fahrvergnüegen*.

Traditionally, you can differentiate here between functional, emotional and experiential benefits, each supported with so-called reasons to believe (RTBs). This way, you could structure your brand strategy in three building blocks, each with a strong benefit statement and its support points. We've often done it that way and it works. But...

What we think about RTBs you have already read in Part One of this book, or our previous one. We prefer stories to believe (STBs), as they create a narrative, which is automatically less technical or 'marketing-y' and more human and emotional. And for that very reason we're also often not happy with splitting functional and emotional or experiential benefits. Everything you do should work on all three levels – functionally beneficial, emotionally engaging and experientially intriguing, so dissecting it is usually difficult and not necessarily helpful. Especially if your brand isn't a single product brand. Once you have multiple 'functional' benefits with their respective emotional and experiential ones, you're better off organizing your building blocks around those different areas and uniting the three benefit dimensions including their STBs into multiple, integrated benefit stories.

Another thing we've had some good experiences with in defining your 'What' is to work your building blocks two-pronged, towards your commercial promise and your societal pledge – see Figure 8.2. This works particularly for brands that do have a dual Mission, a business and an ecological or ethical goal, like Patagonia, REI, Everlane, Etsy or Ben & Jerry's. But, speaking of Ben & Jerry's, even for big multinationals like Unilever or luxury groups like Kering, who are increasingly putting their holding or corporate brand forward with strong sustainability or social objectives, this makes increasing sense (Sherman, 2019).

FIGURE 8.2   It can help to break down your Mission into two pillars to organize your 'What'

SOURCE   The authors (2020)

HOW DO YOU DO IT AND HOW DO YOU COME ACROSS?

The second big set of questions in turning your Mission into a clear brand strategy revolves around How: How do you do it? How do you source, produce…? How are you organized? How is your culture? But also: How do you talk? How do you look and feel as a brand?

The first set of 'Hows' pertaining to how you go about your business are traditionally included in the RTBs, the reasons to believe. This is where you'd talk about 'This deep black stone, a rare and fascinating mineral extracted in Russia' like aforementioned L'Officine Universelle Buly does. Or you'd present your trainers as 'one of a kind rock star instructors' like SoulCycle does (SoulCycle, nd).

But these examples already show that the traditional thinking in RTBs and the separation of functional, emotional and experiential benefits we discussed above don't really work anymore. Modern, successful Ueber-Brands weave them all into integrated stories – the different What dimensions and even the Hows. Function, emotion, experiences, support points, design aspects, recruitment criteria, cultural traits… all is rolled into simple, compelling narratives. A perfect example is SoulCycle, because after introducing the instructors they continue like this:

> They guide riders through an inspirational, meditative fitness experience that's designed to benefit the body, mind and soul. Set in a dark candlelit room to high-energy music, our riders move in unison as a pack to the beat and follow the signature choreography of our instructors. The experience is tribal. It's primal. It's fun.

The second group of Hows deals with what's varyingly called brand character or tonality or personality. A great example here is Southwest Airlines, promising that its service is delivered with a sense of 'warmth, friendliness, individual pride, and Company Spirit'. Or Ritz-Carlton which claims they are 'Ladies and Gentlemen serving Ladies and Gentlemen' (Ritz-Carlton, 2020). You'll find more on this in Step 4 (page 98).

But again, looking at these in traditional terms as brand characters or brand tonality descriptors doesn't suffice anymore. Because it implies something 'put on' vs something lived.

With Ueber-Brands the behaviour is the brand – and behavioural traits are thus not 'just' the brand tonality. They are an integral part of the package, intricately linked with What you do and Why you do it. They are part and parcel of your Mission brought to live in a credible, unique manner.

Hence: Yes, do think about your brand strategy as translating your Mission into What building blocks and How aspects, explaining How you make what you do and How you are while you do it. But then integrate it all into compelling storylines that take your Mission into action – functionally satisfying, emotionally engaging and experientially intriguing. We are living in the experience economy, after all.

Internal feedback

This last step in developing your Brand Mission and your brand strategy is optional, but often advisable. Like the stakeholder interviews, an internal feedback round might not only provide great learning, it also helps to give the organization, or at least those parts whose feedback you seek, a sense of ownership.

A beauty client we recently worked with did a series of workshops to involve different teams in different markets and gain their buy-in before finalizing and deploying its new Mission Statement. The overall idea and statement didn't change, but it brought valuable improvements on some of the ways we laid out our Whats and Hows.

Whose feedback you ask for and how many people you involve in this is completely dependent on the company, its size, its organization and the situation at hand. There are no recommendations possible. Perhaps just a general tip: Here groups do work better than single interviews, or even digitally administered surveys.

RECAP: TO DO – STEP 1

- Investigate your brand/company – with an open mind.
- Dive into your archives – if you think you don't have any, raid the 'junk' cabinets.
- Interview key stakeholders – C-suite to workbench, senior to junior, internal/external.
- Compare with your realities – sourcing/production, organization, budget...
- Summarize in 5 to 10 beliefs – as unique and controversial as possible.
- Analyse market and competition – where do you/can you make a difference?

- Check against your consumers and trends – category and culture at large.
- Discuss all in Mission Workshop – and ideate Mission Directions.
- Phrase into snappy Mission Statements – big and bold, yet specific and ownable.
- Translate into full brand equity – including What and How.
- Optional: Collect feedback from key staff not involved yet.

Step 2: Write Your Myth

The first myth ever written with a mission is probably the *Aeneid*. Commissioned by Augustus and created by Virgil, its purpose was to heal years of civil war and legitimize the new emperor by providing a shared sense of past as well as future, pride as well as perspective. And it worked perfectly.

Of course, it's a bit long for today's attention spans with its 12 books, but it's amazing how its famed opening almost captures the whole purpose in a few words: 'I sing of arms and the man whom fate had sent' (Ferry, 2017). Virgil subtly links the very real Octavius with the legendary hero Aeneas, presenting the former as the latter's logical heir. And it is written in a way that draws us in, so intriguing and full of suspense that our cognition and critical thinking are immediately suspended.

And those are the two main points that are crucial in writing your Myth: Fuse truth with vision, not to say fiction. And tell a winning story we want to believe in, or 'a public dream', as Joseph Campbell calls it (Campbell, 1988).

With truth and vision

The first thing to understand and make sure in writing your Myth is that your history is not necessarily a story. The two can have a large degree of overlap, but usually you want to focus on a select number of facts only.

Nobody cares about a perfect timeline with every innovation or move you ever made. What turns history into an intriguing story is that you pick those true points that naturally connect into a narrative, the narrative that feeds and leads to your Mission. And that you leave out those that don't fit or are irrelevant.

And then you work it. Embellish a bit, dramatize, wring it with a fair dose of creativity and your eye on your vision. Don't lie! But massage the truth if necessary so the message gets clear – and interesting. There's always multiple ways to look at a 'fact' and interpret it.

So, let's see how to find and pick those facts that you can build your story around...

Founding Myth

It all starts at the beginning. We have yet to work on a brand where the founder, their ideas and the circumstances of founding the company are not the most inspiring and influential moments. Besides, you'd be hard-pressed to spin a credible story by ignoring or going against those aspects.

That doesn't mean you're stuck with the founding story you have. This is where selection and perspective come in. Let's take Acqua di Parma again to illustrate this (see also interview with CEO Laura Burdese in Part Three): The key historical facts haven't changed with the newly developed Mission and strategy, but the way they're being used has. In the past, for example, the brand focused on the founder being a noble man and the product initially sold at high-end haberdashers to support a luxury positioning, in communication often translated into classic codes of an aristocratic lifestyle and distinction. Now, the same facts are looked at differently. Yes, Carlo Magnani was a nobleman, but what's much more interesting is that he created the original Colonia for himself, which gives the brand authenticity and intimacy. Yes, the personal fragrance did grow into a brand through tailors, and its clients were naturally more often well off than not. But this also proves that the brand's genesis is intricately linked to Italian sartorial cunning and style, which gives its Mission of 'Celebrating the sophisticated lightness of Italy' credibility and historical grounding – way beyond fragrances.

Another example, from the opposite end of the spectrum, is TerraCycle. Read in Part Three how Tom Szaky talks about growing up in communist Hungary and being mesmerized by the sheer wastefulness in the United States, finding his first TV set in a junkyard, or how his initial employees were spineless, were treated like dirt and were not paid a dime – because they were worms. Both aspects became, in his own words, 'part of the Brand Myth attracting human resources and creating a place people want to work'. Because they immediately – and entertainingly – convince us that this young, well-educated *émigré* from Hungary is best equipped to change our perspective on waste.

FIGURE 9.1   Ben & Jerry's 'Cowmobile', now permanently parked in front of its visitor centre. An icon of the brand's social-activist nature from the founding days, when it was used to distribute free cones, also at protests

SOURCE   JP Kuehlwein (2014). Reproduced with the kind permission of Ben & Jerry's Homemade, Inc.

Apart from this, TerraCycle is also proof that a great story does not require a long history. Actually, we have often written stories solely focused on the founding of a brand, the zeitgeist, which incited it, and the inspiration, conviction and vision of its founder(s).

Culture query

The other two ways to find interesting angles and aspects in developing your mythical story are closely linked. Let's start with a look at the 'soft factors' of your organization, because that's what culture query means.

Basically, it's the same as digging up the Founding Myth, only that this time you look at the entire organization over time. What were its seminal moments? What anecdotes are still talked about? Which elements or stylistic idiosyncrasies first come to mind? What corporate social responsibility (CSR) programmes do you have? How to you pick your suppliers? Or your distribution? What are your human resources (HR) criteria? What do your Christmas parties or summer outings look like? What special 'rules' are in place, explicit or implicit? Or which ones are not?... The questions are endless, and often best researched by talking to employees, longtime ones as well as new arrivals (see also 'Stakeholder interviews' in Step 1, page 55, and the Airbnb case in Part Three). Because it's in the 'collective memory' of your brand that you'll find the core of its mythical power – as well as its manifestations, from which you'll need to write a vivid story.

But, again, be mindful which 'manifestations' you choose in building your Myth – not all are equally important or inspiring, and neither will all of them serve the tale you want to tell. And be clear how to interpret them. Look at them through the eye of your Mission to decide if and in what way they are helpful in elevating this Mission to a Myth, or if they are irrelevant or even misleading.

Look at Chobani, for example. What do you know about the brand? Greek yoghurt, relatively new, probably started in the 2000s, premium, one of the initiators of this category, good quality, high price… But… you've probably never heard that Chobani is Turkish for 'shepherd'. Or that it's the hardworking and compassionate spirit of these Kurdish mountain farmers that inspired the brand's founder, a Kurdish immigrant himself. And that this spirit permeates the company to this day, all the way to the preferred hiring of refugees or first-generation immigrants, the advocacy of its cause and the 'tent' and 'shepherd's gift' foundations to help local communities. If you're really interested, you can find information on all this on the brand's website (Chobani, 2020). But if you're like most of us, just a consumer of its products and communication, chances are you have no idea.

And that's the problem. Because this is a great case for a brand story *not* written, the culture *not* queried and reflected in the brand equity – a potential Brand Myth being underutilized, not to say unused. Just imagine if Chobani connected all the dots and told its tale loud and clear: How it could bolster product quality and drive distinctiveness, substantiate the premium pricing and make the company's philanthropy part and parcel of the whole endeavour. The brand could and would stand for so much more than just good yoghurt, like Ben & Jerry's does, for example. Or Whole Foods or Method or… It would gain much more equity, loyalty and stability in its premium position, never mind a great platform for communication and stakeholder engagement.

Semiology

Semiology or semiotics is the study of signs and symbols and thus naturally part of the above. But since it's such a special aspect in the context of brands and branding, we gave it its own section. Also, whereas you can easily do a culture query by yourself or with designated project leaders, a semiotic analysis is definitely something you need expert help with.

So, what happens during a semiotic analysis and what will you get out of it? In essence, you'll look at all signs connected with your company and brand. But this does not only mean signs in the colloquial sense of the word, ie billboards or icons, but anything that signifies something – ie it denotes or connotes something beyond itself. And that's pretty much everything from the name of the company to the way it's written, to your products, their names and design, their scent, texture, colour, their packaging... all the way to your communication and all the words, taglines and imagery you're using or have used prominently in the past.

And what do you get out of it? A semiotic analysis can be very helpful in deciding, for example, if a certain element you're intending to highlight in your Myth does indeed fit. Or it can help you evaluate different designs or names, checking what you communicate or associate beyond the obvious. It can also alert you to potential pitfalls in your communication. But, most of all, we like to use semiotics as an eye- and mind-opener, a way to see the often all-too-familiar with different eyes, uncover things you never knew were hidden or discover potentials that actually are in plain sight – once you know about them.

The following quotes give you a better idea of what we're talking about – and what you should be looking for. They are from various studies we've done over the years, anonymized of course. All thanks to Dominic Pettman, Professor at The New School University in New York and one of the world's master semiologists:

> Brand XYZ captures this powerful lifeline threading the primeval with the postmodern... a timely combination for today's bobos and urban nomads.
>
> The power of water can never be over-estimated, since it can save you, free you, or claim you.
>
> The word [ ] progresses in the same direction as a welcoming smile: The tongue pressing against the front teeth, and then opening into a gesture of appreciation or welcome.
>
> The emphasis on 'care' need not anchor the brand exclusively to maternal signifiers. This can be re-constellated to map on to younger motifs, such as 'intimacy', 'love', 'protection'... or 'stewardship'.

One last watch-out: *Nomen est omen*, your name is a sign, whether you want it to be or not. With a name like Hermès (messenger of the gods) it'll be hard to end up in the gutter – though there is a logistics company of the same name, but with a very different look and feel, obviously. If you call yourself 'L'Officine Universelle Buly à Paris' you have sophistication and the

FIGURE 9.2 L'Officine Universelle Buly celebrates its name and Napoleonic heritage

SOURCE: JP Kuehlwein (2019)

beauty of complexity basically written above your door (buly1803.com). Or just remember the example of Chobani and how the name tells an entire story – if only it was unlocked.

To higher ground

As summarized in Part One, Myths are Ueber-Stories, stories on higher ground – or those that take you there. They talk about that which words alone cannot express, about something bigger and more meaningful than the stories themselves. They explain the world and the way we like to see it. They are our way of making sense when science and reason can't make sense anymore.

And in this, Myths can let us 'reach beyond' the obvious, the physical, the 'real', to provide explanation and reassurance. Or they can 'guide us' in our actions and interactions, speak of values and show us ways to live up to them. Both directions are highly interesting for brands and often employed, though rarely with clear intention.

Consequently, the first thing you need to do in writing your Myth is to decide which route you want to follow.

Myths that reach beyond

'Remaining unknowable is the only true way to be known.' Colum McCann assigned this wonderful *bon mot* to the famous ballet dancer Rudolf Nureyev (McCann, 2003). I'm not sure if Nureyev was indeed that eloquent, but since we're talking myths... it's a great way to summarize the point and the power of this first direction you could take.

Brands that try to 'reach beyond' build their mythical story by tapping into that which can never truly or completely be known to us yet is essential to our lives. And they thus often prefer themselves to be shrouded in an aura of mystery, interacting in more subtle, sometimes even cerebral tones – without limiting the strength of their proposition. Actually, the opposite: They draw us in exactly because they give us a sense of connecting with something sublime. And that's hardly ever a shouting match.

The example par excellence in this is Crème de la Mèr, the high-end skin care brand from Estée Lauder, which sells itself as based on a magical broth made of kelp from the sea, the source of all life.

Another, shiny example is Swarovski, the global leader in crystals. Its superiority is clearly driven by innovative, precision glass-cutting technology – highly functional, man-made, here and now. Yet, they don't mind a connection with the eternal, mystical allure of naturally occurring rock crystal, being formed under pressure over eons of years in majestic mountains like the Alps.

Swarovski Kristallwelten is a great 'brand experience centre' that indirectly makes that connection and builds the Myth of Swarovski in a myriad of facets, so to speak. As of 2019 it's been visited by 15 million people from all around the world and has become one of Austria's top tourist destinations (Wikipedia, 2020).

From outside, the Kristallwelten (crystal worlds) look as if they were carved into the mountain. You actually walk into a giant's mouth – like a hero in a fairy tale. Inside, you move through a string of 'caves' designed like modern versions of 18th century curiosity cabinets, all filled with artistic installations around crystal and its fascinating sparkle and shine. And while it's clear that the products at the 'gift shop' are man-made, you can't help but imbue them with the magic of the mountains you just walked through, leaving you with the feeling that their sparkle is precious and powerful at the same time, and that the little pendant you admire will put light in your hands, connecting you to that which is normally beyond our reach.

For an example of a Brand Myth that reaches beyond in a radically different way, actually by denying 'a beyond' at all, read about the ATHEIST brand

FIGURE 9.3 The Swarovski Kristallwelten let visitors experience the mythical power of crystal in cavernous 'Wunderkammern' you enter through a 'giant's mouth'

in the following box. It's a great story, but it's also the perfect case to under-stand what lies at the heart of this direction and which you must be aware of, acknowledge and accept: When you follow this route you are tapping into people's beliefs – or, as in the case of ATHEIST, their lack thereof.

'Reaching beyond' is the polar opposite of the beloved business fable of the market participant as *Homo economicus*. It's not about rational decision-making. It's about going straight for the heart, or the soul rather, not even bothering with our cognitive system – or at least that part which economic Nobel prize winner Daniel Kahneman calls system two (Kahneman, 2011). It's all about system one, the fast-moving, intuitive part of our brains that doesn't believe much in thinking but thinks mostly by believing. It's about connecting with people's deeply held convictions or unquestioned 'truths'. And that's what makes it so powerful. You either buy into it or you don't. But if you do, man, you'll have loyalty beyond belief – pun intended.

'REACHING BEYOND' TO THE HERE AND NOW: THE SHOE BRAND ATHEIST
Founder and CEO of the ATHEIST brand, David Bonney, shares how he built a brand based on a myth – or rather the rejection of one, namely God

ATHEIST Shoes is a backwards brand. It was founded as an ideal first – a big, lofty, polarizing, terrifying, passion-arousing, argument-instigating ideal first – and product only second. We were itching to create a brand we really believed in. And what did we most believe in? Nothing.

We wanted to see more atheism in the world. And, as an afterthought, we would connect that cause to a product vehicle we found amusing and felt could carry the ideal well.

We could have chosen easier categories. But in our brazen naivety we chose the hardest product category there is... difficult to buy online, crazy complicated to make... But what conveys identity better than one's footwear? If the shoe fits...

Since 2012, our shoes have carried a message of atheism around the world, creating friendships amongst strangers, even a few one-night stands and a couple of marriages. The blunt whimsy embossed on the soles of our shoes – ICH BIN ATHEIST – is a little connector, an invitation to join a patently absurd club of non-believers... and people want to join.

The brand speaks deeply and honestly, with values that are shared strongly by a minority of people. But it follows that those same values make us the antichrist for a whole lot more people. As the authors of Ueber-Brands write, a principle is only a principle if it costs you. And our branding has cost us dearly. But what we've missed in number of customers, we've gained in depth of connection with the customers we don't turn off.

Myths that guide us

'When a person (or a brand) becomes a model for other people's lives, he has moved into the sphere of being mythologized' (Campbell, 1988). That's the thought behind Ueber-Brands that guides us with their Myths, the second route you can take.

Simply said, it's about setting an example in behaviour for your fans and stakeholders to rally around. It's much easier explained, understood and achieved than 'reaching beyond' with your Myth. But it's very much harder to execute and maintain, because in this case all you do will be constantly checked against what you set out to stand for. You not only have to practise what you preach, everywhere and anytime, you also have to check if your practice and your preaching are still in synch with your community's values and the latest developments in your field. Meaning you have to literally be on top of your game all the time.

And you have to be prepared to potentially stoke controversy. Because for this direction to really be effective, you had best take positions that aren't widely accepted yet. Only then will you really 'activate' those that believe in you – look at the ATHEIST case above, or think about the s... storm even something as benign as Gillette's contemporary interpretation of 'The best a man can get' created (Vizard, 2019), never mind the outcry caused by Nike's truly divisive Kaepernick ad (see above and Kelner, 2018).

In recent times, this direction has been played a lot in the context of socio-ecologically driven brands like Tesla or Everlane, the 'normcore' eco-star, or Brave GentleMan, the sustainable men's fashion brand by Joshua Katcher. The latter actually has a well-articulated Mission Statement that also found a good way of pre-empting potential critics or shortcomings in its last sentence:

> We don't believe animals belong in the fashion production system, or any industrial system for that matter... We believe that ecosystems should not be destroyed in order to make fashion. We believe that the increasing velocity of 'fast-fashion' is one very visible manifestation of a much larger and deeper problem. We don't think Brave GentleMan is a final solution, but it is a means by which to replace more problematic systems.
>
> (Brave GentleMan, 2020)

All that is still lacking is translating this Mission into a great Myth...

But that gets us to another important point if you want your brand to become a Guiding Myth: In this case it's usually less about the story and more about the wo/man. The narrative is often carried by a person as living proof and hero, writing your story in real life, real time. In all three of the above cases, and many others, it's the founder who naturally becomes this person, the example others want to follow:

> Preysman [...] embodies Everlane's ethos. He sports a trim beard and wears the same outfit almost every day: Jeans, a black, long-sleeved, wool button-down and black sneakers. He keeps other aspects of his life equally simple. His most expensive possession is the bed in the rented loft apartment a block away that he shares with his wife; they don't own a car.
>
> (Segran, 2018)

But of course there are plenty of examples that do without this personification, like the already mentioned Nike, or Gillette, Always, Dove... And, anyway, at one point every brand will have to face the finality of its founding face. Chanel and Apple are two very well known and successful examples that prove this is possible. They have both kept their flame burning and their Founder's Myth alive long after the founder passed away. Yet, they also managed to carefully liberate the Myth from its hero or heroine and transfer it onto the brand per se.

In this, the concept of archetypes can be very helpful. According to CG Jung, who brought this term to the forefront in psychology, archetypes are pre-existing forms or themes within the collective subconscious that help us shape our identities and that of others (Jung, 1936). Simply put, they are prototypical characters that help us define and understand ourselves, literally role models like the hero, the villain, the sage, the magician...

You can find more on archetypes later when we talk about defining your Ueber-Target. For now, suffice it to say that these constructs can be very helpful in understanding what Myth you want to project – what type of mythical character you want to stand for and use as a guide. Better, however, are what we call 'kenotypes', because these are less limited and more specific to today's culture. This is how Patagonia, for example, comes across as the 'reluctant activist explorer', or we defined Fekkai hair care as the 'French lover' in a workshop we did.

Your Brand Myth as your meta story

So, what makes a story a Myth? Not you, unfortunately. Or at least, not you alone. It's your audience that makes it – or not. If they don't 'hold the belief', embrace the narrative as meaningful and enlightening or view it as aspirational, something relating to their dreams, you'll never reach mythical power, no matter how beautifully you craft and spin your story or present your mythic guide.

Which gets us to one of the most important and unfortunately also most often disregarded to-dos: A Myth cannot develop in hiding. There's a widespread but false belief that your Mission aka purpose and certainly your Myth are at best instruments for internal use. You share them with your employees, trade partners or other closely connected stakeholders, but you do not share them with your consumers, let alone the public at large. The opposite is true.

This does not necessarily mean that you take your newly developed narrative, perhaps with some pictures and illustrations, and put it on your website. Sometimes Brand Myths are written and designed in a way that you could do that. But it's more likely that you need to and want to adapt it, depending on your audience and the task at hand.

The Brand Myth you are about to write should be looked at and written as something of a meta-story. The story of all the stories you want to tell or have told. It's the overarching narrative that everything you'll do or communicate from now on should ladder up to, written and styled in a manner that appeals to your sense, motivates your people, from employees to partners, but also captures all the strategic core points of your brand. As such, it must be creatively written, but it's ultimately a business-building document. And that balance is usually not so easy to master, especially with your brand or business and the story you want to tell. Etsy provides a rather simple example. Its Mission is to 'Keep Commerce Human'. And its Myth goes something like this:

People make Etsy possible. We provide a meaningful space for sellers to turn their creative passions into opportunity. We enable buyers to discover unique items made with care. And we treat our employees and our community with respect. We're here because the world needs less of the same and more of the special.

(Etsy, nd)

It's not a true mythical story. But it's ok in that it threads the key points into a cohesive narrative that makes sense, is easily understood and connects to the age-old mythical high-ground of 'hand-made = heartfelt humanity vs soulless technology'.

You see how we summarize it in our 'buzzword way'!? You or others would have probably captured it differently. And that's ok, actually it's essential. All your stakeholders should be able to tell that narrative – but in their own words. It should never be something they'll be spoon-fed, something they have to learn by heart like we used to learn poems at school. It must be something that intuitively makes sense to them, something that they automatically feel when seeing your logo or conclude when looking at all your actions and communications.

But it never hurts to give people some support. And so, getting back to the question 'Is my mythical story for internal use only or should I put it on my website?', the answer is: Neither. It should be shared and celebrated widely. But it should also be adapted depending on the audience and its context. This means on your proverbial website you might consider putting a short video that tells your story in a simple, entertaining way. In the next sales presentation you might have a chart with the Myth summarized in five sentences. For your anniversary coffee table book you might turn it into a beautifully illustrated short story. And in your annual report it could appear in the form of an executive summary, more factual and news-oriented than poetic and emotive, or, indeed, as a historic recount, timeline and all.

Now, how do you actually 'Write Your Myth'? Most likely you'll have to hire a professional writer for this – though not necessarily an advertising copywriter. But we'll give you some pointers for developing the plot, extended from the system we shared previously (Schaefer and Kuehlwein 2015).

Seven steps to heaven

In his Mono Myth Model, Joseph Campbell describes 17 steps in three chapters, based on analysing most of the world's big mythical stories (Campbell, 1978). This already shows that building a good Myth – or any story for that matter – takes time. There are usually lots of twists and turns that drive the drama and keep you engaged. And this is important: Yes, you should have the short version, the elevator pitch that summarizes the whole in a few words. Like you can summarize any old fairy tale: Bored princess encounters a frog, which turns into a perfect prince once she kisses him. But this already shows: The bare bones are hardly ever exciting, you need the meat – and the fat for flavour. Only then can you 'get lost' in the narrative and gobble it up with gusto, leaving your critical thinking behind. Something to also remember by the way for your next communication development and testing, where the story is often killed in an attempt to 'save' and focus on the high attention points. Simply put: The short cut is faster, but you miss the story that unfolds along the way.

Having said all this, 17 steps is a bit indulgent. That's why we developed a streamlined version of just seven steps. It kind of goes with the widespread theory that there are only seven basic plots in all of the stories we tell (Booker, 2004). And, if you read our first book, you know how we are partial to the magic of seven anyway.

1 CALLING

Every mythical story starts with a 'calling', a challenge in need of a hero. This is basically your Founding Myth (see above). And, as always, if you get this right, you'll already have at least half of your entire Myth.

2 INSPIRATION

The 'calling' is answered by the 'inspiration' – your product or service idea. Not your actual product or service in all its glory, that comes later. But the idea behind it. YouGov, the research and polling innovator from London, is an interesting case here. On its international as well as its UK site you'll find only institutional big-talk like 'Our mission is to supply a continuous stream of accurate data and insight into what the world thinks, so that companies, governments and institutions can better serve the people and communities that sustain them' (yougov.com). Funnily, on its German site, the same thought is expressed in a much more inspiring and human manner: 'From the beginning we're driven by a simple idea: The more people are heard in the decision making of companies and organizations, the better the decisions will be' (yougov.de, translated by authors). Now that's an idea you can build a big company (and Myth) on.

3 CHALLENGES

This is 'the meat' we talked about earlier, the twists and turns necessary for the drama. It's about the 'fight' to make your idea become real, getting it financed, translating it into a product, how you almost failed, lost all and made it after all. 'When you tell the story of your struggles against real antagonists, your audience sees you as an exciting, dynamic person,' says Robert McKee, one of the world's best-known screenwriting lecturers from LA (Fryer, 2003). Overcoming challenges is what turns your narrative into a true story, keeps it from being bland and makes it credible.

4 BELIEF

Where the 'challenges' are often a challenge for marketing people to talk about, the next three steps will come much more natural to most. Belief is basically the part where you form your convictions. We talked about this in Step 1, 'Set Your Mission' (page 53). The key here is to stick to a 'normal' language and not end up making grandiose marketing statements. And make sure these are unique to you, questionable or even controversial, and not commonly held truths that everyone would nod to and fall asleep.

5 APOTHEOSIS

A big word, but appropriate to the position it marks: This is the climax we're talking about, the seminal moment when your brand proves itself and you become acknowledged as the hero you set out to be. It's when, where, how and what made you famous, your first or most iconic product. Your Porsche 911 or Burberry trench coat, basically. No more explanation necessary, no!?

6 PRINCIPLES

This is what we like to call 'building blocks'. All you learned and perfected over the years, the standards you set and translate into everything you do or offer.

Isn't that like the beliefs? Yes and no. The beliefs are your philosophy, the way you look at the world, what you think is right or wrong. A client of ours, for example, a Charter school, was founded on the strong belief that a school should not just teach calculus and grammar but also morals. You could also call that a principle, but when we say 'principles' here, we mean the actual, tangible things that take the belief from theory to action. In the case above, for example, the way they recruit teachers (hire for heart), the way the curricula are built to provide for learning about values (integrated and personalized), the values they recite on the hallways of every school and live every day (seven!) …

FIGURE 9.4 Seven steps to build your Brand Myth, shortened from Campbell's Mono Myth Model

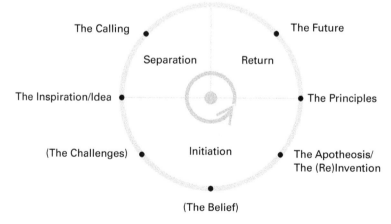

SOURCE The authors (2020)

In most cases, 'principles' will thus mean the unique ways in which you do what you do, 'how' you make things from sourcing your ingredients to structuring your organization or establishing processes. For example, the fact that you only produce regionally, in ethical and fair ways, or the innovative, patented technology that allows you to wash everything brighter than anyone else, or your craft, your unparalleled ingredients, your recipes, your heritage, your style…

7 FUTURE

At last you're back where you started, but really see the place for the first time as TS Eliot famously summarized his idea of exploration (Eliot, 1952). It's the world according to you, with and through you. Hopefully a tiny bit better, or at least somewhat more comfortable, convenient or colourful. And, of course, it's never the end, but the beginning of the new or next future, like Joshua Katcher said about his Brave GentleMan brand: It's not 'a final solution, but it is a means…'.

RECAP: TO DO – STEP 2

- Look at your founding story – and how to make it the ideal starting point for your Mission journey.

- Explore your company/brand culture and history – and pick those aspects that could help to build a narrative.

- Conduct a semiotic study – to uncover new ways to look at your brand and its 'signs'.

- Coalesce all into a mythical storyline (plot) – either to 'reach beyond' or 'guide us'.

- Write it out as your meta-story – the narrative to guide all you do and which all communication shall ladder up to.

- Potentially use the concept of archetypes – to define your hero self.

- Use facts and imagination in doing so – but stay truthful.

- Follow the Separation, Initiation, Return Model – and don't short shrift the challenges.

Step 3: Realize Your Dream

'Today, most successful businesses are storydoers,' claimed Ty Montague a while ago (Montague, 2013). And we still couldn't agree more.

As important as it is to set your Mission and write it into a Myth (Dream) or to find your Ueber-Target and ignite them together with all others (Dare), what we talk about in the following two chapters (Do) is probably the most critical for your success. Strategy is nothing if not implemented. That was always true, but today more so than ever.

Today, your behaviour is your brand. Any discrepancy between Mission and action or any misdeed is immediately spotted and spanked. Your brand (and your Myth) must be built inside out: How you make what you offer and how you share it.

BTW: The fact that these chapters may be a bit shorter than the others should not mislead you. It's in the nature of doing that talking has its limits. And, of course, we don't want to keep you from getting to work longer than necessary...

The creation

Before we get into action it's helpful to be aware of the differences between physical products or services and elements that represent your brand in a more indirect manner. Based on the famous semiotic triad introduced by Charles Pierce (Pierce, 1983), we distinguish three different kinds of 'signs':

- Icons: Represent the brand directly, often famous, 'iconic' products or offers as well as their pictures – eg Porsche 911.

- Indices: Indicate the presence of the brand but are not the brand itself – eg the cinnamon fragrance pumped into malls by Cinnabon to lure people to the store.
- Symbols: Known to signal or 'symbolize' the brand, are associated with it – eg the Intel Inside sound logo.

It's not important to be pedantic about using the proper terms – invariably you'll find people talk about 'icons' while referring to visual brand symbols, for example, like the Nike swoosh or the Apple apple. But it is important to understand the different levels on which these three operate, because only then can you develop and utilize them appropriately.

Products and services

For Ueber-Brands, the product or service isn't simply proof of promise, it's the manifestation of their ideal or dream. Sounds melodramatic? It should. Because at the end, you only become 'ueber' if your products and services are up to it. They need not be perfect in every respect – though that certainly doesn't hurt. But you must ensure that you really practise, or rather produce, what you preach, in every detail; that's essential to your Mission.

SELECTION AND EVALUATION

The first thing to do is assess your entire portfolio, assuming you already have one, with your new Mission and Myth in hand. Does everything you make and sell really live up to both? And we don't just mean in terms of the final product, but ideally in every respect of the four lifestyle stages. Because even if you do not build your Mission on socio-ecological issues, any brand today must show responsibility for what they make – from beginning to end.

Some of the key questions to ask yourself are:

- Where do you source your ingredients? Quality? Special region? Sustainability?
- How do you produce? Ingredients? Methodology? H&M, the Swedish fashion giant, now has a full transparency layer, giving you details on the production of each item on its website (Paton and Maheshwari, 2019).
- What benefits does it offer? How can and how do people actually use it and how does it improve lives? Or the world? Possibly you might want to dig a bit deeper here, if you haven't 'Set Your Mission' yet (page 53). 'Cultural coding' through ethnographies or anthropological studies can sometimes bring amazing insights.

- What happens at the end? Could it be a new beginning? Have you thought about full-cycle business models? A client of ours, for example, has been providing repair parts and services for up to 20 years, long before the EU passed a respective regulation in 2019 – a competitive advantage that was never highlighted.

One thing to note while assessing the 'Myth-fit' of your portfolio: As with your fact search in 'Setting your Mission', the results here are not necessarily top or flop only. Very often, all you need to do is tweak or change certain aspects or look at them from a different angle, to make things 'Mission compatible'. And equally often, this can actually unearth a competitive advantage heretofore unnoticed or underutilized.

For the complete misfits you only have two possibilities: The ideal way is to discontinue or suspend them, until you get them 'right' – how FRoSTA did as we described in Part One, Principle 7. And, as incredible as it sounds, this must not be to the detriment of your business, as the famous example of Patagonia asking people to 'not buy a jacket' has proven. The alternative of course is to deprioritize them, if that is possible from a business volume perspective. Or, if the 'deficits' are substantial, at least contextualize them, so you acknowledge the product's shortcomings and pre-empt any critics like Patagonia did, when its sourcing of duck feathers and whether they might come from force-fed ducks was a potential issue. It took several years to establish a certified, cruelty-free supply chain, during which it alerted buyers of potential issues (Patagonia, 2020).

What you should never do in any case is to present these 'less than ideal' offers as your icons, your hero products. But if you've followed all steps so far, there should be no danger of this, hopefully.

FIGURE 10.1   Even if your brand is not built on sustainability, it must act responsibly along the entire value chain

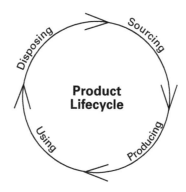

SOURCE   The authors (2020)

INNOVATION AND IDEATION

As shown above and recently proven during the COVID crisis, potential 'issues' with existing products can actually be a blessing in disguise as they often inspire innovation and new business possibilities. New sustainability challenges in particular can be a true innovation engine: 'There's a century old mythology around the idea that animal-derived materials are the pinnacle of quality, but now exciting fabric innovations are setting a new luxury agenda,' says Joshua Katcher, founder of the ethical menswear brand Brave GentleMan (Abbott, 2018).

The important thing to note here is: Where traditionally innovation started by analysing markets and consumers for potential gaps or unmet needs, today's Ueber-Brands usually begin ideating around their Mission. The guiding questions are: What products serve our brand's purpose? What are we here for? What do we get inspired by? What do *we* think the world needs? vs the classic approach following questions like: What do consumers think they want? What is the market doing? What are opportunities to sell with maximum margins? What else can we produce with existing capabilities?

Of course, it doesn't mean that the latter questions are suddenly irrelevant. It's basic business to ensure your offers are marketable with sufficient margins, that you optimize production, etc. But with brands that are Mission and Myth driven, the starting point is different. They are more guided by ideas or even ideals rather than commercial calculations. Those still come into play, but after the ideation, not to inspire innovation but rather to evaluate potential ideas regarding marketability and profitability.

The optimal way to innovate is if the two directions, Brand Mission and customer desire, are naturally one, for example because your brand as well as its products are inspired by your fans, community developed, so to speak. A very successful example of this is the aforementioned beauty phenomenon Glossier with products 'inspired by the people who use them' (intothegloss, 2020). And it's been a runaway success ever since, thanks to the upward spiral of 'blog feeding products praised in blog feeding more products', as of 2018 even with its own 'community' temples on Los Angeles' Melrose Ave and in Lower Manhattan (Lam, 2018). A perfect case of the brand being its own medium.

Design

In markets where basic functional needs are largely taken care of, design is a key differentiator. More importantly, however, for Ueber-Brands, it is a way to show their superiority as well as their aesthetic sophistication. Apart from functional features, this is often the best way to express a shared sensibility with their Ueber-Target, reflecting their evolved tastes and styles as well as their interest in distinction.

Naturally, though, your design must not only be refined, it must primarily follow or, better yet, spring from your Mission and Myth. A good example is Camper: 'From the beginning, the word "casual" has meant something special to us. We create relaxed yet refined styles that exist between the realms of sneakers and dress shoes.' And it has stuck to it 40 years and counting, creating many designs that have become icons, like its 'twins', for example, where the right and left shoe are not identical, but are variations of a shared 'DNA', like non-identical twins. Same with its sporty casual 'The Runner' and bowling-style 'Pelotas', featuring 87 balls on their outsole (Camper, 2020).

What these examples also show, however, is that having a distinct design language does not mean being pigeonholed or even formulaic. Rather, you need a clear list of dos and don'ts, a design language defining core principles that give you a sharp direction yet allow for variations and adaptations. As famous designer Joe Doucet said in our interview: 'You must stay on your feet with technological possibilities evolving so quickly. But also keep up with the changing styles of your avant-garde target.' (Doucet, 2019).

Naming

We already talked about this in the context of developing your Myth. Your brand name is a key asset, a brand symbol, often directly expressing, sometimes connoting and in certain cases also confining your brand's aspirations. The same holds true for your product names. Every strong Ueber-Brand has a very clear naming strategy.

Apple is a well-known case. As is Ben & Jerry's – its ice-cream flavours' names like Cherry Garcia or Empower Mint not only express the brand's tongue-in-cheek attitude but also its political stance, often in an outright activist manner like Pecan Resist, donating $100,000 of the proceeds 'as a form of peaceful resistance against the Trump administration' (Rose, 2018).

There are many other examples in all categories from beauty brand Benefit and its cartoonish naming (BadGalBang or PoreProfessional), part of an overall 1960s design by the way, to the new craft beer brand BrewDog's rocking Elvis Juice or Dead Pony Club, or the Fortnite 'battle

FIGURE 10.2 Joe & The Juice spices up its products – and its prices – with fun-funky names

SOURCE JP Kuehlwein (2019)

locations', which are always alliterations like 'craggy cliffs', 'frenzy farms', 'misty meadows'.

Interestingly, the absence of a 'name' can be just as strong a statement, as Muji shows through its purely functional descriptors, in line with its minimalist strategy. Or you can go for numbers, as most prestige car brands have done for decades, expressing technology over phantasy and thus superseding often short-lived lifestyle names of their less prestigious competitors – where are those blasts from the past like Opel Manta or Ford Escort?

A celebration

This is about dramatizing what you do, the way you talk about it and make it feel really special, an aspect that is much more important for Ueber-Brands than for regular ones. Because the challenge is not just to put your products out there – you need to put them out there on a pedestal. Not literally, though, because today you must find more subtle and intelligent ways to imbue them with a significant aura and a sense of superiority. You have to be much more inspiring and more experiential.

There are three main ways of doing this, of celebrating and elevating your products into *manifestations* of your ideals rather than mere functional fulfilments.

From RTB to STB

RTB is the standard way of substantiating your product: The reason(s) to believe in its superiority. These can be special ingredients, a unique technology, your craftsmanship... or simply your heritage or your established name and reputation. Though be careful: The latter are basically milking your brand. Without renewing and re-investing in new RTBs periodically, you will soon look very old. Myths have become Myths because they occasionally get a facelift, a re-telling in a contemporary context, with fresh eyes.

Which gets us to STBs: Stories to believe. Ueber-Brands don't just talk left brain, they don't just convince rationally. They must lure you emotionally. And for this, stories are much better than 'reasons'. What your Myth is for the brand overall, your STBs are for your products: Stories that provide a narrative that pulls your heartstrings as much as quell your critical mind.

L'Officine Universelle Buly talks about its massage stones: 'A touch of mineral rawness brings serenity and balance to the bathroom: Stones and their beautiful jagged contours hold virtues that should be unceasingly resorted to' (https://www.buly1803.com/en/54-stones).

A very different example is frozen food brand FRoSTA, decidedly not a highfalutin' French beauty brand: It talks about the products as 'wholesome meals like grandma would have'. Emotional and evocative right there, opening a narrative in a very simple manner with a few well-chosen words. But it gets better. Instead of calling out 'no additives, preservatives etc', as most other do, it wraps those RTBs in the historical and very highly regarded story of the *Reinheitsgebot*, a 1516 Bavarian Beer purity law to only use unadulterated, natural ingredients without flavour enhancers, substitutes, etc, which is deeply rooted in German culture and everyone knows and appreciates. You can get the full story at the in-depth interview with the CEO of FRoSTA on the Ueber-Brands podcast at ueberbrands.com (ueberbrands.com, 2019a). Scan the QR code at the front of this book for a direct link.

What both examples show is that it doesn't take much to romanticize your RTBs into STBs. Just talk about your products like normal people would; ok, like a decent writer would. No institutional speak or marketing jargon or hyperbole. You can boast, but do so in more imaginative ways using metaphors, historical references, sensual comparisons... a language that's emotive and humane, showing that you care about your product as well as the person you talk to.

Rituals

> I don't go to church on Sundays anymore, but I try never to miss Laura Crago's Survivor ride at SoulCycle. It is everything that I loved about church as a child. First, there is pageantry. We enter a darkened studio. Candles burn. Music booms. People are dressed funny. We follow a celebrant (Laura), who leads us through a prescribed series of acts while perched atop a sacred platform. This is theatre!
>
> (Vincent, 2017)

There's hardly a better way to express what 'ritualizing' can do to your product and its users than how this fan of SoulCycle explains it.

The power of rituals is that they can make an everyday activity feel very extraordinary. They can lift your product into the realm of something almost 'sacred' or at least dear to you. Using it becomes less of a mundane act or a chore and more something that you cherish because it allows you to get in touch with yourself or your memories, gives you a respite, stimulates you, calms you, etc. Rituals are thus the opposite of routines. Where routines are purely functional, something you do repetitively and thus efficiently without much concern, rituals are very intentional and highly emotional, an activity with purpose and meaning. And they transfer exactly that to your product and brand – and make your users loyal 'beyond belief'.

The above church reference is the standard example. Religion thrives on rituals. But there are lots of worldly activities as well, like the opening of the Olympic Games with its fire-running, flame-lighting, marching-in rituals, the iPhone swiping, pinching, flipping, the T-Rex dinosaur popping up on Google Chrome when you're not connected to the internet or the ever-changing 'emote dances' on Fortnite. Or… the use of your brand/product?

What do you have to do to 'ritualize' your product's use? Well, it's like mythologizing your brand – ultimately it's the users, your fans, who 'do' it. But you can inspire them. For that you must do three things:

1   Think about the role your product and its use can or does play in people's lives. When is it regularly used? How? What does it feel like? What could you compare it to? What benefits does it provide? What does it do to people? What do you want it to do to people? Ethnographies or cultural studies can help here, as can extended interview sessions with your hard-core

fans – possibly yourself or your employees or friends. Usually these are better when using projective and associative techniques, because of which we recommend a trained moderator for this part.

2 Set a special technique or sequence of steps for the usage of your product. This can be a unique tech innovation like the iPhone touch screen swoosh, or a special way to apply your product, as beauty brands often do, or simply the way it gets delivered, like the black Peloton trucks with their stylish staff, also clad in black. Or it's something inspired by the actual use of your products in certain circles or cultures, like the Corona lime wedge or the Tequila orange/lemon slice and salt ritual.

3 Put it out there and penetrate it – but with the feel of an insider tip. Stick to it and repeat it incessantly. Start by convincing and 'converting' your Ueber-Target. And inspire them to share their 'secret' know-how with others, turning themselves into brand intimates and making the followers who adopt the ritual feel like insiders. But support throughout, don't just rely on it happening by itself. BTW: It usually is even more convincing if you present the ritual not as something you came up with, but something 'discovered' by expert users or R&D folks, etc.

Information and education

The third way to celebrate your offer is to provide context and depth. It's about information and education but way beyond the usual usage instructions or manuals. Because it's not about familiarizing people with product features or functions. That factors in, but it's mostly about dramatization and validation. And, in the case of truly innovative products or category approaches, also transformation – attitudinal and/or behavioural change.

You want to give your brand authority, perhaps even imbue it with a special aura, but at least express its relative superiority or specialty. The very welcome side effect: You thus often automatically connect it to a higher level of sophistication and connoisseurship. Which makes your Ueber-Target and your strategic targets feel somewhat advanced, ahead of the mainstream – in knowledge and in style. And that is something most people are willing to pay for.

A good example is the global leader in high-end paper Gmund. 'The seminars we offer you can't find anywhere else in the world,' says CEO Florian Kohler. And that's why many blue chip CMOs from Siemens to Hermès travel to the tiny town near Tegernsee, Bavaria – and become key accounts (Markert, 2019).

FRoSTA is another case, though its connoisseurship would never be called that. Here you'd talk about mindfulness, responsibility because its aim was to educate the public, politicians, regulators and consumers about the drawbacks of industrially made foods and about viable alternatives. Which was and is essential for its business, to make people appreciate their additive-free products and willing to pay a premium. But, of course, the reality is that it has also built itself into an authority along the way, factually, in that it learned a lot in the process, but not least also in public perception. And that doesn't just reassure its now 'educated' users about the product quality and ethical brand fit; it also gives them the very welcome feeling of being more aware than and ahead of the rest.

Another, more experiential way of educating or rather 'edutaining' your targets are brand experience centres, for example from Porsche. Its PECs, from LeMans to Shanghai to LA, are for many 'just' an exciting outing, akin to an amusement park for grown-ups. But beyond that they are mainly built to fuel the fascination with the cars and turn its fans into what they most like to be: Petrolists, car aficionados, experts who are acknowledged as that and often asked for advice by their peers. 'Many Porsche clients are perfectionists,' says Michael Seifert, Head Instructor at PEC Hockenheim. 'That's why our trainers must be much more than good driving instructors. They

FIGURE 10.3   The 'White Coats' of beauty retailer Kiehl's Since 1851 is famous for providing hands-on product education and plenty of hand-picked samples to its customers

SOURCE Reproduced with permission of Kiehl's Since 1851 (2020)

have to really know our products, to answer Porsche drivers even the most intricate questions about their cars, to make them the essential 5% smarter than others' (Giese, 2019).

And, as this quote shows, educating people about your product and thus elevating your brand is hardly easy or cheap. It does require quite a level of investment, certainly persistence and sometimes even a thick skin. FRoSTA's educational campaign is still going on, cost a lot over time and made some bitter enemies in the industry. The same holds true for Patagonia. But the executional demands are getting more and more advanced as well. It's no longer enough to put out white papers, write articles, release studies, etc. Even if you don't go to the extreme of building costly real-life learning and experience centres, people want their attention sparked and sustained with well-made videos, often also called 'epipheos' (videos to create an epiphany), that are more comparable to action films than classic documentaries. Milla, for example, a German initiative of Modular Interactive Lifelong Learning for All, hires directors of photography or writers from Netflix and other entertainment professionals (Fahrun, 2019).

All in all, 'doing' your Mission and Myth is much harder than setting or writing it, but also more rewarding eventually. 'It's a marathon, not a sprint,' as Dr Jens Mueller-Oerlinghausen, expert in organizational and performance management, said in an interview recently (Mueller-Oerlinghausen, 2019). The next chapter will most likely drive this home even more clearly.

RECAP: TO DO – STEP 3

- Look at everything your brand does through the eyes of your Mission and Myth – including icons, indices and symbols.

- Assess your portfolio according to its 'Mission fitness' – along the entire lifecycle.

- Look at all products and services from different perspectives – facts can be interpreted.

- Select the heroes – amend the products and services that are ambivalent, deprioritize the 'misfits'.

- Uncover hidden assets and new opportunities – 'inspired' by Mission-musts.

- Ideate and innovate based on your ideals – potentially in new ways (crowd-sourced).

- Define a unique design language – and design accordingly.

- Develop a naming strategy – consider 'no names' or numbers.

- Substantiate your products with STBs – vs simple RTBs.

- 'Ritualize' your products – elevate the role they play in people's lives through special techniques.

- Celebrate the superiority of your products and services – develop information and education strategies.

Step 4: Live Your Dream

'Don't fuck up the culture,' said Peter Thiel, billionaire entrepreneur, venture capitalist and significant investor in Airbnb when Brian Chesky, founder of Airbnb, asked him for his single most important advice (Chesky, 2014). And Thiel is not known to be mushy or cushy.

This is what we'll talk about in the following pages: Culture. The chapter will touch on other aspects as well, but ultimately this is what it's all about. Your company or brand culture is your single most important asset. It sums up and echoes everything you are or do, from your production to your organization to your identity. And it directly informs and moulds your presence and the way the world will experience you. Everything you do should – must – be a reflection and an expression of your culture: 'As Gen Z shoppers enter the market, their purchases show they care more about founders' biographies and what a brand stands for and less if a line is categorized as "mass" or "prestige"' (Strugatz, 2019). Or, as Oliviero Toscani, the photographer who famously created the first purpose campaign for Benetton, said in a recent interview: 'Every company is a socio-political institution, closely interwoven with societal structures' (Strasser, 2020). And as such you cannot hide behind closed doors. Especially if part of your allure is built on sparking those societies, even guiding or at least nudging them, as is the case with most Ueber-Brands.

Inside out

'It used to be all about the outside, now the inside must be transparent,' said Michael Burke, CEO of Louis Vuitton (Griese, 2019).

Ueber-Brands radiate inside out. Their 'image' is no longer just that, a shallow projection of what they like others to see; it must be grounded in and substantiated through the way they are. Their appearance and their essence must be one.

Practically all our guest authors make this point in their chapters in Part Three, as well – without prompting. So of course, we'll start this section of 'Live Your Dream' with what you must do and how you must be internally – the kind of company you build, how you organize and structure, all the processes, your HR, your KPIs, your culture...

Culture

Culture eats strategy for breakfast. Because any strategy is only as good as its implementation, and that means as good as your people are. They must embrace your strategy to execute it seamlessly. And in order to embrace it, they must not only understand it, but also feel it. That's why one of our clients, for example, makes a point of 'hiring for heart', rightfully convinced it's easier to teach skills than change character (Reinik, 2018). But your employees must not only feel and fit your Mission, they must believe in it as well. And for that they must believe that you believe in it, proven by the culture you foster. Motivation needs trust and trust needs honesty. It's as simple as that.

Chris Dale, Global Head of Communications and Public Affairs for YouTube, calls YouTube's culture a 'culture of expressing yourself' in our interview in Part Three, perfectly reflecting its Mission of 'Broadcast Yourself'. Just think about this seemingly simple set of words – how crucial and far-reaching they are. How could a company become the global beacon (and behemoth) of self-expression if not by fostering that exact culture internally? How could they win the right employees and ensure they'll keep this Mission in mind in everything they do, every time they talk to someone, be it a partner, customer or the public? How could they convince all of us that freedom of expression is not only a human right, but can be a boon, fun and enriching to all of us, if they didn't live it every day?

The same holds true, of course, for more traditionally 'cultured' businesses like Ritz-Carlton for example. That's why staff members don't just think of themselves as 'Ladies and Gentlemen serving Ladies and Gentlemen' (Ritz-Carlton, 2020), they actually address each other exactly as that, an indication of how seriously Ritz-Carlton translates its Mission into operational credos and guides, including its 'Three Steps of Service'. It set out to truly empower employees vs managing them. Headed by 'I am Proud to be Ritz-Carlton', the service values, for example, include statements like 'I am empowered to create unique, memorable and personal experiences for our guests', or 'I own and immediately resolve guest problems', all the way to 'I am involved in the planning of the work that affects me' (Ritz-Carlton, 2020). No surprise that Ritz-Carlton has meanwhile spawned a profitable division to teach and train other hospitality businesses in operational excellence.

Cycling brand Rapha, on the other hand, adopted its self-motivating mantras aka values from a fierce sports mindset, including, for example, 'Suffer – Good Enough Isn't' (Rapha, 2020), creating an atmosphere that attracts but also emboldens a passionate 'biker spirit' among their staff, which in turn connects it immediately and deeply with their Ueber-Targets. It practically hires and builds its Ueber-Target in-house first to radiate out and naturally draw in its followers and fans.

And that's exactly the point why it's all about culture with Ueber-Brands: Yes, it's a matter of credibility and transparency, and yes, it's also about

FIGURE 11.1 Women activist investment brand Ellevest inspired and expressed its culture through this presidential commentary on New York bus shelters

SOURCE JP Kuehlwein (2017)

employee pull. But ultimately it is their way of building thriving businesses: Celebrating and living the aspirations of their targets within their organizations. And thus not only being much more authentic, but also having more product authority, building deeper, lasting customer connections and saving lots in process and control as well as communication – internal and external. Their culture is directly linked to their equity, operational excellence for them must mean cultural excellence, their behaviour is their brand. Peter Thiel understood this early on, or felt it instinctively, which either way makes him the great businessman he is.

Four things are important in building the right culture for your brand:

1 RECRUITING

More important than perfect skills or experiences is the mindset of your employees, their attitudes but also their interests. You never create passion for your brand if you don't have it in your brand. Rapha thus hires only biking fanatics. Netflix looks for people who are curious and courageous so 'every person at Netflix is someone you respect and learn from' (Netflix, 2009). So, ask yourself: What people do you choose? Are they people your target would like to hang out with? Someone whose judgement they'd trust?

2 ENABLING

Normcore brand Everlane built its headquarter next to an autobody shop in San Francisco's most 'normal' Mission District (Segran, 2018). Estee Lauder and LVMH give their 'maisons' (brands) as much independence as possible, allowing for different cultures between, say, Bobby Brown and MAC, Rimowa or Louis Vuitton (see also the box in Part One, Principle 6, page 34). Other companies offer in-house childcare to empower their parenting staff, or allow in-office skateboarding to stay young (Red Bull). And then there's the trend towards Strategic Brand Venturing by consumer packaged goods (CPG) companies to (re)capture an entrepreneurial, disruptive spirit and culture (Van Rensburg, 2014). Whatever you do, your set-up should enable the aspirations you cater to and the culture you're trying to create. Think about where you want to be – uptown, downtown, out of town, what dress code you establish (if any), if you'll thrive in open plan or individual offices, if pool tables and micro-kitchens are good for your Mission and Myth as they are for Google and YouTube, or if your culture would benefit more from elegant communal spaces or group outings, like REI does.

3 INSPIRING

Speaking of REI: Apart from doing all to enable your specific culture, you must also inspire it through symbolic acts. A great example is #OptOutside. In 2015 REI started closing all shops, including the online one, on Black Friday, providing paid leave for its employees to live up to the company's Mission and spend time outside with their families rather than shopping or selling. What's amazing: This wasn't only an uplifting lighthouse act for its culture, it was also an instant business success, creating enormous awareness, goodwill and additional revenue. In a similar way was Elon Musk's publishing of Tesla's patents not just a culture and PR stint, it ultimately helped build the category and thus disproportionately the business of its leader, Tesla (Peterson, 2016). Culture needs inspiration and that starts at the top.

4 INCENTIVIZING

'The actual company values, as opposed to the nice-sounding values are shown by who gets rewarded, promoted or let go' (Netflix, 2009). Hardly ever were truer words spoken. And yet, the reality is vastly different. How often have we worked with clients on Mission Statements, translated into new structures and strategies, just to find that HR plans and criteria, benchmarks and key performance indicators (KPIs) were left unchanged – and thus still driving 'old' action, anti-Mission. If you cannot incentivize on or benchmark against a certain strategy, don't pronounce it. If you have to stick to certain KPIs against your Mission, be at least honest about it and explain why. If your career management doesn't allow for immediate adoption of Mission-congruent and culture-fostering policies, show a timeline for how you'll get there.

Let's end this with another, we find perfect, way of expressing what this wobbly construct 'culture' is, why it is so hard to grasp and why it's so crucial at the same time. Doug Atkins calls culture 'the social soup of shared assumptions that an organization has about how its members should behave, relate and decide things together'. Now, if that doesn't tempt you to read more about his experiences and insights at Airbnb in Part Three...

Organization

Who do you feel better about: Lyft or Uber? Based on the Uber scandals regarding the CEO's behaviour as well as its driver treatments and remuneration strategies that came to light in 2018/19, most will probably answer 'Lyft'. This shows how important organizational decisions are – and not only in creating the desired culture (see above), but also for your public standing and your target relevance.

Assessing how far away your structures and processes are from your newly set Mission and cultural ideal is 'very important, if not crucial' according to performance management expert Dr Jens Mueller-Oerlinghausen (Mueller-Oerlinghausen, 2019). As is setting a plan to close the probable gap.

If you need to secure exceptional craftsmanship, an alienated worker in a low-wage country will most likely not do: 'We'd never think of having someone just do all the sewing and then another person do the hardware... You put your mark on it from start to finish; it is yours', says Hermès' Céline Rochereau, who organizes its artisans (Hass, 2019). Equally, the fact that Netflix talks of its organization as 'highly aligned, loosely coupled' makes sense, considering its cultural mantra of 'Freedom and Responsibility' (Netflix, 2009). But it's not only about structure and processes, it's also about policies like Netflix's 'No vacation policy'. The idea: Just as people work anytime and anywhere to get their job done, they should also be able to take off when and where they want, as long as they get their job done. No limits, other than your performance. And the 'boss' shall lead by taking enough weeks themselves so they return visibly recharged (Netflix, 2009).

More radical organizational concepts to facilitate a Mission-appropriate company culture and behaviour are those of Freitag, which we already talked about in Part One and BrewDog, the Scottish craft beer cult. BrewDog started in 2007 to 'revolutionise the beer industry and completely redefine British beer drinking culture'. Today it is one of the fastest growing food brands in the UK. And the company is rebellious from the ground up. Decidedly independent and community-minded, it is crowd-funded by over 70,000 shareholders, 'radically transparent' in its operations as well as finances and celebrates a punk culture all the way down to a monthly 'beer allowance' for every employee (BrewDog, 2020a). That's truly and successfully living and radiating your Mission inside out.

What all these examples shall show you is that it's not only important to re-think your organization in order to walk your Mission talk. It can simultaneously drive efficiencies, increase employee ratings, community acceptance... and be a lot of fun, apart from the mess and stress that a re-org definitely always is.

Identity

Most everybody knows Chanel's classic visual identity in stark black and white, Cs interlocking. Truly everybody knows the colourful Google logo and the fun spirit and endless doodles it sparked. Both examples show how a clear Mission can inspire a unique, recognizable identity even decades past the founding personalities who originated them.

But these identities don't just radiate out, they also have a re-affirming effect on the cultures that gave life to them. They aren't just symbols, they often also function as symbolic acts, like the ones we talked about in the discussion on culture (page 99), sending a signal to all employees as much as the world about what kind of spirit this brand wants to live. Take the Google doodles for example. They immediately communicate creativity, joy, liberty, curiosity, innovation – all in a playful manner. A constant reminder for everyone what this brand wants to stand for. But then there's the story of how it all started. And that makes it a powerful mnemonic for every employee of the culture and spirit they never want to lose: The first doodle was created in 1998 when the two co-founders wanted to signal their temporary absence, having joined the Burning Man Festival. Let that sink in for a second. Both founders of a start-up that had just done a $1 million finance round, out at the same time to party their heads off at what was then a truly wild festival in every sense of the word. If that's not a symbolic act for daring entrepreneurship and limitless curiosity… daily re-asserted with a little doodle.

Speaking of symbols: Remember the three kinds of signs, based on Pierce!? Your brand identity lives on three levels:

1 Symbol level.
   This is what most people mean when they talk about Brand or Corporate Identity (CI). The Google doodle or the Chanel b/w double C … your logo and the look and feel around it, including special colours, naming systems or shape language (Apple rounded edges).

2 Index level.
   Often confused with the above, these are things that stand for or indicate the brand. You can feel it already, but you're not really experiencing it yet. Like the first scent of spring or the atrocious scent assault of A&F stores during the brand's demise, the sounds of Hôtel Costes in Paris, made famous through numerous CDs and playlists, or the swirly-striped tents of Cirque de Soleil.

3 Icon level.

Now you're at a tangible, experiential level. Usually here you have iconic products that stand for the brand, *pars pro toto*, like Levi's 501 or the Porsche 911. Or the beefy 'bros' in Joe & the Juice smoothie bars. You can't take 'em home, at least not officially, but they're part of the fun, what draws people in.

You should think about, design and play with all three levels. But all must start from one point, your brand character. We already talked about this in 'Set Your Mission'. Your brand character is part of the How of your brand equity: How you want to behave and be seen? How you want to come across? It's the personality you define for your brand.

Many companies use personas for this, often created around archetypes. They define themselves as 'kick-ass coach' or 'tireless hero' or 'wild child', which is usually helpful, as it gets you to a more pronounced, sharper 'personality'. The alternative is a combination of adjectives. 'Naughty but nice' or 'peculiar and eccentric' are good ones here as they give you a fairly clear idea of the kind of character you want to have. But unfortunately, all too often you end up with bland passe-partouts like 'reliable and confident'.

In that case, what you should do is write down not only the adjectives you want to project, but also those you reject. What you are and what you're not. And if you then end up with 'confident but not arrogant', you know you're nowhere. Which brand would not want to be confident? And arrogant – why not for an Ueber-Brand!? It'd be much better already if you'd go for the classic line from Sister Sledge's 'Greatest Dancer': 'Arrogance but no conceit…'.

Outside in

A brand's identity not only shines to the outside, it just as much reflects to the inside, reminding all internal stakeholders what they work for and hopefully reigniting them each time anew. The same holds true for your 'go-to-market' moves that bring your brand to life, the Brand Experience. Their primary purpose may be external, to market, but they also are a way for your employees to see the result of their work, instil pride and inspire. Like symbolic acts, they work both ways, which is why we headed this section 'Outside in'.

Brand Presence

Distribution is important, not just to reach your targets, but also in building recognition, the right kind of recognition. Luxury brands always knew this and have thus been fighting to tightly control their retailing, many to this day, by negotiating strict and exclusive depot-contracts, curtailing grey distribution or putting offenders on blacklists, like Patek Philippe apparently still does (Koch, 2020). Oatly, the upscale oat milk from Sweden, decided for this reason to enter the US market not on supermarket shelves, but through specialty coffee shops, enlisting the sensual spaces as well as their baristas to 'position' the brand appropriately – and help educate about it as well (Wertheim, 2018).

And Nike and Birkenstock leaving Amazon wasn't for economic reasons alone, either. Both CEOs made it amply clear that the fact that Amazon does not protect, let alone build its brand equity was the key factor (Novy-Williams, 2019). In the case of Birkenstock the pull-back had come in stages over years, largely driven by Amazon being too cavalier about counterfeits (Salden, 2017; T3N, 2017).

Inversely, many online or direct-to-consumer (DTC) brands are moving into real-life stores, which they helped kill in the first place. The do-good optical brand Warby Parker was one of the first. Many have followed, like Allbirds, opening stores in metro cities like New York or Berlin, all verticalizing not the least to unfold the brand in all its glory. The Elyx house in LA, swanky club of Absolut's eponymous premium label, is certainly one of the more interesting ones to note. It's actually the home of Absolut Elyx CEO

FIGURE 11.2 Allbirds, the New Zealand wool-shoe company, is moving offline with remarkable speed

SOURCE JP Kuehlwein (2020)

Jonas Tahlin. Or think of gaming giant Fortnite holding its championships in real stadiums – with all the action still virtual though.

All this emboldens Gary Friedman, CEO of Restoration Hardware, who evidently sinks a lot of money into his shiny, multi-storey 'brand houses', often cum club and fancy roof-top restaurant, as in Manhattan's Meatpacking District. In a recent shareholder letter, he was happy with a 3 per cent net for 2019 and going 'contrary to conventional wisdom', not overly concerned to tip the scale substantially off-line, leaving Restoration Hardware's online business failing, according to Gartner L2 (Danziger, 2019).

Traditionally, there was only one thing that mattered in making distribution decisions: Reach. Gain the biggest exposure possible to maximize sales opportunities. In building an Ueber-Brand, however, you should at least consider three aspects:

1 Location?

Of course, reach is still a key factor. But Ueber-Brands are also aware of what a certain location says about their brand. The 'company they keep' is critical in building or undermining their equity, making Amazon, for example, questionable in some cases, as said earlier. And for many if not most brands a multi-sensual offline presence in a suitable environment is still indispensable, even if it's only one or a handful around the world.

2 Penetration?

Same as with reach, penetrating a market is not necessarily such a good thing for Ueber-Brands. Overextended, on every corner, it's hard to keep control of your brand experience (see also the Starbucks case in Part Three). And it certainly doesn't help elevate the brand. Even the big luxury houses had to learn that lesson. Blinded with yuans during the noughties goldrush, they opened shop in every glitzy Hong Kong or Shanghai mall, just to cut back a few years later. A much better strategy is to do pop-ups in enchanting places, embedding yourself into your target's life rather than them searching for you God knows where. 'Our customers are migrating birds,' Simon Sproule, CMO of Aston Martin, told us in a recent interview. Aston has a very limited number of brand experience centres or flagships, but 'pops up' often where things are happening for Ueber-Targets, like in Courchevel, where you can rent special Aston Martins for a mountain drive or in Carmel, where it runs a club house with movie theatre and all during the annual Monterey Car Show. You can also listen to the full interview with Simon on ueberbrands. com. Scan the QR code at the front of the book for a direct link.

3 Distinction?

Does the place allow you to present yourself in a unique manner, according to your Mission? No matter if you're considering a stand-alone store, a shop-in-shop, a digital presence or a true cross-channel venture, whatever you do should build your brand, not just sell it. Check out the Hermès online flagship, overhauled in 2018. It's simple, intuitive, functional yet in the brand's unique elegant and precise manner, including inspirational videos and product lay-downs. Or think about the pioneering Virgin clubhouses. And then look at the United or Lufthansa lounge on your next flight, yes, also the newer ones. We don't want to pick on Star Alliance, but what a lost opportunity in brand building! Could one of the reasons be that they are not as clear about their Mission, Myth and brand character?

In summary: A Brand Presence must be about utility, especially online. And it's about memorability. But most of all, it should help build your brand. All must be looked at through your distinct equity.

Brand experience

Have you ever thought about your cashier set-up? Considered it not just under efficiency aspects but as part of your brand experience? Well, you should. Look at the hand-held pads showing an open check-out at Trader Joe's or, on the other extreme, the discreet backroom operations at Prada *et al*, to which your platinum card is taken on a silver tray while you have a coffee in the comfy club chair. Both 'closings' say a lot about their respective brands. And that is our point in this last section of 'Live Your Dream': When you create an environment or touchpoint for your brand, make sure it's not just well done, welcoming etc. Make sure it reflects and builds your Mission and Myth. All your stores, service stations, shows, outlets should never simply be appearances but always true experiences of your brand.

Ok, we agree, it can get a bit annoying that every hole in the wall, pop-up, mall outlet or poorly designed e-commerce platform touts itself a 'brand experience centre' these days. And that's not what we mean. The last thing we'd recommend is upping everything with some 'experiential' hocus-pocus, dipping every touchpoint deep into the brand chocolate, so to speak. But what we do advise is that you think hard about how you can make all your brand interactions and environments work harder for you. How you design the things you have to design anyway in a manner that makes them 'flash' your Mission and add another couple of words to your Myth each time.

The Trader Joe pads are a perfect example in this way. They are simple, old-school, human, natural… all things that perfectly fit the brand. They are the absence of bells and whistles and that makes them sing the Trader Joe 'song' so much louder, in a quiet way. Everlane's 'pay-what-you-want' approach to surplus items works in a similar way: A simple twist, that not only makes sales much less 'selly', it lets its ethics and its Mission shine straight to the heart of its Ueber-Targets, who often actually end up 'over-paying'. Or think of Cire Trudon, the venerable Parisian candle brand, and how they invented 'les cloches', bell-shaped covers to conserve the scent of its test-candles and exude it when lifted. A highly functional necessity that elevates each 'sniff' to an almost spiritual experience.

But depending on the brand's Mission it can also mean going all out, operating operatically, if you will. L'Officine Buly, the already mentioned beauty brand from Paris, relishes anything baroque. Its counters are Brèche de Bénou marble, its soaps come in little boxes you might normally find at an antique store, everything is wrapped in its custom Gazette paper and there's a calligrapher to write your personal notes (*mots doux*) on gorgeous gift cards. It can get a bit much, especially when you read the description of an online order process (Buly1803, 2020). But at the end it leaves you with exactly the feeling the brand wants to stand for: Artisanal, hand-made, natural beauty products steeped in history and made with 'audacity and precision in a winning and innovative spirit' (Buly1803, 2020). That simply can't be austere.

What's important is that you think about aspects material to your Mission and Myth. And that you find little, surprising twists in the ordinary processes that can turn them into extraordinary moments. Memorable moments. Moments that pay into the equity of your brand as life goes on.

Let your fans and customers take the lead role in your 'play', not your brand. But do design the 'set' and inspire them (if not to say 'direct them'), by acting appropriately yourself. Your behaviour talks louder than any billboard ever can. All your acts communicate, whether you want to or not. So, you had better make sure they say the right thing, in the way Virginie Viard did, Karl Lagerfeld's right hand and successor at Chanel. Her spring 2020 couture show in the Grand Palais, one year after Lagerfeld's death, definitely made a mark yet in a very respectful and quiet way, bowing to Karl and starting a new era at the same time. It continues to build the Brand Myth by referencing Gabrielle's formative years at Aubazine Abbey as much as it talks about the here and now, and all that in a very simple but grand gesture. Mission accomplished.

RECAP: TO DO – STEP 4

- Take a close look at your culture – and ensure it reflects your Mission in the best way.

- Define values and desired behaviours – codifying the culture you want to be lived.

- Recruit accordingly – make passion for your Mission a key criterion.

- Enable the culture you're after – with respective structures, processes and policies.

- Develop inspirational, symbolic acts – which can actually ignite your business at the same time.

- Adapt your benchmarks and incentive programmes – they must reflect your values.

- Assess your organizational structures – and adapt as necessary.

- Define your brand character and craft your identity to reflect your Mission – inside and out.

- Check your distribution strategy online and offline – evaluate not only reach but also equity fit and distinctiveness.

- Design your brand experiences to live your Mission and Myth – starting with standard operational aspects.

- Focus on those details that are critical to the story you want to tell – finding unexpected twists.

Step 5: Find Your Ueber-Target

The fact that this topic is the penultimate chapter should not be misinterpreted as 'this is the (second to) last thing to think about'. Our target – and particularly your Ueber-Target – must be the benchmark throughout; it is the one you design for, hence it is often also called 'design target'.

Ueber-Brands, like any other enterprise, must be successful and that means being relevant for their targets. But, as we explain in 'Start with yourself', one of the key differences of Ueber-Brands is that they are more Mission- than market-led. Their impetus is normally not consumer research defining a market opportunity, but their founders having an idea, seeing, discovering or inventing something that could improve our world, or at least their category. And only then researching whether this concept could pan out economically. Some don't even do that, being so convinced and gutsy about their Mission.

Ueber-Brands are built inside out. And that's how we have built our how-to model – with targeting next to messaging, where it belongs.

Understanding

If the risk for Patagonia is to be seen just like any other company – one that cares as much about profits as the environment – then the comparable risk for The North Face is to be associated with suburban parents and college students whose greatest trek is across the quad, rather than trail runners, mountain climbers and the occasional well-dressed rapper.

(Meltzer, 2017)

This nicely captures the conundrum of most premium-priced brands. And this is where Ueber-Targets come in. They help mitigate the balance between distance and proximity so essential for Ueber-Brands. They are crucial in making your brand aspirational yet keeping it approachable. Give it credibility and authenticity, but without ever letting it become so 'authentic' that it loses all appeal.

As such, your Ueber-Targets are often the people closest to your brand, your most early adopters or fans, the ones that really dig you from the start. In a way, you could call them the 'lowest hanging fruits'. But what makes them an Ueber-Target is that they are actually the 'highest hanging fruits', the ones in the sun that make your brand shine. They just fell in front of your feet, to ride that metaphor to death.

What target?

We distinguish two basic types of targets: Your Ueber-Target and your strategic target. The latter can be subdivided into core target and wider target. The differentiation user/non-user is parallel to this, on a different level.

It sounds more complicated than it is, as Figure 12.1 shows. Your strategic targets are basically everyone who could potentially buy your product or enlist your service. They can be broken down into your core target, the ones you should focus on as most promising, profitable, likely to be won with less effort/expense and your wider target, the ones further out, who are less interesting also because they will use your products less frequently and take the most to convert.

Your Ueber-Target is your brand's and its strategic target's dream target, your muses – the people you probably had in mind when you conceived your brand and who personify your ideal user above and beyond. And the people your strategic target is inspired by and aspires to, the ones they look up to as most competent and cool in the context of your Mission.

You can have users across all three targets, but probably least in the wider target, especially early on in your lifecycle. For non-users it's inverse: Ideally you should have very few in your Ueber-Target, because your Ueber-Target can only play its part if they are perceived as using you. As you move further out in your strategic target you actually want to have a decent percentage of non-users, as they are your source of business and growth opportunity.

FIGURE 12.1 Your Ueber-Target leads all

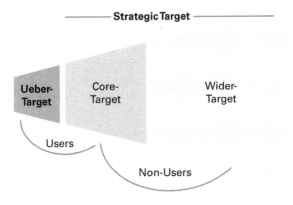

SOURCE The authors (2020)

A good brand to exemplify this is Rapha, the premium cycling brand. Rapha's Ueber-Target is the 'Sophisticated Cyclists', sometimes also called 'Gentleman Cyclists'. These cyclists are athletic and cultured, and love cycling because it combines physicality with worldliness, allowing them to discover new countries and cultures while they push themselves up the hill. Many are cycling pros or semi-pros.

Its strategic target, on the other hand, is all the people who cycle and are willing and able to spend on their outfits – as simple as that. Its core target within this is what some dismissingly call MAMILS (middle aged men in lycra). Often accomplished, upper-middle class guys with an urge to re-kindle their youthful self, athletically and aesthetically, with varying degrees of success, one should add. The wider target includes everyone on two wheels, even those who only bike occasionally or to the city's next green market, use e-bikes and rarely splurge on expensive gear.

It is important to distinguish from all this the influencers, advocates or ambassadors (IAA). Influencers are people who are active on social media and have a fairly large following. Advocates are category experts who speak highly of you. Ambassadors can be either, but are paid by you. Naturally, both your Ueber-Target as well as your strategic target can be or become any of these three, but that's not essential. They work on different levels. IAA are tactical – you look at them to grow your brand, drive recognition and reach. Your Ueber-Target, on the other hand, is strategic – you look at them to build your brand, as inspiration and aspiration for yourself and your strategic targets.

But sometimes you're lucky and it all synchs up. As On shows, the Swiss sneaker brand that is currently going global. Roger Federer has been a friend and fan of the brand for a while. And as a sports legend with style, he was clearly an Ueber-Target for On. Now he's become 'investor, contributing product designer and representative for the brand' as well (Paton, 2019). Literally a matter of stars aligning: Roger Federer is now On's Ueber-Target, influencer, advocate and ambassador, all in one. The fact that he's also vested in the company could work either way – increasing his credibility since he has 'skin in the game', or undermining his endorsement value by being partial.

One more thing before we move on to researching your targets: Most brands have one kind of Ueber-Target, to help focus the brand. But sometimes it's in the nature of the Mission or the category that you (must) have two or multiple Ueber-Targets. An example of the first is Aston Martin, which equally sees 'Old Money Collectors' and 'Young Active Curators' as Ueber-Targets (ueberbrands.com, 2020). A case for multiple targets is YouTube, whose creators and content are as varied as the world, thus invariably forcing it to subdivide strategic targets as well as Ueber-Targets, as You Tube's Chris Dale explains in our interview in Part Three. However, splitting your Ueber-Targets proves difficult and ineffective more often than not. You're much better off setting your eyes on one group, aspirational across all.

Who and how are they? And how many?

Your main job at this point in the process is to clearly understand and define your Ueber-Target, as everything else, including your strategic target, should 'follow' from there. But, as you've seen, it all hangs together, and you will understand one much better when compared with the other.

The best and easiest place to begin digging into the reality and psychology of your targets is always your community, if you already have one. If you're only starting out, it can also be your personal friends and followers, the ones who are as obsessed with the category or concept as you are. Or it's the kind of already out-there groups and forums you'd like to win over. Either way, the people within your real or imagined community are the ones you should first check out and listen to – in person or via social media. Not only are they a big pile of data to crunch and analyse. They can really teach and inspire you if you look and listen closely, with open eyes and ears.

This was exactly how Seedlip found its Ueber-Target. Seedlip is a wonderful Ueber-Brand. Its Mission is to 'change the way the world drinks with the highest quality non-alcoholic options' or, in better words: 'Solve the dilemma of what you're drinking when you're not drinking' (Seedlip, 2020). As Ben Branson, founder and CEO of Seedlip, told us, in the early days of the brand, when he was trying to understand more about his still limited number of buyers, he noticed one place in particular ordering disproportionate amounts of product, so he got in the car and drove over to check them out. What he found was a revelation, then a very new concept: 'Daybreaker parties' for people who like to dance but not to drink, and preferably do so before they go to work as a kind of fun morning exercise class. Seedlip's Ueber-Target was clear from that moment on: Daybreakers. Cool, fun-loving party people who don't need or want alcohol to enjoy themselves. You can listen to the interview we did with Ben on ueberbrands.com (ueberbrands.com, 2016e). Scan the QR code at the front of the book for a direct link.

Of course, it's usually not as easy as this. And if anything, it works better with a polarizing and passion-driving Mission like Seedlip has. You usually have bigger followings, the conversations are deeper, and the engagement is higher. Though even then it's often hard to really get to the nuances and truly understand mind-sets, motivations and hiccups, let alone have an Ueber-Target jumping out at you like the Daybreakers did.

But what social listening and trying to analyse your communities can almost always do is help develop initial ideas and hypotheses how to cluster or segment your targets.

SEGMENTATION

We can hardly make this into a class of consumer or market research; actually we wouldn't even want to. But some particularities are important, so we touch on those.

Segmentation studies are usually costly. To parse the market, which is their job, they need a fairly big number of respondents. And: The more particular the market or consumer, the less incidence, the more it costs – and the less likely you'll find it readily available. Many institutes like TNS or Euromonitor provide general social or consumer segmentations for purchase, and there is a lot of topic- or market-specific research to be found online, some for sale, others for free. Before investing in a custom study, those are the ones you should start with. Their validity and reliability may be sometimes sketchy, but that's not so important for our purposes. We're looking for inspiration, not validation. Meaning: We don't want to know at this point how big exactly our targets are, how much potential they hold or where geographically or demographically we'll find most of them. What we want first is to identify them. Get an idea of who our Ueber-Target could be and how our strategic target could be cast. The rest you'll do once you have a clear hypothesis, because that's much cheaper than searching for needles in the global haystack of 7.8 billion.

Sometimes you're really lucky and you come across a study that immediately makes your nebulous target vision stand right in front of you, readily researched and vividly labelled. The 'Aspirationals' were such a thing for a client of ours (Globescan, 2019), the 'HENRYs' were it initially for Acqua di Parma (Danziger, 2019).

More likely, you'll find a social or category segmentation somewhere that doesn't quite cut and cluster in line with your concept. But it inspires something, a way of looking at your targets. And often that's all you need to narrow the search or get a better sense of direction.

What you have to do, then, is develop this further through online research or group discussion. Imagine who these people could be, what they would love or hate, how they live, what they buy… And with this as your brief, you can then go to a good research company to suss it out in detail, qualitatively and/or quantitatively.

QUALITATIVE

This is the part where you want to dig deeper, understand an underlying motivation, find the truth behind a public behaviour or attitude, the psychology of a category… that's why it's called qualitative. That and because you look at a very limited, non-representative sample in a relatively expansive way.

Many skip this stage because they feel clear about the 'psychograhics' of their targets, but from our experience, this is a pity. Even one group session or a dozen netnographies often yield amazing insights that can illuminate your thinking about your target but also about your business. And, it's a good regulator to check your developed ideals or phantasy Ueber-Targets against the realities.

There are many different methodologies, from one-on-one interviews to focus groups to cultural or anthropological investigations. Our recommendation is that you invest in an expert who is psychologically trained, experienced in the use of associative and projective techniques and knows how to moderate versus transcribe verbatim.

QUANTITATIVE

The main thing with quantitative research: Your sample must be big enough to allow for sub-clustering and cross-tabbing. Say you're researching something like the 'Suburban BBQ Hero': In this case you need a pretty wide age-range, because you want to see which cohort over-indexes, young fami-lies or 50+, you need men and women as gender proclivities may differ between age groups or regions, you need richer and poorer, you need those that have bought high-end grills and those that are 'passionate but prag-matic' in their tools, the first possibly as the core and the latter as the wider target… The list goes on.

This is what makes quantitative research often quite costly. Therefore, use it cautiously. It is expensive and if you cut corners you may end up caus-ing problems for yourself. Numbers can trick you by feigning accuracy and reliability where there isn't any, as said before.

The good news: Online research has brought costs down substantially. But again, be careful. Complicated questions usually aren't sufficiently answered with simple methods. If your budget is limited, it's better to try to validate your targets indirectly. You can look at existing studies and see if they corroborate your ideas. You can try to deduct the size and value of your groups from other category research. You can approximate, you can use common sense… or you can ask an institute with a study that might cover your interests if they can dig in their data and look for answers to specific questions. They usually accommodate you gladly, if the existing studies are not custom ones. And the costs are still much lower than commissioning your own research.

What's actually most interesting in terms of insights and effectivity are inventive qual-quan options like the CAPO methodology from &Equity (Equity, 2020). They unite the validity of quantitative with the depth of qualitative research, at least to a certain level.

One last point: It's not the focus yet, but you can certainly learn a lot about potential influencers and advocates throughout the above process, perhaps even identify one or the other already.

Personifying

Once you have a pretty good idea of your targets, especially your Ueber-Target, and they have been vetted and scaled, it's time to bring them to life. Transcreate the research findings and the type of person that it gave rise to into something that feels real and can inspire all your stakeholders going forward.

Because this is what this next step is for: Develop your Ueber-Target To Go. A distinct kind of personality and a format to share it in. The benchmark against who everything will be checked going forward – from your innovations to their production to your communication. The 'person' you will always ask if you are in doubt whether something should be done or not and in which way.

And for this it must be sufficiently vivid and detailed. It must be creatively inspiring enough to ignite the heads and hearts of your designers and marketing people. But it must also be real and specific enough for your R&D to gain direction from or your more economically minded trade partners to 'see' it. It should lead many different people and professions with many different perspectives and questions over a long period of time. And for that it must be quite robust.

There are many ways to go about this. Here is one instrument that might help you to refine your Ueber-Target ideas.

Archetyping/Kenotyping™

According to CG Jung, who brought the concept to modern day psychology, archetypes are pre-existing forms or themes within the collective subconscious, which we use to give us guidance in living our lives as well as shaping our identities and looking at others (Jung, 1936). They are behavioural patterns, pre-scripted scenarios that help us act faster and, it seems, more intuitively in any given situation because they are deeply ingrained. We don't think everything through but run on autopilot.

In our efficiency driven business world, this rather layered and complex theory has been often reduced to a set of prototypical characters, basically role models like the hero, the villain, the sage, the magician... (see among others Mark and Pearson, 2001).

How can they help? Two things: First, you should look at them as a bit of a crash course in human psychology, mapping different motivational structures and personality types. A good exercise, forcing you to think deeper about what drives your Ueber-Target or what type of soul your brand has. Just keep in mind that the number of archetypal motives (because the concept applies not only to characters, but also to events, situations, scenarios) is limitless and not confined to the 12 that are often quoted. And they are regularly mixed. Only in poorly written stories are characters cookie-cutter, one-dimensional. In reality, we are much more complex, for better or

FIGURE 12.2 The 12 iconic archetypes are a good starting point, but don't limit your thinking to these

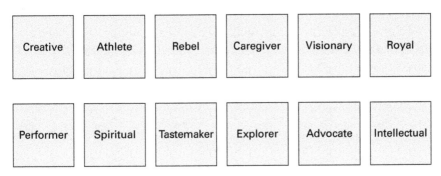

SOURCE The authors (2020)

worse. Nobody is ever consistently and exclusively, say, the hero – in a given situation, let alone throughout life. We mix and match different archetypal concepts like a bit of hero with the face of a jester, a dose of sage and a scenario of doom.

And this is exactly what you have to do for the 'archetypes' to serve their second purpose and help define your brand character or personify your Ueber-Target. Use the iconic 12 as a starting point only, to inspire your thinking, but mix and match them to your liking or needs, give them additional dimensions or contemporary twists. Otherwise you won't really get anywhere, especially in our postmodern age, where eclectic tensions, hybrids and layers rule. Apart from the fact that having such a limited number, often only three or four that fit a given category, would make it quite difficult to differentiate brands.

For our work we have thus evolved Jung's idea of archetypes a bit further into what we call kenotypes™, in cooperation with Dominic Pettman, aforementioned Professor for Culture and Media. 'Keno' is Greek for new, and this is what they are – typical blends of archetypes that you'll find in today's culture, researched across different countries. They can run the gamut from Zen Girl to Ice Queen to Soul Sista. And you can map them and track their evolution. At the latest count we are at around 30 females. Still a manageable number, but one that avoids building clichés. Besides, even those are constantly advanced, combined or sharpened. It's a living system, just like our societies are.

Another interesting way to bring the archetype concept in line with current culture is what Professor Dr Jens-Uwe Pätzmann from Hochschule

Neu-Ulm did. Together with his team he analysed 50 of the most recent blockbuster movies to see what forms the traditional 12 archetypes have taken (Pätzmann and Hartwig, 2018).

And that is what you can do, too. Don't bother with Jung and archetypes and all that if you think it's too complicated. Just pay attention to the hottest Netflix series or Hollywood movies or, better yet, read good novels. You'll find plenty of well-conceived characters to inspire you and give ideas how to shape your Ueber-Target. Also, you can always look at the real-life avatars of those fictional characters, the celebrities. Among them you'll find many examples that can bring your Ueber-Target to life.

Imagining

The most important part in imagining is actually naming. What name or title you give your Ueber-Target but also your strategic target is about 70 per cent of what you have to work on at this stage in the process. Because, remember, we're building a guiding personality, a conceptual character for the entire organization to embrace and work against. And that isn't always unfolded and examined with a 10-page booklet in hand or watching a two-minute video. It's often just referred to by a shorthand, its name.

The other aspect: Where images present a complete picture, words let you create your own. The positive of this is that it is less confining and forces people to use their imagination, which is the whole point. The downside is that it has yet to give you a shared sense of direction in a few words. And that is hard.

That's why this part will probably take the longest and the most discussion. After all it can make a huge difference if you call your Ueber-Target 'Metro Mobiles' or 'The Movers' or 'Forerunners' or 'Work hard, travel harder', as we debated recently for a client. A good example for an evocative yet directive name is 'Kitchen Hustlers', which the cooking brand Haven's Kitchen uses for its Ueber-Target; these are people who like to cook but also have other obligations and hence like some support, tricks or shortcuts sometimes. You can listen to our interview with Haven's Kitchen founder Alison Cayne on ueberbrands.com (ueberbrands.com, 2019e). Scan the QR code at the front of the book for a direct link.

But, of course, as important as the name is, it's not enough by itself. It needs an underpinning, covering or, better, uncovering of as many details and aspects of your Ueber-Target as necessary. The core aspects you need to touch on usually are:

- general outlook on life;
- lifestyle, demographics;
- family situation;
- cultural and commercial interests and hobbies ('avid opera fan and hard-core shopper at TJ Maxx');
- relationship to the category at hand.

To these you can add lots of details that seem interesting or enlightening in your particular case. A good idea is to string all the important aspects together by telling a little story, like 'A day in the life of XX'.

Important to keep in mind: Even if you've researched it all and you could fill every pore of this person with data, don't! Leave room for imagination, because that's what this Ueber-Target is mostly needed for.

And don't worry too much about being 100 per cent 'correct' all the time. It is ok to exaggerate here and there, for creative effect or clarity. As long as it doesn't become a parody or satire. You're not making reportage here, you're concocting your muse, so a little licence is ok.

In terms of formats: Anything goes. It largely depends on the kind of organization, ie what format works best for whom, but also the kind of Ueber-Target you talk about. How you present your personas says a lot about them as well. If you're talking about an erudite, sophisticated target, a linen-bound mini-book may be a good idea. If you're talking about a young beauty target, a fantasy Insta-Account would probably be a better format.

Choose whatever brings your Ueber-Target to life best. Mood boards or swipe-videos (made from existing material) are standards and they always work. The latter, apart from being more fun and shareable digitally, also give you two more dimensions to unfold your character: Sound and motion.

But again, it doesn't hurt to be a bit more creative, like shooting a little video-story, creating a flip-book, designing a lenticular or pop-up book... we have even created 3D rooms for clients, so all their country managers and salespeople could literally immerse themselves in the life of their Ueber-Target.

RECAP: TO DO – STEP 5

- Define your Ueber-Target – in contrast to your strategic target.
- Align those with existing or desired users – as well as non-users.
- Start by looking at and listening in on existing communities – your own, or the ones you want to win.
- Check out existing segmentation studies to parse your market – and build on those to 'imagine' your targets.
- Use qualitative research to dig deeper – enrich and corroborate your imagination.
- Use quantitative research to validate your ideas – using existing studies or commissioning your own.
- Collect information and thoughts on potential influencers throughout – as well as brand ambassadors.
- Craft all this into a persona – possibly applying the concept of archetypes.
- Make it come alive – in a format that fits who you're talking about.

Step 6: Ignite All Targets

You've come to the last step of building your Ueber-Brand: Sharing it with the world. Partially, this was already the topic of 'Live Your Dream', in the sense of curating your Brand Presence and experiences. Now it's about igniting and engaging your targets, from 'Ueber' to 'Wider'. And, actually, not just those, but all your stakeholders, from employees to investors. Apart from the fact that all you say and do communicates way beyond the intended 'targets' anyway, you obviously have a lot more interactional groups besides your consumers.

But let's stick with those for a second. We don't really like the term 'target'. It's too martial. It's outdated, implying a subject–object relationship. It's just wrong, as if you were out to hit or even kill someone. But we couldn't really think of anything better – 'audiences' or 'recipients' being equally passive, 'stakeholders' being bulky, never mind 'communication partners'.

So, we stuck with targets. But we must highlight that in today's brand interactions, none of the word's connotations are valid anymore; their opposites are. It already starts with 'interactions'. Today's brand relations, including mass communications, are by and large interactive, the 30 second commercial monologue yesterday's hero. But those interactions have also become more complex in recent years. In particular, Ueber-Brands are expected to connect with their audiences through inspired and shared experiences. Proclamations are reserved for truly big, world-changing news, preferably of the sustainability kind.

But, these days, the targets are also offering more in exchange for the goods than just their hard-earned cash: Knowledge, credibility, status, social currency, followers, advocacy… The good old transaction 'merchandise–money' has truly turned into a multidimensional interaction.

On top of all this, Ueber-Brands always have to target in a non-targeting way. Their style must live up to the sophistication they aim for. They must seduce. Because selling, just like targeting, is far too direct and banal... non-experiential.

We saw a nice Chaumet print ad the other day that, albeit a bit restrained, sums up in an almost Emily Post kind of way what people want from their 'Ueber-Brands' and which we'll talk about in the following chapters in some way or another: Grace and character. Good luck!

Myth to stories

The first challenge is how to take your Brand Myth into actual communications. Because this is the goal vs traditional brand communication, which has too often been too tactical. Your Myth is the meta-story that all you say or do should ladder up to. All your communications should tell mini-stories that are part of or derive from your overall Myth.

That does not mean you should always say the same. You'd be dead in no time if you did. It doesn't even mean you should be totally consistent all the time. Predictability is not very exciting, which is why many Ueber-Brands have a lot of 'soft assets' to play with – iconic signs, colours, shapes... that make your brand communication recognizable but not formulaic.

No, what your communication should be is not consistent but coherent. There should be a connective narrative running through everything, threading it all together and always leading to your Brand Myth. At the same time, however, it should always feel fresh and surprising, letting people see your brand and its Myth in new ways. Just like a good soap opera, basically, that has a clear theme and cast yet can let these live through ever-new twists and turns to keep you hooked. You see, in a way we're going back to the beginnings of TV advertising ... soap opera 2.0 so to speak.

A good CB

No matter if you work with external partners or in-house teams, the work you get is always only as good as the brief you give.

There are hundreds of briefing formats in the world of marketing, starting already with how to call them: Creative brief, which the acronym CB traditionally stands for? Communication brief, acknowledging it's not only a creative challenge? Or brand brief, because communication may be just one solution, next to action, etc? And that's just the beginning.

We like 'creative brief' because creativity is what you always want – a creative solution, no matter if it's a campaign, a promotion or a store opening. And that it should be strategically smart and pointed – well, that's the point of the brief.

Regarding format: It doesn't really matter. If the agency you work with, for example, is partial to one particular format, go with it. If you've used one in the past, fine. There are five things, however, that every brief has to talk about – even if its format gives you only three boxes:

1 Objective. Why are we writing this? What do we want?

2 Target. Who are we addressing? Who do we want to do, think or feel what?

3 Insight. What do we know about them? What's inspiring them, holding them back?

4 Message. What information, idea, act, fact... could most affect this target? How could we nudge them towards the objective?

5 Technicalities. CI guides, timelines, budget...

The example in Figure 13.1 is one that we have worked with in the past. It's a bit more elaborate than just the five musts above, but it's still pretty straightforward. We particularly like that it puts action and communication on an equal footing, not presuming communication is the only solution. And that it includes questions regarding our effectivity, how we will gauge success or failure.

The good thing about writing a brief is not only that those briefed get direction. It's almost more important that it forces those who brief you to think things through. Is it an action we want to incite or an attitude we want to change? Is communication really the best way to go? Are we really clear about the targets? What are our KPIs? Or does success show in 'soft' factors?

The other thing that gets forgotten all too often: As the one who briefed, you are responsible for the project and you should lead throughout, support with additional information, answer questions, check in, discuss potential thoughts... A brief is never the end of a job, it's always the beginning of one – 'theirs' and yours.

FIGURE 13.1 An example of a creative brief that inspires thinking beyond communication as the only solution

MISSION
Why does the brand exist? And what is its story?
Everything we do should further our mission and reflect our myth.

What is the issue?
Why do we have this brief in the first place? What is the business problem?

APPROACH
How are we likely to solve the issue?

Is it about the brand taking action to bring its mission to life?
Or is it about getting other people to act? Making them buy/buy into?
Or is it about getting the world to listen? Confronting an attitude?

Remember – the solution may not be (just) communications.

RALLYING CRY/SPARK
What is the key idea, inspiration or insight?
What one thought seems more important than any other? What feels like the best inspiration we have right now – may be an idea or an example or a sketch…

Is there any support for that key 'something'?
Show us why it's important.

PEOPLE
Who do we want to engage with?

And what do we know about them that is important in this context?
Any insights? Barriers? Traditions?

SUCCESS
In the end, what do we want to achieve? What do we want people to do or think or feel?
What's our end-game? And how is that different to what our target does, thinks or feels today?

How will we measure success?
New behaviours, sales, free coverage in newspapers, new customers, fame… there are many possible measures…. best ro use a variety.

Anything else….?
Space for random inspiration, ways in, gut instincts, observations on competition, watch-outs….

SOURCE The authors (2020)

Agency or in-house?

This didn't use to be a question, but with communications having become more manifold and digitalized, and brands becoming media themselves, things have changed. Many companies no longer have one or two key external partners over time, but instead work with many agencies from design to PR to advertising to performance, often even competing ones in a given field. And they've started taking things in-house and/or set up custom teams with marketing networks, covering all disciplines, uniquely for them, like an outsourced in-house team.

What to advise? Generally speaking, we're Solomonic: A mix is best. It makes sense to keep community and content management close, in-house or custom-built, long-term connected. The knowledge needed and gained is so vital to your brand, it doesn't make sense to completely outsource. Who else but you could best answer critical posts in forums? Who but your staff has all the inside know-how to decide what to share and when? Apart from the fact that your social media and your customer relationship management (CRM) should be closely linked anyway, feeding each other. Two wheels, with your organization as transmission.

The same holds true for strategic partners. Their value builds over time. The more they know about you and your category, the better they can help.

But for creative jolts and certainly for the 'big jobs' it makes more sense to get the calibre needed externally. Apart from the fact that you can't commit to and pay certain talent permanently, it's harder to think out of the box when you're in it all the time. The value of your in-house teams is their involvement and intimacy with the brand. But that makes it hard to then forget everything, step outside and think different and anew.

Being in-house brings depth, of head and heart, knowledge and commitment. Ideally. Going out gives you width, perspectives and horizons, inspiration and stimulation. It's as simple as that.

Actors and symbolic acts

Why 'actors and symbolic acts'? Because that's what influencers, etc are: They act on your behalf. And that's what all your stakeholders should do, acting in favour of the brand – no matter if they work for it, talk about it, invest in it or buy it. A community of more or less active 'agents' inspired by a shared Mission and Myth.

To achieve this, your brand, however, has to act first. You have to produce and provide for real, but also for inspiration, in so-called symbolic acts. This can be anything from staging big events like salesforce' Dreamforce, the annual symposium for change in San Francisco, to turning your founder's villa into a museum, like Louis Vuitton did in Asnières (Louis Vuitton, 2020) or sponsoring the Tribeca Film Fest (Montblanc) and supporting a cause. You have to set the stage, so to speak, with backdrops and props for all the action in your favour to take place.

BTW: We talk about 'action' and 'actors' because today's communication is more visual and experiential than talkative. It's about showing, proving and doing things rather than just claiming them. But communication it still is, of course. Just louder, as images supposedly talk. And more engaging, as acts hopefully are.

Employees, ambassadors and influencers

The best is always when others talk you up. Ideally without ulterior motive, like an endorsement contract. But that's hard. And requires a lot of good and inspiring things to be done, like the just mentioned symbolic acts. To resonate, you need to be an agitator, perturb, push, proffer our culture at large or at least the category you're in (see also 'Interaction', page 135). To create word of mouth you must give people something to talk about or say something meaningful and unheard of. Or you're lucky and have a product that creates exceptional passion, including the urge to share that passion.

ROLES AND CIRCLES OF INFLUENCE
The matrix in Figure 13.2 details the different roles all these 'actors on your behalf' can take.

Looking at it closely, you'll conclude easily that a good employee covers all four quadrants. And that's exactly why we always say that Ueber-Brands must radiate inside out.

Your employees are your best spokespeople; ambassadors, influencers, experts and advocates all rolled into one. If you hire well, that is, choosing those that are not just looking for a career but care about your Mission. Tom's story about TerraCycle in Part Three is a perfect example of how to build a true movement from employees to partners around the world.

One of your employees is you, of course, the CEO and/or founder. The head of the company is its biggest influencer – and should act like one as well. That was always true for business-to-business or investor relations and

FIGURE 13.2 It's important to be clear about which role an influencer will play for or with your brand

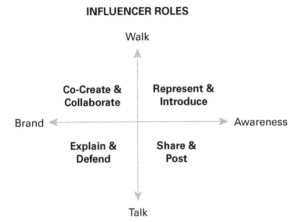

INFLUENCER ROLES

SOURCE The authors (2020)

becomes more and more expected in business-to-consumer relations as well. Though it can get tricky sometimes, especially when communication isn't that person's strongest skill.

Next stop are your customers, particularly the Ueber-Target ones. Assuming your customer satisfaction is good, brand users make the most convincing ambassadors. Yet, they are regularly under-utilized. WornWear from Patagonia is a great example of how to create a forum for your fans and tease advocating stories out of them. It's all about repair and re-use/re-cycle of Patagonia garments, so full on the brand's Mission, but with that come lots of adventurous tales from the product's 'first life', showcasing its durability and the fun you can have along the way.

From this group you should ideally also choose your 'professional' influencers, people you pick for their expertise or reach, or both, to endorse your brand. Everybody knows by now that these people get paid for their favourable communication, just like brand endorsers or those giving testimonials always have been. So, don't even try to pretend otherwise. What can still make the conceit credible is when they are true fans/users of the brand or category competent experts, who conceivably could be users – without them being undiscerning and over-used marketing sluts, of course.

More and more, however, it's advisable to go for micro vs macro influencers. 'Macros' are nothing but celebrity testimonials – as expensive and effective as they've always been, or not. Good micros, on the other hand,

FIGURE 13.3   Ueber-Brands must radiate inside out

CIRCLES OF INFLUENCE

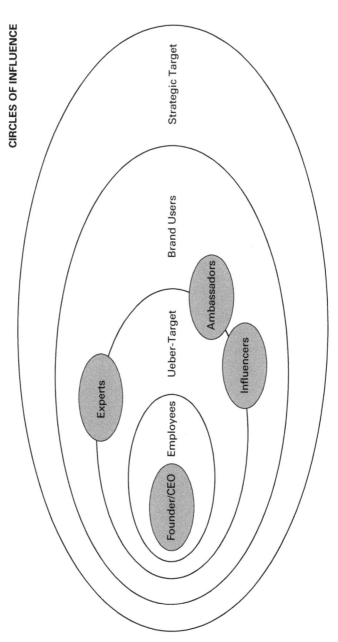

Strategic Target

Brand Users

Ueber-Target

Employees

Experts

Ambassadors

Influencers

Founder/CEO

SOURCE The authors (2020)

still have the social connection with their followers, the expertise and the credibility, which let the whole concept get so high-flying in the first place.

And that basically gets us back to why your employees and users are your ultimate micro-influencers. They are the most credible, are accessible and are socially connected with 'normal' users, and they are far less costly.

HIERARCHIES OF ACCESS

If you want to learn about the way our societies congregate around gods and gurus, and brands for that matter, Neil MacGregor's book *Living with the Gods* is a great starting point (MacGregor, 2018). Among other things, he shows how all cults are built on differing degrees of access. Direct admission to the holy grail is only granted to the priests, your employees so to speak. They should ideally be recruited from your Ueber-Target, like the Vestal Virgins, who tended to the sacred fire in Rome and were always chosen from 'founding' families, known to care about continuity.

A more contemporary and worldly example is the biking brand Rapha. We already explained its 'Sophisticated Cyclist' Ueber-Target and how it cascades into the biking market at large ('Live Your Dream'). Now, let's look how it creates different degrees of access – and admiration – through what we call the 'Velvet Rope' (see Part One, Principle 2, page 11).

Simon Mottram, who founded the business in 2004 in London, was inspired by the gritty but gentlemanly world of road cycle racing back in the 1960s. The brand name itself is borrowed from a somewhat mystical but short-lived team on the Tour de France (1959–61). Mottram created high-performing apparel with a unique modern-vintage aesthetic reflecting the 'hard-working and fulfilling character' of his favourite sport and he quickly found that plenty of other *vélo* enthusiasts shared his sentiment. And this is where the Velvet Rope is drawn – just like in front of any self-respecting club, separating the ones 'in' from those 'out'.

On the 'in' side are committed Rapha Cycling Club (RCC) members who regularly meet up in shop-clubhouses around the world and organize 'Gent's Races' like the 'Leave No Gentleman Behind, Bavaria' (Schott, 2014). They call themselves 'Raphia' and they inspire many more occasional racers to buy a RCC membership, plenty of branded gear and to buy into the philosophy, symbols and rituals: their motto is *ex duris gloria* ('glory through suffering'), they always help struggling members push over a hill and they recognize their sub-tribes by customized caps on their handlebars and on their heads that are accessible to RCC members only (Richardson, 2017).

On the 'out' side of the Velvet Rope, the Rapha bunch is sometimes referred to as MAMILs, and other riders smirk when they see them pull up in what they perceive as outlandishly expensive gear. Yet, they are still connected to the brand, because they are part in. They form the hard-core followers from whom the next insiders, aka RCC members, will be picked. And they thus still wield 'influence' over all those outside, the ones on the sidelines, drawn to the spectacle, but mostly spectators, hardly ever actors. In marketing speech: Our wider target or occasional buyers.

Sounds crazy? But it works, as it has since the beginning of human culture.

The Rapha or Raphia example explains one other thing quite well: Just as you should choose your influencers for their commitment to the brand, you cannot look at them as only means to an end. You must respect and ideally involve them as partners to be really effective. Juergen Habermas, the preeminent sociologist, calls this 'communicative action' (Habermas, 2011), meaning you discuss with mutual respect, in search of the best solution, vs trying to push your own opinion through and direct others. An ideal, sure, but worth striving for. And it can actually be fun and pragmatically done. Fashion brand Alexander McQueen does it in its London flagship, where it sometimes opens up the normally private second floor for creative (design) students to discuss and 'move from a very exclusive and maybe too-transactional space into a highly inclusive and inspirational one', as its CEO Emmanuel Gintzburger says (Amed, 2019). The new level of Ueber-Brand building involves stakeholders and especially Ueber-Targets in the brand creation and evolution, as we can also see in the YouTube interview in Part Three. The brand not only feels 'made for me' but is 'made with me'.

Sponsorships and CSR

The terms 'positive luxury' or 'conscious luxury' refer to high-end brands that have embraced sustainability as (part of) the new quality. And the world of mass is not far behind: Most brands have understood by now that certain ethical and ecological standards must be upheld to not become the next scandal and risk their followers' goodwill, especially that of the younger targets. Sustainable success is almost impossible today without a certain level of sustainability.

The boundaries between sponsoring and CSR have become blurred in this, if they weren't always, which is why we lumped them together.

Traditionally, sponsorships were acts of patronage, a way of 'giving back' by those blessed with success in a preferably public manner. It was used haphazardly and more tactically. Internally it was classified as PR, usually on corporate rather than brand level. The connections to the company or brand purpose were often none or very loose ones, because the primary purpose of most businesses was simply being profitable. And sponsorships were a way to legitimize that profit, as well as the less agreeable actions presumably needed to achieve it.

Corporate social responsibility (CSR), on the other hand, was born more principally. It's inspired by the Kyosei philosophy conceived in the 1990s and calling for businesses to build symbiotic relationships. The idea is that a company has certain responsibilities towards the societies it lives in – and from. The concept is by definition more integral, ongoing and strategic. It's not something you can do – or not, like sponsoring. It's something you must look at and commit to, at least on a certain level.

And now it's all become one. Because the concept of having a Mission or purpose requires you to look past the balance sheets and behave in line with your Mission across the board – commercially as well as societally. At least for Ueber-Brands. It does not mean that we must all be out to change the world, eradicate poverty or limit global warming. Simply changing or elevating your world, ie your category, can still be a big deal and business. But it means that Ueber-Brands have to live their Mission – internally in the way they produce and organize themselves (CSR) as well as externally through symbolic acts (sponsorships).

REI, the outdoor apparel brand, gives back 80 per cent of its profit to outdoor communities. It's an incredibly hefty percentage, but when you look at it as a re-investment it seems smart and not so astounding anymore. These 'sponsorships' or 'CSR acts' help REI to create word-of-mouth (WOM) marketing much more effectively and directly in the right places. And: This engagement isn't arbitrary or immaterial to their business. It is directly linked to the company's Mission, creating awareness and engagement, branding and selling in one swoop. It is truly a business-building investment, and definitely not some kind of patronage.

Chobani, on the other hand, still follows a more traditional model. Ten per cent of its post-tax profits regularly go to its foundations, supporting refugees, immigrants and generally those less privileged. There is a connection between these 'sponsorships' and the brand, but only in the form of the founder's personal background and the brand's name 'Chobani', referring to nomadic mountain shepherds in his native Kurdistan. But hardly anybody knows this. It is not woven into the Mission and Myth, and certainly not into the product marketing. It lives in the fine print at the bottom of Chobani's webpage, perhaps more nobly, but definitely less effectively so.

Important for you, en route to elevating your brand into an Ueber-Brand: Choose your Mission wisely (see 'Set Your Mission'). Don't stray too much from what you're actually doing, don't go too high-ground, because then you'll have trouble creating symbolic acts (eg sponsorships) that effectively connect with and further your business as REI does. Test-run your Mission by checking what kind of sponsorships, commitments or advocacies you'd take on – and think about whether this is in your – and the brand's – heart.

Of course, you can sell ice cream as a means to further your socio-ecological agenda or shoes to advocate atheism. But chances are, you'll have to come up with some complex three-part Mission as Ben & Jerry's does with its 'interrelated product Mission, economic Mission and social Mission' to connect it all. And it will still always be flimsy and questionable. Far from the effectivity of a well-rounded Mission that unites commercial and societal interests, as Jim shows with Burt's Bees in Part Three.

FIGURE 13.4   Burt's Bees model 'The Greater Good' connects its product, profit and societal Mission

SOURCE   Reproduced with permission of Burt's Bees (2020)

Interaction

'Courage comes from caring,' said Lao-Tse, supposedly. And he was right, even etymologically, without speaking English. Courage comes from cor, Latin for 'heart', as still evident in our idiom 'having the heart for something'.

Why are we telling you this? It's good for cocktail party conversations. But beyond that it also captures neatly this last chapter in elevating your brand: When you're driven by a Mission and follow your convictions, you naturally 'have the heart' to do things, which may seem daring to others. Ueber-Brands grow on their readiness to go places that others don't dare, do the new, the less expected, the courageous. They lead and dare all of us to follow. And this must be your attitude in designing your interactions.

A good case in point is the recent collaboration between the venerable German porcelain brand Meissen and Supreme, the streetwear superstar (Waters, 2019) mentioned in Part One. There is none to extremely little overlap between the two brands' targets. And their equities are dissonant at best. Yet Meissen agreed to this controversial venture, probably in a move to regain some edge and younger audiences, as did Supreme, flaunting its collaboration power and trying to prove artistic substance, we assume. And guess what – it seems to have worked. Never mind that the porcelain cupids in a Supreme T-shirt, which weren't exactly cheap at over €4,000 retail, are already offered for over €7,000 on auctions. All the PR and awareness this garnered is priceless, at least for Meissen, Supreme being seen as a media darling. Meissen is talked about, comes across as gutsy and proves willing to re-assert its long-lost role in contemporary culture – and not just the high kind.

Tonality

In our first book we spoke a lot about how Ueber-Brands must 'un-sell'. It basically means that overly promotional communication is usually avoided in the interest of creating an air of cool. Applying more seductive techniques like staying a bit veiled and mysterious, having a highly confident tone, even arrogant to some, being courageous, provoking and teasing, yet holding back at the same time. Playing hard-to-get rather than hard-selling yourself. And, if you've got to be pushier here and there, at least be tongue-in-cheek about it.

This basically leaves two big tonality routes, as well as mixing them, if you want to 'Ueber' your brand: 'Stand strong' or 'Stay schtum' as Molly

Flatt calls it (Flatt, 2012). But before we get into these, let's look at an Ueber-Brand that screwed this up royally, not doing either and creating a major s$%& storm, including a 15 per cent share drop.

'It's just a terrible commercial' (Mautz, 2019). That's one of the headlines written about the Peloton Christmas ad 2019. And it sums it up quite well. We don't even want to get into the whole debate of whether the ad is truly sexist (it is), mysoginist (it is), fattist (it is), patronizing (it is)… the list could go on. What's most worrying to us is that this piece of communication is so utterly cheesy, so out of touch with contemporary culture, it couldn't even dream of inspiring it. Yet that is exactly what Ueber-Brands should aspire to, and Peloton actually does in most everything else.

We heartily disagree with Mark Ritson and 'the Sharpists' (Ritson, 2019) who claim salience is all that matters in communication. This may be arguable for regular mass brands, but it certainly is not for prestige ones like Peloton. Detail and design matter more with Ueber-Brands than with regular ones. How they do – or say – something is just as important as what they do or say. Their appeal rides heavily on their perceived cultural cool and sophistication. And anything that puts this with-it-ness and wit into question is potentially lethal. Because style you either have always – or not.

STAND STRONG

Probably the best and most effective way for Ueber-Brands to communicate is full-on Mission, with heart and courage.

Square, the mobile payment system, does this in a charming and droll way (thanks to the namesake song from the 1940s) in its almost anthemic 'thing-ummy-bob' commercial (tvadmusic, 2018), celebrating the often-overlooked craftsmen and -women, and their value for our everyday lives. Its series of small entrepreneur and city portraits takes this further and tells edutaining stories in more depth, close up and human. In all this, it brings its Mission 'We believe everyone should be able to participate and thrive in the economy… we believe in fair and square' (Square, 2020) to life. And it does so in an intelligent, humorous, warm-hearted and even artistic way.

BrewDog, the Scottish beer rebel, is another great example. Much rowdier and grungier in style, but thus equally true to its Mission, showing a knack for today's (sub-)culture and its Ueber-Target's ideals and aspirations. Check out its 'Decade of Dog' review of its mythic story on YouTube and you get a good idea (YouTube, 2020). Then look at its more product-focused 'This punk's for you' video and you'll see how you can sell in an un-selling way, including a very effective spoof on what's called 'ingredient porn' in marketing lingo.

STAY 'SCHTUM'

Of course, no brand can afford to stay totally schtum. After all, they're created to move us – and their merchandise. But being a bit enigmatic or even esoteric can do an Ueber-Brand a lot of good, especially if it's of the artsy and luxurious kind.

Jil Sander, the high-end conceptual fashion brand, hired famous German independent film director Wim Wenders to create five short films for its 2018 and 2019 collection. Beautiful but certainly not shouting at you. All its other 'communication' is similar, rather cerebral, sometimes surreal, always artistic – completely in line with its equity, but far from traditional notions of advertising.

Those are examples of how golden 'silence' can be in the case of Ueber-Brands. Acting in a controlled way imbues you with an aura of control, speaking softly makes people listen, staying above shouting matches builds authority. Apart from the fact that these are all also Ideas That Do. And the quietest action will always speak louder than the mightiest megaphone.

FIGURE 13.5 This frame is empty because Burning Man does not see it as culturally appropriate to share pictures in 'brand' contexts, as they told us. It is one of its core principles – 'decommodification' – to restrain communication from and about the event

BRANDS AS MEDIA

'The medium is the message.' When Marshall McLuhan coined this famous marketing mantra in the late 1960s, he was talking more about the socio-logical aspects of media, namely TV. But it holds true for today's Ueber-Brands as well. The How is as crucial for them as the What. And this means channel and context matter – in building their presence as well as in choosing their ways of communication.

As an Ueber-Brand you can never assess anything, including your media or placement choices, purely on efficacy. You always have to factor in how it reflects on your equity, what message your media sends.

This is why magazines like *Vogue* or *Architectural Digest* still pull quite a lot of advertising. 'Being seen' there builds cachet; it's the fashion and design world's equivalent to the *Good Housekeeping* seal. And this is also why brands have more and more become their own media. They occasion-ally splurge on 'big' campaigns for reach and broad awareness. But they mainly try to pull their followers through their Mission or non-traditional and self-disseminated communication in the interest of more engaging and equity-building target interactions. The latter is often called native content, especially when it looks like it was 'born' online, isn't overly 'selly' and comes with a less polished, homemade feel. 'Non-traditional' means 'wild-postings' or other creative outdoor/in-life placements and cooperation.

And then there is truly becoming your own medium. RedBull is the ulti-mate and well-known case here, its media-arm (Red Bull Media House) having taken on such dimensions that rumour says it might be severed soon. But there are also other ways, like creating your own 'world' to showcase your brand and let your fans dive into it. Swarovski Kristallwelten and Porsche Experience Centers we already talked about. Other examples are retail flagships cum restaurants, café or bar. Or brands that go all the way out into the hospitality business like Armani, Bulgari or Mini did. Latest entry in this is Shinola, the watch and accessory brand from Detroit, which recently opened its own boutique hotel. But careful, these are investment-heavy and can easily feel arbitrary and gratuitous if the link between the 'hospitality' offer and the brand's Mission isn't as obvious, as in the case of Rapha, for example. You 'borrow interest' and thus imply that you don't think your brand and its original offer suffices.

The point in all this: As much as you are creating your brand based on your own Mission and beliefs, you should communicate in an original, idio-syncratic manner. And that includes your media choices – or better yet your own media.

It's all digital

Someone recently said 'Having a chief digital officer is like having a CEO – a chief electricity officer'. In the past decades our lives, and certainly the world of brands and marketing, have been digitized to such a degree that it doesn't make sense to have a separate 'digital department' anymore – or a chapter on digital for that matter. It's all digital, at least at a certain point in time. Your wonderfully personal experience in that old-school bakery in a cobble-stone street of Stockholm's Gamla Stan ends with the receipt being e-mailed – followed by newsletters, rebates... a never-ending slew of CRM. The artisanal wood bowl you bought in that Soho 'gallery' has a QR to watch a film about it being made in a Kenyan women's co-op. The custom blend colour kit that makes you uniquely you is only available online DTC, just like the love of your life or your next hot date.

It does not mean that everything should 'feel' digital, like a soulless row of 0s and 1s. Not at all, as trends like 'technomysticism' or 'netromancy' (Wortham, 2015) show. Our technological rage has created the opposite, a shift towards the artisanal, the handmade, the soulful, the natural and traditional.

And it certainly shouldn't mean that your budget should go full on performance marketing or social, as we have already discussed.

But what it does mean is that all you do as an Ueber-Brand should no longer follow a binary mindset – online vs offline, mass vs prestige, old vs young, men vs women. Instead, embrace your self-created Mission and Myth cross-channel, cross-line, cross-culture. The only thing that matters is that you are true to yourself and your followers.

RECAP: TO DO – STEP 6

- Translate your Myth into many stories to tell – or do.

- Be coherent in all your activities – but not necessarily consistent.

- Always develop clear creative briefs – not the least to discipline yourself and think things through strategically.

- Decide what to do in-house and what to outsource – probably a mix of both.

- Choose influencers and ambassadors – and decide their respective roles.

- Start with yourself and your employees – then your Ueber-Target users.

- Set up different 'hierarchies of access' – tiering along the Velvet Rope.

- Define and develop 'symbolic acts' – often sponsorships or CSR activities.
- Be aware of your 'style' – for Ueber-Brands the How is essential.
- Stand strong, interact with courage – or stay schtum, exuding quiet authority.
- Be your own media – digitally integrated.

Summing up

The Ueber-Branding Model

Here we summarize all the steps and their action points in overview – structured in the three phases Dream, Do, Dare. But as we said going in: This is the logic flow in theory. In practice, things often happen in parallel. And that's ok, because ultimately they're all interrelated, as Figure 14.1 shows.

FIGURE 14.1 The three phases (six steps) of our Ueber-Branding Model capture all seven principles of Ueber-Brands as laid out in book one

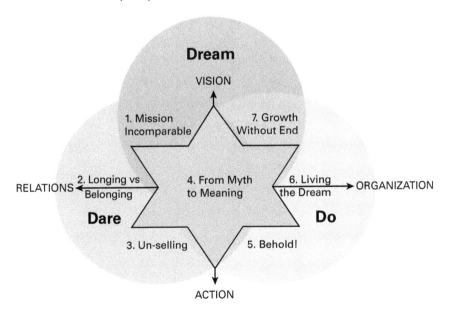

SOURCE The authors (2020)

DREAM

Step 1: Set Your Mission

- Investigate your brand/company – with an open mind.
- Dive into your archives – if you think you don't have any, raid the 'junk' cabinets.
- Interview key stakeholders – C-suite to workbench, internal/external.
- Compare with your realities – sourcing/production, organization, budget...
- Summarize in 5 to 10 beliefs – as unique and controversial as possible.
- Analyse market and competition – where do you/can you make a difference?
- Check against your consumers and trends – category and culture at large.
- Discuss all in Mission Workshop – and ideate Mission Directions.
- Phrase into snappy Mission Statements – big and bold, yet specific and ownable.
- Translate into full brand equity – including What and How.
- Optional: Collect feedback from key staff not involved yet.

Step 2: Write Your Myth

- Look at your founding story – and how to make it the ideal starting point for your Mission journey.
- Explore your company/brand culture and history – and pick those aspects that could help to build a narrative.
- Conduct a semiotic study – for new ways to look at your brand's 'signs'.
- Coalesce all into a mythical storyline (plot) – either to 'reach beyond' or 'guide us'.
- Write it out as your meta-story – the narrative to guide all you do and which all communication shall ladder up to.
- Potentially use the concept of archetypes – to define your hero self.
- Use facts and imagination in doing so – but stay truthful.
- Follow the Separation, Initiation, Return Model – include the challenges.

DO

Step 3: Realize Your Dream

- Assess your portfolio according to its 'Mission fitness' – along the entire lifecycle.
- Look at everything from different perspectives – facts can be interpreted.
- Select the heroes – amend the products and services that are ambivalent, deprioritize the 'misfits'.
- Uncover hidden assets and new opportunities – 'inspired' by Mission-musts.
- Ideate and innovate based on your ideals – validate afterwards.
- Define a unique design language – include naming.
- Substantiate your products with STBs – vs simple RTBs.
- 'Ritualize' your products – elevate the role they play in people's lives.
- Celebrate the superiority of your products and services – develop information and education strategies.

Step 4: Live Your Dream

- Take a close look at your culture – to ensure it reflects your Mission in the best way.
- Define values and desired behaviours – codifying your culture.
- Recruit accordingly – make passion for your Mission a key criterion.
- Enable the culture you're after – with respective structures, processes, policies.
- Develop inspirational, symbolic acts – which can actually ignite your business at the same time.
- Adapt your benchmarks and incentive programmes – to reflect your values.
- Assess your organizational structures – and adapt as necessary.
- Define your brand character and craft your identity to reflect your Mission – inside and out.
- Check your distribution strategy online and offline – evaluate not only reach but also equity fit and distinctiveness.
- Design your brand experiences to live your Mission and Myth – starting with standard operational aspects.
- Focus on those details that are critical to the story you want to tell – finding unexpected twists.

DARE

Step 5: Find Your Ueber-Target

- Define your Ueber-Target – in contrast to your strategic target.

- Align both – with existing or desired users – as well as non-users.

- Start by looking at and listening in on existing communities – your own, or the ones you want to win.

- Check out existing segmentation studies to parse your market – and build on those to 'imagine' your targets.

- Use qualitative research – to enrich and corroborate your ideas.

- Use quantitative research to validate your ideas – using existing studies or commissioning your own.

- Collect information and thoughts on potential influencers throughout – as well as brand ambassadors.

- Craft all this into a persona – possibly applying the concept of archetypes.

- Make it come alive – in a format that fits who you're talking about.

Step 6: Ignite All Targets

- Translate your Myth into many stories to tell – or do.

- Be coherent in all your activities – but not necessarily consistent.

- Always develop clear creative briefs – not least to discipline yourself and think things through strategically.

- Decide what to do in-house and what to outsource – probably a mix of both.

- Choose influencers and ambassadors – and decide their respective roles.

- Start with yourself and your employees – then your Ueber-Target users.

- Set up different 'hierarchies of access' – tiering along the Velvet Rope.

- Define and develop 'symbolic acts' – often sponsorships or CSR activities.

- Be aware of your 'style' – for Ueber-Brands the How is essential.

- Stand strong, interact with courage – or stay schtum, exuding quiet authority.

- Be your own media – digitally integrated.

LIKE WHAT YOU READ? – WANT TO KNOW EVEN MORE?

Remember that you can access multi-media materials relating to the content of this book, as well as additional or updated case studies, podcast interviews, commentary and more at our website, www.ueberbrands.com. Or simply scan the QR code below to be led right to the Bonus Material page for the book.

We value your comments on the models, methods and cases we share in the book and would love to hear about your own experiences in elevating brands. We encourage you to discuss them with the Ueber-Brands community on our blog at ueberbrands.com or to write to us directly at authors@ueberbrands.com. Chances are we will want to interview you for the podcast or for our next book.

Lessons: Ueber-Branding in action

Practitioner perspectives and insights

In Part One we summarized and illustrated the seven principles we have found to drive the success of Ueber-Brands through our research. Part Two provided an in-depth review of the three phases of brand elevation and six associated steps we recommend you take to get there, based on our own experience and that of best-in-class peers.

For this final Part Three of the book, we invited seven practitioners to tell you directly about key aspects of brand elevation and how they are brought to life in their companies.

You will read from the founder of TerraCycle about how he transformed the recycling company's Mission into a Myth and movement. The CEO of prestige beauty brand Aqua di Parma talks about how the mythical core allows her to grow the brand's equity and business, concurrently. Burt's Bees is premium priced but now part of a large consumer goods group and operating in the popular segment. Yet the brand has succeeded in growing purpose and profit in harmony right up to today, as Jim Geikie, GM throughout the whole transition, recounts.

Starbucks has become a global brand behemoth, and that requires harking back to your brand DNA to stay strong as you grow, as the ex-CMO Europe, Samantha Yarwood, who was responsible for the project explains. How do you 'shine from the inside out'? As the, then, Global Head of

Community at Airbnb tells us, defining a purpose for Airbnb was one thing, but launching and truly living it as an organization is quite another. You will read how they succeeded in doing it. Lakrids is the dream of liquorice lovers come true. But how to scale such a dream, internally and externally? This is what the high-end candy's Global Director of Sales at the time will tell us about.

And finally, we look out into a future of brands as media and as cooperative platforms. And for that, we turned to no lesser than Chris Dale, YouTube's Global Head of Communications to learn about how to be a brand when you are not one but many.

Each of the seven stories comes in its own style and form to capture the unique experiences and insights in their most genuine way. The majority were written by the practitioners themselves; others however are recounted or transcribed by us, and one is even a direct dialogue.

For all seven we asked our contributors to provide a brief bulleted summary to make things even easier for you.

Enjoy – and be inspired!

Case 1: TerraCycle

From Mission to Myth to movement, or:
How to 'eliminate the idea of waste'

Many business-to-business companies do not go much beyond seeking a recognizable, visual identity when it comes to brand-building. The often technical focus of their offers as well as the presumed mostly functional brand–customer relations seem at odds with more emotional or even seductive marketing or brand-building efforts. TerraCycle is one to prove this wrong. A waste management company and thus literally at the bottom of it all, is evolving to become an Ueber-Brand of sustainability by applying most of our seven principles, from Myth to Ueber-Targeting to radiating inside out. Winning over the hearts and minds of its employees, consumer packaged goods (CPG) companies, suppliers and the general public by rallying them behind its Mission of 'Eliminating the idea of waste'.

In this article Tom Szaky, the iconic founder of TerraCycle and cheerleader-in-chief, tells us first-hand how he and his passionate waste worriers make everyone buy into material recycling and join in to create a global movement. You can also listen to an interview we did with Tom on ueberbrands.com (ueberbrands.com, 2019c). Scan the QR code at the front of the book for a link.

Tom Szaky

Tom was a 19-year-old freshman when he dropped out of Princeton University to fully dedicate himself to his idea of converting food waste into 'earthworm-poo-fertilizer' and using this to fill recycled soft drink bottles for sale. Fast forward 20 years and Tom can claim to be CEO of 'the coolest little start-up in America' (Burlingham, 2016) but, more importantly, to be the engineer and leader of a passionate alliance that unites consumers, 'Big CPG', recyclers and some 200 million volunteers behind TerraCycle's Mission, transforming it into a powerful movement. Below he shares this incredible journey and what it taught him about Ueber-Branding.

What separates garbage from gold is a matter of perspective. Our greatest challenges (and achievements) have not been necessarily finding the proper scientific formulation for turning toothbrushes into playgrounds but creating a brand mystique that attracts people to fulfil our purpose. Using Myth as a branding strategy, we have managed to make garbage cool, aspirational, even sexy by sparking curiosity with very visual, memorable and easy-to-understand concepts and stories that are at once special and accessible.

Today, corporations, municipalities, small businesses and individual consumers bring TerraCycle's programmes to 21 countries while manufacturers use them to source unique, story-driven materials for their production. With more than 200 million people collecting today, the company has kept nearly 8 billion pieces of traditionally non-recyclable material out of landfills so far.

How to build a thriving organization: Turning Myth into a culture

There are three core buckets of constituents to which TerraCycle sells its brand, all of whom must buy in in order for us to do the real, impactful work of recycling, waste management and creating new systems for the circular economy. The first are our employees and staff, as attracting talent, retaining that talent, and motivating them to fulfil our purpose is essential. And we haven't done badly. In the past year alone, TerraCycle has doubled our number of employees worldwide (including the expansion of our human resources department!).

Who on earth would want to work in waste? Me, TerraCycle's first employee, for starters. One publication recently referred to me as the company's 'shaggy-haired, enigmatic founder' (Idle, 2019), which I suppose is somewhat accurate. I live near a forest, don't own a suit, have been known to wear a uniform of T-shirts and hoodies, and am always the point person, travelling 'somewhere' to sell.

Creating a thriving company culture implicitly goes back to the core values established by its creator, and without ego, I can say I am part of the TerraCycle DNA, and more importantly, its brand mystique. The world

FIGURE 15.1 The 'messiah of waste-management' Tom Szaky – part of TerraCycle's Brand Myth and spreading the gospel among its stakeholders

SOURCE Reproduced with permission of TerraCycle (2020)

loves a college drop-out story (much like the respective founders of a certain social network and software corporation), and whether I meant it to or not, it's one that inspires and attracts.

Way before I cut my sophomore year short to focus on TerraCycle, I was born in 1982 to two physicians in communist Hungary. Shortly after, the Chernobyl Disaster destabilized the region, and we left the country as political refugees. Fleeing to Germany and Holland before settling in Canada, where I am still a citizen, it was in capitalist North America I went to public school, taught myself to code at 14, and learned about business and entrepreneurship.

Having come from a country with little, to a world where over-consumption was the norm, I was astounded by the things people trash; the first television set I ever saw was one being thrown in the garbage. I became fascinated by garbage.

This sort of 'Creation Myth' is an essential piece to any successful brand. Be it an event, the invention of a machine, or a superhero in a comic book, people want to know how it started and what human thing triggered that series of events. With this origin story comes a promised authenticity, accessibility and truth that help people feel connected to a Brand Mission.

And the story continues: In the beginning, most of our employees were spineless; they were treated like dirt, and we didn't pay them a dime... because they were worms! Originally, TerraCycle converted garbage shovelled from the cafeteria dumpsters into organic fertilizer by feeding it to worms, taking their castings and turning it into a product. TerraCycle's vermicompost, which my friend back home in Canada proved made fabulous plant fertilizer, was a submission to Princeton University's annual Entre-preneurship Club Business Plan Competition, which caught my attention with a grand prize of $5,000.

Attracting and retaining purpose-driven people, we unwittingly created a brand early on. This happened nearly as organically as the fertilizer we were producing. Those first days slinging worm poop were thin on cash. But what we were filthy—pun intended—rich in was authenticity and people enam-oured with the Mission of making garbage the hero. Plus, it was pretty fun! Those first years were close to a party doubling as a manufacturing operation.

With the money from our first investors, we rented our first office space on Nassau Street, where we outfitted the space with discarded furniture that was garbage as far as most were concerned. We hosted art parties on the week-ends, which gave our broke, exhausting days, and the walls, some colour.

As demand grew, we needed more space, but our workplace design remained an expression of our Mission and Myth. Photos of our offices reveal open floor plans and themed conference rooms; the Travel Room features a world map made of corks and the Media Room boasts a table supported by media equipment like VCRs and stereos. In fact, all our offices around the world are designed entirely from repurposed and upcycled 'waste' items. Trash, basically.

Our desks are made of doors, there's overstock carpeting on the floors, and our exterior and interior walls are covered in ever-changing graffiti from local artists. The gravel of our 'cork-yard' at headquarters is made of corks and flip-flop pieces repurposed as soft, colourful gravel where, with concrete, we've used recycled glass beer and wine bottles as retaining walls for garden beds. Our Bottle Room is one of the larger conference spaces, its walls erected entirely of two-liter soda bottles suspended from the ceiling from wires such that they move and you can walk through them. My own office is similarly constructed, as are that of the CFO and lead legal counsel, creating an environment of literal transparency from the executive team.

Now, most of the people who work for TerraCycle today aren't college drop-outs, but they have chosen to work here out of everywhere else. Our lead scientist of R&D spent six years at Johnson & Johnson, was employed at The DuPont Company and Xerox Corporation, and holds three US Patents and seven World Intellectual Property Organization (WIPO) Patents. Our CFO comes from the American Red Cross having also worked with Clorox and Procter & Gamble, huge conglomerates with whom we are partnered today. Folks have interned here while in school, worked with their departments to extend their terms by semesters, and accepted offers right out of college.

FIGURE 15.2 Living the Mission and spinning the Myth: A TerraCycle meeting room with walls made of PET bottles and a table made of recycled doors. More symbolic than practical

SOURCE: REPRODUCED WITH PERMISSION OF TERRACYCLE (2020)

The TerraCycle brand mystique is attractive in a world fed up with 'business as usual'. But this attraction means nothing without retention, and there are many aspects of our culture that add to this. The dog-friendly aspect is a major stress-reliever (eliminating the idea of waste is intense!), and, going back to my hair, our dress code is very casual, nary a suit or slack in sight; I couldn't care less what people wear to the office, as long as the work is good.

Weekly 'Take a tour with TerraCycle' sessions call upon the different departments to present what they do to foster a sense of belonging and understanding for new and long-standing employees. Our catered lunch programme recently transitioned to all-vegetarian, five days a week, to demonstrate our commitment to climate action, as well as the preferences of the majority.

Projects have been known to take odd hours (with our international teams and clients on different schedules, calls will happen outside the US workday), and urgent timelines come up, but with a strong benefits package, including a Green 401k with match, 22 days of volunteer time off (VTO), parental leave, healthcare, and development programming, we invest in our employees and value their time.

These are real, important things we find to be effective in selling our brand to our most important stakeholders: Our employees. Leveraging

Brand Myth and mystique allows us to inspire people and be a valuable commodity in a competitive job market.

How to gain customers and their business: Translating Myth into benefits

Bold enough to do things differently, our customers are organizations working with us on solutions for the circular economy. These include some of the biggest companies in the world – manufacturers, retailers and corporations – and consumers that see our services as a value-add in a world yearning to vote with their dollars for a future with less waste.

Well-known partners include Gillette, Herbal Essences, Bausch + Lomb, and Febreze, who bring national access to recycling solutions for municipally non-recyclable items through mail-in and drop-off. Top groceries and store chains such as CVS, Walgreens, Walmart, and Kroger in the US, and Carrefour and Tesco in Europe, work with us to provide in-store recycling stations, retail promotions and downloadable shipping labels.

Gaining these customers is a matter of making them see the value in recycling, taking responsibility for what they produce, addressing the increasing concerns of their own customers and/or all of the above. And what makes our customers want to work with us is that we engage people. Our programmes touch people. This is the 'steak' to our 'sizzle' of Brand Myth. You can't have profit without people, and we have more than 200 million collecting with us around the world.

For example, in order to ramp up the supply of used bottles (trash picking will only get you so many), we started the Bottle Brigade, which would provide the model for the 'sponsored-waste' division now known as National Recycling Programs, our largest, most recognizable and profitable line of business today.

In 2007 we launched our very first sponsored programme with Honest Tea, our longest standing brand partner. Packaging its juices for kids in the popular drink pouch format, the brand wanted to offer its customers a solution for the multi-compositional item, a combination of foils and different types of plastics.

Unsure of how it would be received by the public, we budgeted 100 accounts for the programmes, meaning that only 100 people could sign up with their e-mail. All 100 were spoken for within 24 hours! That year, several other food and beverage brands followed suit.

People want to do the right thing, but they are busy. They have grown accustomed to the convenience, price point and function of many disposable products on the market today, and despite being concerned about pollution and waste, if the solution is not easy-to-understand and available at low cost, they will not engage.

One of TerraCycle's most recognizable promotions is the annual Recycled Playground Challenge, sponsored by one of our largest brand partners worldwide. Through this recycling and voting contest open to schools K–12, the brand donates a playground made of recycled oral care items collected through the programme to the school that garners the most 'Playground Credits' during the promotion.

This rewards the consumer and creates an investment in the sponsor company as a patron of the products, and a patron for a charitable cause. It becomes possible to reap real, tangible rewards when companies administer initiatives that ask the consumer to do more than just buy the product, but also get involved with doing something good for their community. The feel-good notion of giving back helps to close the values–action gap.

Now several years running in the US with iterations in Europe, the contest creates a connection between the stuff we throw away and the things they can become, especially for children, our future stewards.

In addition to recyclability, one of the most important factors consumers cite in their selection of eco-friendly products is the use of recycled content, specifically post-consumer recycled (PCR) resin, which TerraCycle is primed to provide from our collection programmes (Pierce, L, 2017).

Currently, CPG companies generally use generic recycled materials (ie 'rPET' or 'rHDPE') aggregated from one or many municipal recycling facilities. These contain plastics from many different types of products and packaging, come from any number of places and have no traceability back to the original product or where the material was generated or collected.

But TerraCycle is able to offer its customers special materials that tell a story, providing the exceptional opportunity for manufacturers and major brands to differentiate and command a premium. The traceable, 'origin story' component can be communicated clearly and effectively to today's consumers, who will find value in their ability to relate to the product and the story behind it.

The highlight of our work with storied plastic is our beach plastic division. It started when we worked with Procter & Gamble to create the world's first fully recyclable shampoo bottle made with beach plastic for Head & Shoulders, the #1 shampoo brand in the world. Hand-collected by a myriad of dedicated NGOs and volunteer clean-up organizations already picking up litter in marine environments, plastic originally headed for land-fills was used to establish a new supply chain.

Once people understood that they could unlock tremendous opportunities in reverse logistics, our NGO partners came through with enthusiasm and tireless dedication. Ocean and shore plastic is an environmental problem they connected to, so they helped P&G integrate it into our packaging – and they continue to supply our production to this day.

Sold in France, the bottle was made by collaboration with SUEZ, Europe's top waste management firm playing a key role in collecting, sorting, and ultimately delivering high-quality plastic pellets. The project would go on to win a United Nations Momentum for Change Lighthouse Activity Award, which we were honoured to share with our collectors.

That we are able to help brands recycle and be recycled is a huge part of the TerraCycle magic for people, planet and profit, but when it comes to eliminating waste, we've sought to go deeper. Recycling solves for the symptom of waste, but doesn't get at the cause of waste: Disposability.

TerraCycle's new circular shopping platform Loop works with companies (many of which also have a recycling programme with us) to create durable versions of their own goods previously housed in single-use packaging. The products are offered in a combination of glass, stainless steel, aluminium and engineered plastics designed to last at least 100 uses; when they do wear out, TerraCycle is able to recycle them.

FIGURE 15.3 Rallying stakeholders behind a shared Mission and Myth: TerraCycle customers and volunteers collecting plastic on the beach

SOURCE Reproduced with permission of TerraCycle (2020)

These sorts of close, continued collaborations create a strong position for benefits and profit. Reconciling innovation and short-term growth with sustainability is not easy, and requires boldness above all investment. Dialogue with all stakeholders (brands cannot succeed in Loop or with TerraCycle recycling programmes without cooperation from retail) yields information and de-risks the endeavour.

Marketing and public relations have always been an integral force for building our business, providing credibility and generating return on investment for our customers. Last year, approximately 21,000 media placements included TerraCycle globally (both ones we generate and ones that come over the transom) and save putting press releases on the wire or boosting posts on free social media platforms such as Facebook; none of them are paid for.

Brand partners who post about our partnership on social media receive higher engagement rates on TerraCycle and Loop content as compared to their average post with drastically higher likes, comments and shares across platforms.

These metrics and feedback are examples of what we have since described in new business development as the 'TerraCycle magic' – it influences customer perceptions, drives audience engagement, and boosts brand equity... not to mention, helps our customers get lots and lots of 'likes'.

This social benefit creates a mystique around TerraCycle that makes people want to be a part of the movement. In the same way luxury and lifestyle brands can command premiums and represent an aspirational set of values, we've been able to market a Myth that brings real meaning to people's lives.

Our customers, manufacturers and brands are always looking for new ways to engage the world with products and services that people want to buy. Plain and simple, this is the purpose of business: To be a reflection of our desires. By working with us, our business-to-business clients allow their customers to be a part of something big.

How to unite and activate partners: Sharing in the Myth

Creativity and community are at the core of what we do because solving the complex problems of waste is a feat of collaboration. We work with a number of processors, plastic vendors, producers and developers to make the magic happen, and engage more than 200 million collectors, including businesses, schools and individuals, recycling worldwide.

The leading recycling company in every country we operate in owns a majority stake in our operations there. In Europe, this is SUEZ, who worked with us on the beach plastic bottle for Head & Shoulders and purchased 30 per cent of TerraCycle France, UK, Sweden, Finland, Belgium and the Netherlands.

These partnerships may not seem as glamorous as the ones with big brands and retailers generating media buzz, but they are some of our most important. Recycling and circular management of resources suffer due to the sheer fragmentation of systems worldwide. With the common goal of improving practical recycling, our partners unite complimentary management and logistics expertise to produce first-of-their-kind solutions.

Once collected, the items need to be aggregated, sorted and processed in order to prepare them for recycling. That's where our network of warehouses and materials processors comes in. Because of the complex nature of our collection programmes for products and packaging that require special handling, the people we work with need to have the capacity to handle us.

Our cigarette programme is a good example, as the tobacco, paper, and other organics, such as ash, need to be separated from the cellulose acetate plastics in order to compost and recycle the respective parts. When the waste is 'checked in' to its receiving warehouse, it must be weighed in order to track data for the amount recycled through the programme, as well as allocate the proper amount of TerraCycle points to the collector who shipped it.

We've launched the first ever national programmes for items such as razor blades and industrial adhesive packaging, which have unique needs of budget, invoicing, data management, pricing and regulatory matters. Every processor is different, and we work with several vendors with different systems that are applicable for various parts of the business. Some are more manual or automated than others, as some waste streams require more handling and accounting.

Handling complex waste streams requires custom solutions, and that's a lot of work! Our vendor partners need to be creative, nimble, adaptable, and above all patient, and wouldn't do the work unless we were a value add for them.

Having a regular customer like TerraCycle is a pro in a competitive market for materials processing, which often comes down to price. The companies we work with can command a premium and report to potential customers and stakeholders their work with a purpose-driven, and often demanding, organization.

Some of the operations vendors we work with also handle our fulfilment for custom collection bins, such as for the razor recycling programme, as well as for our comprehensive recycling Zero Waste Box system. For the Zero Waste Boxes in particular, we have people in charge of fulfilling for consumers, as well as for big partners like Subaru and other companies who use our boxes to divert waste in the front and back of their operations.

Packaging producers, plastic pelletizers, and lumber and moulding vendors help us create playgrounds out of toothbrushes, personal care and beauty packaging out of beach litter, and benches out of cigarettes. Working with unconventional materials is always a risk, and quality can be hard to maintain, but as with our processors, our relationships have made for learnings for both parties, which is the magic of collaborative work.

An important thing to remember is that supply chains are about people, not just processes. What's interesting is the higher up the waste hierarchy you move (from litter to landfill, waste to energy, to recycling, upcycling and re-use), the more jobs you create in the process. In terms of injecting value in moving from the linear to the circular economy, this is a positive most of us can agree on.

Ultimately, creating mystique for our collectors and allowing them to share in our storytelling is our greatest work. With all the processing, separating, aggregating, bailing, pelletizing, extruding, and injection moulding going on behind the scene of our recycling, we've been able to create smooth, unified experiences for the people collecting. Yet, we've also protected the trade secrets about our operations, while keeping transparent. Because this aids with our brand mystique, which is important to our customers, suppliers, vendors and investor stakeholders. No other company does what we do because no other company has the same relationships. We put ourselves out there but don't show all our cards.

Consumers are thus empowered and educated but also intrigued and seduced. TerraCycle allows the world to teach each other about the fissures in our global system, provides the tools to start the conversation about responsibility, and offers a road map out of the mess – yet the system is never fully unveiled and totally understood, its complexity and mystery being one of our biggest draws.

What other garbage companies are so extensively covered by the media? Credibility and prestige come from our high value, negative cost marketing, and more and more, high-value press hits come through from imprints like *Vogue*, *Harper's Bazaar*, CNN, NPR, and *The Washington Post*, bringing our Mission in front of more people every day. We've had the opportunity to turn waste management into something cool.

For example, our reality TV show *Human Resources* (once described as '*The Office* meets *Project Runway*') used the mass appeal of the format to de-operationalize waste management and make recycling accessible. It brought viewers behind the scenes and into the fast-moving environment of the TerraCycle office. Shot on location, it featured real employees (including myself), and used no scripts. Definitely more *Real World* than *An Inconvenient Truth*.

Through my books and blogs, I've created access to the CEO of a growing company, allowing people to empathize, connect and be inspired by our Mission. Our presence in schools and stores makes us part of the lives of the average consumer, yet we are viewed as a disruptor in the space. We bring big concepts down to earth, and turn something most of us try not to think about, garbage, into the hero.

Selling is the opposite of seducing. It's not sexy. Letting the message speak for itself without huge advertising spends has allowed us to build our business from the ground up and at low cost. Our collectors perceive us to be authentic, cool, resourceful, and ground-breaking, and build us up as a prestige brand at every level.

FIGURE 15.4   United in their mission – mother and daughter collect 'toys waste' to be sent to TerraCycle for recycling. Toymaker Hasbro is one corporate sponsor of the programme

SOURCE Reproduced with permission of TerraCycle (2020)

Having a strong, clear purpose costs nothing and has the potential to mean everything to people. TerraCycle is doing real work to eliminate waste equivalent to hard numbers for items diverted from landfill, thousands of dollars of material captured, and appreciable sales lift.

With hope, as we continue to grow (and we are still growing!), the magic of our Brand Myth will change shape in the light, and keep on attracting the energy of the people who make it possible.

RECAP: TERRACYCLE

The principles that drive the success of TerraCycle in leveraging Myth to make recycling a movement:

- *Have a good origin story.* Knowing where something comes from vests a person, place, or thing with credibility, authenticity and trust.

- *Bring pie in the sky ideas down to earth.* People long to belong, understand, and learn new things that allow them to connect with others and the world around them. Make the complex seem simple, the intellectual seem accessible, and the impossible seem possible.

- *Turn the taboo into something interesting.* Taboo is just that which people don't understand, and it's just on the edge of being cool.

- *Be shareable...* It is possible to create access while maintaining mystery.

- *... but don't show all your cards!* Watering down your language or credo in order to be understood and well liked is not the way to go, and neither is too-eagerly over-explaining why you are important. Telling your secrets will not create the intimacy with your audience that you seek. Allow the strength of the Mission to speak for you and maintain a cool head about messaging around the Myth, and all the stakeholders you are trying to reach will clamour to share in it.

Case 2: Acqua di Parma

The power of a mythical core, or: How to build your business and your equity simultaneously

Acqua di Parma started as a very personal Colonia of a noble man from Parma and grew over more than 100 years into a truly iconic, global brand. Today it reaches from eau de toilette celebrating the Mediterranean Eden, to artistic reflections on rare ingredients, from grooming products to soul-crafted accessories and services. Since 2001 Acqua di Parma is part of LVMH.

In 2017, Acqua di Parma CEO Laura Burdese asked premium brand building agency Select World to help re-ignite this iconic Italian legend. Wolfgang Schaefer led the project agency-side as then Chief Strategy Officer. How this great iconic brand was (re-)strengthened and expanded around the classic Colonia, is a fascinating story. It proves once more that a strong Mission and Myth will liberate you while at the same time holding everything together, taking your business further with every step while bringing your brand closer to its core.

The following are excerpts of a talk between Laura and Wolfgang in which Laura shares exclusive insights about strategy and process and reasons why the new Barbiere line as well as the project as a whole is deemed such a success.

Laura Burdese

In a career spanning more than two decades, after completing her studies in international economics, Laura gained extensive experience in the beauty industry first (with marketing experiences at Beiersdorf and L'Oréal). She then moved into the watches and jewellery business by joining The Swatch Group, where she successfully developed her career for over 18 years, growing in different positions before being appointed President and CEO of Calvin Klein Watches and Jewelry Co in 2012. In October 2016 she was appointed President and CEO of Acqua di Parma.

Wolfgang Schaefer (WS): Welcome, Laura. Why don't you start by telling our readers a little bit about the situation when we started the project. What did you see as the biggest challenges?

Laura Burdese (LB): From the research we had done it was very clear that Acqua di Parma had some incredible assets. First and foremost, our iconic beautiful yellow colour, the logo itself and an amazing product. On top of that, it had a strong legacy – a long history of over 103 years. But the main challenge was clearly how to bring this beautiful little rough diamond back to light and to life again. We felt that the years had almost covered up its beauty and the brand had become unable to fully show its power and express its potential. We were in front of a challenge: Using this amazing legacy as a springboard, not a cage, bringing the brand to another level, maintaining a strong base of loyal customers while attracting at the same time new ones.

WS: Recruiting new customers while keeping the old ones is always the biggest challenge, so we set up a process that was actually quite robust.

LB: Yes, it took a lot of time and efforts. We deep dived into the brand with studies and interviews. We interviewed a lot of stakeholders of the brand, loyal and new customers, the greatest staff, store managers, journalists, VIPs and opinion leaders in different countries. The resulting research highlighted the strengths and the assets, but also the areas that needed improvements. This process was important to start creating a solid basis. I think without these months of research and studies, we wouldn't have had the very positive results we have today.

WS: Clients often wonder if all this upfront work is really worth it – if it really adds something or just tells you things you already know.

LB: I have no doubt it was absolutely necessary, so it was really worth it. Indeed, some of the points and assumptions were confirmed, but we also discovered a lot of interesting new aspects. I think that without this process, we wouldn't have been able to create this beautiful story, this new narrative in such a solid, relevant and meaningful way. I think I would do it again in exactly the same way. I remember that at that time we were under pressure, because we wanted to start as soon as possible to rebuild and re-shape the brand. Besides, we had a deadline, which was the launch of Colonia Pura in just six months. Yet the few months spent studying the brand, doing research and interviews, were essential to understand which assets it was worth to build on, what needed to be changed, what we had to stop doing and what we had to start doing in terms of brand equity and fundamentals. It was thanks to this process that we came up with a very solid, relevant, meaningful vision, Mission and brand equity in a very short period of time.

WS: First thing we had to do is get clear about your Ueber-Target…

LB: Finding the right target audience to address was probably one of the most challenging things. At the time there was a big gap between the people we were actually talking to and the people we wanted to address. The brand was aimed at consumers who were in their forties and mainly based in the Western part of the world, mainly Europe. Bear in mind that we weren't even present in Asia three years ago, but now we are. We wanted to reach out to a different customer, but we didn't know exactly who. We knew that Acqua di Parma was probably not going to attract Generation Z consumers and Millennials for one simple reason – Acqua di Parma was born over 100 years ago as a personal Colonia, for a grown-up generation of illuminated and discerned connoisseurs. By design, it's a timeless and genderless Maison. Simply, this is a brand for people who know about fragrances and how to choose them. Which is why we also like to call Acqua di Parma 'The University of Fragrances', meaning you arrive at the brand after you've done your primary, secondary and high school. So, Acqua di Parma is a sort of academic validation for discerning consumers. And that's why we settled on the 'HENRYs', 'High Earners, Not Rich Yet' as our initial Ueber-Target. The 'HENRYs' matched the audience we *wanted* to talk to, but, at the same time, they weren't too far away from our usual loyal customers. We therefore decided that everything we did had to be addressed to them. At the beginning, the definition of 'HENRYs' was a little bit wide, but then, through the process, we were able to come up with a more precise description that helped us position ourselves and open up to a specific Ueber-Target for more precise marketing activation.

FIGURE 16.1   Apart from the heritage and authenticity of Acqua di Parma, the fact that it is to this day handcrafted in large part is a key connector to the brand's Ueber-Target

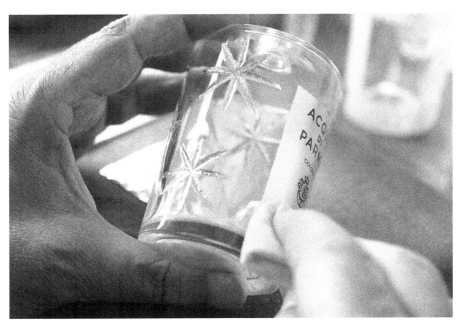

SOURCE   Reproduced with permission of Acqua di Parma (2020)

WS: One of the reasons we thought the HENRYs are interesting is that they have this desire for brands that are authentic or that have a story to tell. They are very quick to find out if something is just a marketing gimmick, or if something is really, truly made with passion and has some authentic history. Isn't that right?

LB: It is absolutely right. Because Acqua di Parma was not born as a brand to be 'marketed'. It was created by a man, Mr Magnani, for himself, and his inner circle of friends and family. While travelling around the world, Magnani longed for Italy, for Parma, for his family and for the Italian sun. He didn't want to create a brand, but something personal. So right from the beginning, the DNA of the brand had this sense of 'un-marketedness'. Acqua di Parma was never conceived as a 'marketing creature', that's why, as the time passed, it turned into a quintessentially Italian experience for all those people looking for an authentic, transparent and genuine brand that really stands for something.

WS: Which were other findings about Acqua di Parma that you would consider most interesting?

LB: We discovered different points. One of the most important ones – and I would go as far as considering it one of the pillars of our strategy for the present and the future as well – is that, by DNA, Acqua di Parma is a unisex, genderless brand. It is true that the original product had been created by a man for himself and for decades it was exclusively sold through men's tailors. But over the course of a century and due to its gender-neutral scent, Acqua di Parma developed into a unisex, genderless brand. Our fragrances are all made with selected and carefully chosen ingredients grown under the Italian sun, but they are not meant to be for men or women, they are just meant to be the best on the market.

That said, by design we are a little bit more 'masculine' and inclined towards men. Male sophistication is ingrained in the brand's DNA and this is what makes the brand authentic and unique compared to all other niche fragrances or lifestyle fragrance brands, which often have a female skew. But that doesn't mean we are 'for men only' – just like traditionally female brands have very successful male fragrance businesses, a 'masculine' heritage can be very attractive for women as well. In our strategy we therefore decided to put men first, yes, but be always also very clear that we are ultimately a unisex label with a very solid and large female customer base.

WS: As so often, the hardest thing in defining our Mission was finding the right words. We settled on 'Celebrating the sophisticated lightness of Italy' to capture that we are not only a fragrance brand but something much bigger, that we stand for the effortless chic of Italian men, which many parts of the world aspire to, and the ease of your wonderful Italian lifestyle per se. Can you explain this concept from your point of view?

LB: The brand has been about Italian excellence, craftmanship and style since 1916. And yes, we wanted to celebrate the sophisticated lightness of Italy, as Acqua di Parma stands for this 'lightness'. But we had long debates about the word 'lightness' because it has different meanings in different languages. In English the word has two dimensions, both of which are highly relevant for the brand: Lightness indicates something that is not heavy, something easy and unburdened, which goes to the 'effortlessness' of Italian style. But it also talks about something luminous, the sunlight in particular. And this is also part of the essence of the brand. Our fragrances are, first and foremost, 'sunlight fragrances', they are not too strong, not too concentrated; they are luminous and bright, made from sun-ripened Italian fruits, flowers and herbs. So, this term 'lightness' really covers 360 degrees – from the lightness of Italian men's style to the luminosity of our scents which never cover or clutter, always letting the essence shine through. The term was therefore the perfect word to really express the soul of the brand.

Yet, unfortunately in many other languages, Italian for one, there are two different words for these two ideas: *leggerezza* and *luminosità*. There is no one term to capture both. And, more importantly, in the beginning we were scared that the term may have negative connotations, since something light can also be perceived as superficial, as something that doesn't have substance and depth. That's the reason we decided to elevate the word and came up with the concept of 'Sophisticated lightness', represented by our trademark yellow. A colour shade that represents an iconic and very important asset: It hints at the Italian sun, represented by the round Acqua di Parma hatbox, the perfect gift. And because handmade is an important feature of our packaging (the labels are still applied by hand), our round hatboxes thus unite all three concepts – the Italian sun, soul and style – the three core values and pillars of the brand.

FIGURE 16.2   The idea of celebrating the 'sophisticated lightness of Italy' led to a distinct way of chiaroscuro photography, playing with light and shadow, as in this ingredient shot

SOURCE   Reproduced with permission of Acqua di Parma (2020)

WS: You sometimes actually even use the metaphor 'Italian sun bottled' when talking about Acqua di Parma. I find that a lovely shorthand, but I also always cringe a bit, because the brand is so much more than 'just a fragrance'.

LB: Yes, that's correct. Acqua di Parma was born as a fragrance, because Mr Magnani wanted to create a scent for himself to remind him of Italy, Parma and his family, but then it has grown into much more than just a fragrance brand. It is a global icon of Italian style and this is exactly what Acqua di Parma is today. Yet, everything still radiates out of Colonia, which represents the sun in the Acqua di Parma universe. We really rotate around this Italian sun, this Italian warmth and luminosity. Everything we do and we have done really radiates from this centre. This was actually another strong finding from our research – Colonia is our pillar and it is located at the core, a key element of our strategy. Everything else radiates from Colonia, even what is really not related to fragrances, everything comes from there.

WS: The brand literally is a bit like a solar system where you have the sun in the centre, literally and figuratively in the form of Colonia, and everything radiates from there. And I agree, this was one of the smartest strategic decisions. Brands are often so infatuated with the new, not the least driven by the market, that they leave their icons behind. But we went the totally opposite direction – and it pays.

Another important strategic point is to translate your Mission and your strategy into a simple, compelling and ownable story, ideally a Myth, so everybody 'gets it' right away and the brand and its products 'talk' to you. The Acqua di Parma Myth we re-crafted is one of my absolute favourites and it's very closely connected to the brand's heritage. Which were the most interesting aspects that we found when we dug into the brand's long history?

LB: There were many different elements. One of the most important points was the idea of timelessness. Though we had to re-shape and re-frame Acqua di Parma in a more contemporary way, we knew that Acqua di Parma has this timeless soul, which was very important to us. This idea of timelessness was therefore crucial right from the beginning. We wanted to be contemporary but definitely not follow fashion trends. Around this we positioned other important points – naturality, transparency, luminosity and simplicity. Acqua di Parma comes from nature and Colonia is the most natural fragrance. All these ideas of naturality: The link with the territory, with Italy, with the Mediterranean Sea and with the Earth; the best ingredients, grown under the Italian sun and then handpicked and carefully mastered by Italian artisans, all these ideas were other key points of the brand that were turned into further pillars.

There was also another concept that emerged and that was somehow linked with timelessness: I've met so many people who told me they may have used the brand once or never used it, yet they all love it. This happens because the brand resonates with people, something that genuinely delights me. It means that Acqua di Parma really has some values, design and essence, which remind people of a shared history, parts where our heritage and theirs are intertwined. And this resonates with the longing for essentiality, for naturality, for true things, which you find across all generations including Millennials. And this was something that really struck me and I realized we could use this strong element for leverage. So, we reinterpreted the idea that the brand is 'old' to let it play into this nostalgia for something that we are missing in today's world and in our lives. We combined all these elements – timelessness, nostalgia, essentiality and respect for values – in a new way, finding that they are even more important today than they were yesterday.

I could list another point that should be added to this list and that's authenticity and the intimate side of this brand. Acqua di Parma stands for authentic values; as I said before, it is not a marketing 'creature', but it is a genuine brand that resonates with people looking for authenticity, content, substance, rather than just a marketing story. All of these points may seem different, but in the end they all relate to a single universe, and they are the basis for the strategy to come. We celebrate nature, sincerity, generosity – a way of life in its most sophisticated form, embracing time and generations. A philosophy of heritage, elevating a ritual into a rite of passage.

WS: Personally, for me one of the most important aspects of Acqua di Parma is that it was created as a personal scent, not for sale. It gives the brand such an intimacy and truthfulness, which you hardly find these days. For the first 60 to 70 years Acqua di Parma was never sold in fragrance stores, it was only sold through tailors, because Mr Magnani, who originally developed this fragrance for himself, had a licence to sell Burberry trench coats and Church shoes to tailors. Tailors liked the fragrance and started using it whenever they had finished a suit. They would sprinkle it with Acqua di Parma to take off the scent of the workshop and make it feel fresh and personal. I think that's a wonderful story that really gives depth to the product, elevating it beyond any other fragrance. And, again, it makes it very clear you are not just a fragrance, you are an icon of Italian style.

FIGURE 16.3 Acqua di Parma's tailor heritage solidifies its status as an icon of Italian style

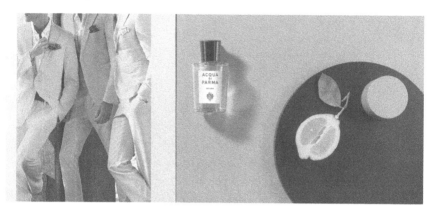

SOURCE Reproduced with permission of Acqua di Parma (2020)

LB: You are right. The fragrance was used by tailors and became the last finishing touch before they delivered a suit to their customers, mainly noblemen in those times. It was a way to elevate their craft to a higher level, as if they were completing their gift to their clients. By the way, it is still used nowadays by selected tailors in Italy, because it's part of our history.

WS: Can you tell us more about the growth strategy that you set forward? How does the brand evolve beyond Colonia?

LB: First of all, the strategic work we did at the beginning to re-launch the brand, the so-called 'Brand Epic',[1] set the path, taking Acqua di Parma from soul to future. We consider it our Bible and it has become a strategic pillar on which we build. One of the key points of the strategy that allowed us to grow in a fast and steady way in these past three years was really to put Colonia at the centre. When we rebooted the brand we had so many products and categories, including lifestyle and leather goods. We felt we had to start not from scratch, but from the beginning, to re-frame the overall theme. So we took Colonia and we turned it into our hero product, and strengthened its world. We also decided to enhance the yellow colour for its warmth and power. From there we launched a more contemporary version of Colonia, called Colonia Pura, and started a communication platform with this new fragrance. Everything we developed from then on was placed under the Colonia frame and colour-coded with our trademark yellow shade. You could say that everything in our strategy has to be seen through the yellow-tinted lenses of Colonia.

That the strategy is successful was proved by the fact that Colonia has been growing double digits and has become our key product.

The next step was taking care of our universe: Acqua di Parma also has the Blu Mediterraneo line, another super important pillar of the brand. This was the second biggest challenge. In some countries Blu Mediterraneo is even more known than Colonia, but it is a lighter and easier fragrance. It is also a little bit younger and, though unisex, it remains slightly more feminine, so it is different from Colonia as it represents the quintessential Garden of Eden of the Mediterranean Sea. We therefore decided to bring it into the orbit of the Colonia world and under the yellow frame of Acqua di Parma, giving it a new role. If Colonia represents the core, Blu Mediterraneo is the entry gate to Acqua di Parma. Results show that this strategy was again very successful.

As a last step, after reinforcing the core and offering customers a new entry gate to our universe, we had another task – elevating the whole Acqua di Parma catalogue. We planned to build a top line as an artistic interpretation of our Colonia: Signatures of the Sun. But some of the

FIGURE 16.4 The Blu Mediterraneo line is lighter, easier and more unisex. It's distinct yet part of the Colonia world, for example through the photographic style and use of the colour yellow

SOURCE Reproduced with permission of Acqua di Parma (2020)

existing products we wanted to migrate into this line were currently in brown packaging. Luckily the products themselves were great and very much liked, but, again, we had to bring them back into the yellow, black and white frame and endow them with the current visual identity of the brand. Launched two months ago, the collection is already a success. To recap things, I would say that one of the main successes behind the growth of the past year was giving Colonia the role of core product, turning Blu Mediterraneo into an entry gate and employing the Signatures Collection to elevate the overall approach of Acqua di Parma. The reshaping of the rest of the portfolio – including lifestyle and home décor products such as candles and the Barbiere line – followed.

WS: ... Barbiere! Please tell us how you started expanding your *barbiere* grooming services and how this strengthened the brand.

LB: Barbiere was a separate line in the Acqua di Parma catalogue, characterized by a different colour and design. It was unscented and it was very small. But we turned it around thanks to our *barberia* (barber's shop) services. We had one *barberia* in our Milano boutique, and it was working quite well, but it was small and wasn't very consistent in the frame of the new strategy. Yet it was clear that it had potential for different reasons: it started as a trend with hipsters, but, as the years passed, male grooming became part of a solid routine for men all over the world. This is a fast-growing market and becoming part of it was another important point. Again, we realized that to reinforce the Barbiere line we had to bring it into the Colonia frame. We therefore proceeded to repackage it with our trademark yellow shade and gave it a scent to allow it to become part of the Colonia family. We also added some new products for the pre- and after-shaving routines and for styling.

Barbiere was also re-launched with a new and beautiful campaign that spoke the same poetic language as the one for Colonia, but tailored for this line. For the general campaign as well as for the *barbiere* narrative we used a real family – a man, a woman and their kid. It was a powerful and emotional message as there was real chemistry between them. A strong brand must be able to convey emotions to people, and when we started studying the situation of Acqua di Parma we realized the brand wasn't reaching out emotionally to consumers. Building a strong emotional bond was also another key point and with the Colonia Pura campaign and then Barbiere we managed to do it. Acqua di Parma has always been about passing values from one generation to the other: Mr Magnani

FIGURE 16.5 Going back to the brand's core opened up a new perspective on its shaving line and service, expanding the brand into a new global business

SOURCE Reproduced with permission of Acqua di Parma (2020)

created Colonia and then gave it to his son who passed it on. The Barbiere story revolves around a father and son, and shaving as a transforming ritual, a rite of passage from father to son, so it tells a wonderful story that talks to the heart of consumers.

WS: Exactly how it all started in the Roman Republic, where the bearded ones were the 'barbarians'. So starting to shave was not only a sign of growing from boy to man, you also started saying goodbye to the barbarian in you... a great historical truth that gives Acqua di Parma credibility, authenticity and the right to own this cultural rite of passage.

LB: Yes, that's right, everyone loves this story! You shave to become civilized and then you're ready to face the world with a different approach.

WS: Apart from being a product line, Barbiere is also becoming a crucial brand experience for Acqua di Parma. Can you tell us more about it?

LB: The name of the line – Barbiere – indicates the man, the barber. It hints at the personal and unique relationship between a barber and his customer. After we re-launched the line, we decided to roll out a series of services that could elevate the products. We started implementing a *barbiere* service in all our boutiques; as soon as we renovate a boutique, we now bring in a *barbiere*. For example, we renovated our Milan-based boutique and installed a bigger *barbiere* service. In the countries where we don't have our own boutiques, we go for pop-ups, shop-in-shops or shared spaces where we offer this service. Usually this means hotels, five-star and luxury centres and airports, but the service must be delivered in the proper way. This helps us increase awareness of the line and the service and of Colonia, of course. So far it has been really good as we offer a tailored service that is completely different from that offered by our competitors. Barbiere is a quintessential 360 degrees service in traditional Italian style, so it offers a series of shaving, facials and hair treatments.

WS: This was quite an investment effort. How did you manage to build the *barbiere* service up from scratch and turn it from one little service in your flagship store in Milan into a global service?

LB: That's a very good question. The Barbiere line and its services have a high-end position compared to our competitors. At the same time, they are not mind-busting. It was very complicated and time-consuming, but we select the best barbers in the world, we train them and make sure that the services are impeccable. As you may imagine, this is logistically complicated and very expensive. When we implemented the service in our

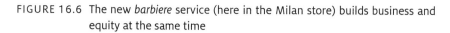

FIGURE 16.6   The new *barbiere* service (here in the Milan store) builds business and equity at the same time

SOURCE   Reproduced with permission of Acqua di Parma (2020)

stores it was relatively easier since we already had the right people, but we had to improve the service. But when we start bringing it into different business models – think about hotels, department stores or airports – and applying the concept to other countries, well, then we have to develop innovative business models, in order to make it work. So, we fine-tuned the business model to make it profitable. We did some tests and some of them were successful, others weren't, but we eventually found a business model that worked. We started building up, for example, an academy of barbers in Milan, in order to have the best barbers around and give them impeccable training. Then we started selecting the proper locations, such as department stores, and we realized that some of them were willing to give us spaces for very favourable commissions. This allowed us to build up a strong relationship with them and develop a win–win business model that proved financially sustainable.

WS: So, is Barbiere really successful or is it still too early to say?

LB: It is successful on two different levels – in terms of expectations and numbers. First of all, we over-exceeded the ambitious target that we had set up for ourselves, so we are obviously very happy about the point. Then it is successful in terms of numbers: The line is appreciated, we have a collection of fantastic products, sales are great, and services are increasing very quickly. So, overall, it is a financially successful operation. But to me there's even more than that: Every dollar invested in Barbiere goes back to the Colonia world. Colonia is going from strength to strength, also thanks to the support we gave to Barbiere. So, we have two different lines, but the investments are very synergic. Today, at Acqua di Parma, it seems that every step we take to build our universe brings us at the same time closer to our core and strengthens it.

WS: That's great news. The brand and business strategy have focused on and nurtured the core, which in turn now radiates a magnetic force, keeping everything together as it unfolds.

LB: You said magnetic!? In Italian I always define Colonia as a *forza centripeta* – a centripetal force.

WS: Like a centre of gravity…

LB: Exactly. Everything goes back there and whatever is not attracted by Colonia, well, we will have to leave it behind. That's why we cut and discontinue some products. We felt that our energies, resources and money had to go towards this strategy based on a strong centripetal force – Colonia.

WS: Laura, thank you so much for this talk! It makes me nostalgic... I almost feel like doing it all over again, it was so much fun, apart from being successful....

LB: When they ask me if we ever did something really wrong in terms of strategy in these three years, I always say no. We are all proud of the things we did and the results we achieved. Barbiere and Colonia are growing very healthily; Blu Mediterraneo is flying, especially in Asia, something that allowed us to bring the line to China, a strategic market. Signatures of the Sun has just been re-launched, but first performance looks promising. Overall, the results are proof that the strategy works beautifully.

WS: I think that whenever you invest time and lay the foundations properly it pays off. It always does. Laura, thank you so much.

RECAP: ACQUA DI PARMA

- The initial research phase took time and effort but was crucial in creating a solid base for the success of the project.

- Without this process it would have been very difficult to create the new narrative in such a solid, relevant and meaningful way.

- At the beginning was the definition of a clear Ueber-Target that was the focus later on for more precise marketing activation.

- Focusing on a gender (men) doesn't limit the brand's target; it's actually what makes it authentic and attractive to women as well.

- Focusing on the brand's core product anchored and opened its Mission, at the same time, inspiring a very unique yet expansive way of looking at the world.

- Diving into the brand's heritage revealed many important aspects that helped build a strong story, often by interpreting points in a different way.

- All this allowed Acqua di Parma to expand the business but make investments synergistic – the brand now works like a magnetic force.

Note

1 Brand Epic is a Select World tool to develop and record the brand narrative visually and verbally. It is then used as benchmark and bellwether for all future innovation and activation. More information at www.selectworld.com (archived at https://perma.cc/WCG6-BSTJ)

Case 3: Burt's Bees

Growing an Ueber-Brand ground up, or:
How purpose and profit can live in harmony

Is it possible to pursue a higher purpose while generating profits and growth? To most brands this seems like an impossible question to answer. But Ueber-Brands like Burt's Bees show that it is possible to grow and become a leading brand in your industry while doing exactly that: Having a Mission while making money. Or 'balancing people – planet – profit', in this specific case, as Jim Geikie lays out for us below.

Jim joined Burt's Bees in a critical phase just before The Clorox Company took over the brand, desiring to scale it further and faster as any mass marketer would intuitively do. He analyses for us how his leadership team and those that came before him managed through these key transitions, coming out in delivering a purposeful proposition and strong profits. You can also listen to an interview we did with Jim on ueberbrands.com (ueberbrands.com, 2017). Scan the QR code at the front of the book for a link.

Jim Geikie

Jim is a consumer products marketer who has focused his 30-year career on the beauty care business. He first became interested in 'Mission-driven' brands when his then-employer, consumer goods giant Unilever, introduced the Dove Campaign for Real Beauty and also acquired Ben & Jerry's in the early 2000s. He became fascinated with how these brands connected with consumers through shared values and beliefs that transcended product features and benefits. Joining Burt's Bees with its earth-friendly personal care positioning felt like a natural next step for him. He worked for the company between 2006 and 2017, serving in a variety of marketing and general management roles. He now is a partner in One Better Ventures, a certified benefit corporation that provides advisory services and growth capital to exceptional entrepreneurs.

Burt's Bees is a personal care brand, known for all-natural formulas and earth-friendly practices, that has become a US market leader in lip care and cosmetic products and is available in 50 countries worldwide. The business was founded in 1984 by two back-to-the-landers – Roxanne Quimby, an artist, and Burt Shavitz, a beekeeper – living a minimalist homesteaders' life in a remote part of Maine. Their values of self-sufficiency and resourcefulness and their belief in the wisdom, power and beauty of nature underpin a business that has succeeded as the product offering has evolved over the course of three decades and as ownership has passed from the founders to private equity and ultimately to a major multinational consumer products company. Burt's Bees is a story of riding a cultural movement from the fringes into the mainstream as well as a lesson on balancing purpose and profit – or selling without selling out – on a journey to global market significance. From its inception in 1984 in an abandoned schoolhouse that the founders rented for just the cost of fire insurance to its current position within The Clorox Company portfolio, Burt's Bees has managed to grow into a market leader while maintaining unwavering commitment to its founding principles, convictions and beliefs.

The founding phase

*Products that enable a life's purpose, and just enough profit
for a homesteader's life necessities*

Burt and Roxanne each had migrated to Maine on a circuitous path, abandoning modern urban life for a simpler, more self-reliant, and more demanding rural life in the wilderness. A Henry David Thoreau quote, 'I went to the woods because I wished to live deliberately, to front only the essential facts of life, and see if I could not learn what it had to teach, and not, when I came to die, discover that I had not lived' hung in Burt's converted turkey coop home and represented their motivation to abandon the comfortable circumstances in which they were raised. They were essentially practising homesteading, a lifestyle of extreme independence and self-sufficiency characterized by growing, making or reclaiming everything you need to subsist. It can also include making and selling craft work to earn enough to buy the few necessary things that cannot be grown, scavenged or created.

FIGURE 17.1 A statement of beliefs rooted in those of the founders

What We Believe

We believe that work is a creative, sustaining and fulfilling expression of the inner being.

We believe that what is right is not always popular and what is popular is not always right.

We believe that no one can do everything but everyone can do something.

We believe that most complicated and difficult problems we face as a civilization have the simplest solutions.

We believe that Mother Nature has the answers and She teaches by example.

We believe that by imitating Her economy, emulating Her generosity and appreciating Her graciousness, we will realize our rightful legacy on our magnificent planet Earth.

SOURCE Jim Geikie (2020)

One day, Roxanne was hitchhiking and Burt offered her a ride. A friendship formed, and eventually they launched their business partnership. Roxanne, ever the artist, helped Burt repackage his honey, which he sold as a commodity in large unlabelled pickle jars, by developing packaging and graphics that would appeal to the tourist trade in Maine. She then discovered a shed full of beeswax, a by-product of the honey business. That beeswax turned into their first product, Burt's Beeswax Candles, and would ultimately become the main ingredient in their iconic lip balm product. Burt had painted his name on his beehives to deter theft, and Roxanne thought it was an ideal, alliterative brand name: Burt's Bees.

The role of purpose

Roxanne is known to be a highly principled person with strong convictions and her personal values underpinned the company. These were published prominently in the company's marketing materials (see Figure 17.1). In 1984, products were becoming increasingly more synthetically formulated in order to achieve greater consistency and lower cost of goods. Roxanne's founding of Burt's Beeswax stood in contrast to the prevailing corporate practices and she rejected the 'better living through chemistry' movement. Her belief that 'what is right is not always popular and what is popular is not always right' put that difference into stark contrast and became a source of authentic credibility when what she believed to be 'right' became increasingly popular after the turn of the century. Believing that 'the old ways are the right ways', she sought to make products that honoured the wisdom, power and beauty of nature. Her goal was to make a modern product but by employing the ingredients and processes that would have been available to Cleopatra. Moreover, because her products took from nature, it was her goal to replenish and give back to nature.

The Mission manifested in the products through three attributes:

1 Natural formulation. The '% natural' bar on the front of every product package became a transparent indication of a formula's integrity. Natural raw ingredients were only part of the formula. She was also deliberate about using 'kitchen chemistry' to process her product. Heating, cooling, blending constituted a more natural and safer processing method than some of the more common industry alternatives that used harsh solvents and were suspected of creating potential human health risks.

2 Environmentally friendly packaging. Her use of glass, aluminium and craft paper packaging reinforced the importance of recycled and recyclable 'earth-friendly' packaging. Her use of clay-coated unbleached kraft paperboard cartons turned inside-out to print on the unfinished side reinforced the recycled image.

3 Differentiation, differentiation, differentiation. In a world of parity consumer products, she strove to make products different and better than what was otherwise available on the market. If a consumer tried a Burt's Bees branded product and liked it, differentiation would ensure they came back and would find it difficult to find a comparable alternative. For those who like the Original Beeswax Lip Balm's waxy texture combined with the prominent tingle of the peppermint flavour oil, there were not any competitors who offered that combination of attributes in the early days. And because beeswax forms a non-occlusive barrier on the lips, the formula did not create the water-logging effect, preventing the circular use-need phenomenon common to most petroleum-based products that consumers term an 'addiction'. Different. Better. Burt became a symbol of both authenticity and difference.

FIGURE 17.2 Mission and Myth manifested: An original Burt's Bees Beeswax Lip Balm in terracotta packaging and the modern logo showing the mythical founding figure and noting the Earth friendly nature of the brand's products

SOURCE Reproduced with permission of Burt's Bees (2020)

The role of profit

The company operated independently, without outside investment and influence, for 20 years. The original ambition was modest. Roxanne assumed if she could sell $20,000 in candles and could keep her costs to $10,000 that would give her $10,000 in profit, which was triple her income from waiting tables. The business was profitable from the outset, and she only made capital investments when there was sufficient cash to cover the expense. Her wholesale customers all paid in advance of shipping – there were no credit terms offered – which helped with cash flow.

There was no tension between purpose and profit, which were intrinsically linked during this phase. The Mission and their methods were consistent with a lifestyle choice that both founders had made and that was bigger and more significant than the business. The primary financial goal wasn't to get rich but to provide for life's necessities.

Roxanne may have been financially conservative, but she was strategically bold. There were four significant decisions in the early years that cemented the foundation – a retail customer, a company relocation, a category choice, and a personnel decision. In 1989, a buyer for a trend-setting SoHo New York boutique called Zona discovered Burt's Bees candles when Roxanne was exhibiting at a western Massachusetts gift show. Her success in this boutique retailer raised the brand's profile and created a wholesale demand for her products which gave her certain leverage to secure favourable terms. The right retail presentation and the right retailer relationship have always been fundamental to the brand marketing and the company strategy. In 1993, she made two bold choices that set the company up for long-term success. First was the decision to relocate the small business from remote north-central Maine to its current home in North Carolina. Roxanne found North Carolina to be more supportive of entrepreneurs, more centrally located for her East Coast distribution, and with more access to skilled workers. She has said that the hard choice to relocate to North Carolina was the best strategic decision she made. Second, she made the decision to focus her product range on personal care and to stop producing products that at the time accounted for 75 per cent of her revenue. The lip balm product was increasingly successful, personal care items enjoy more frequent use, and the profit margins were better. She stopped making the candles, stove polishes and pet care products that comprised her eclectic portfolio, to focus more narrowly on 'Earth friendly natural personal care'. She also decided to buy out Burt's stake in the business and operate without a partner. Burt preferred his life in rural Maine to life in developing North Carolina, so he took the opportunity to cash out and return to the place where he was happiest.

Roxanne was running a thriving business and operating entirely consistent with her values. In 2003, the business had grown to approximately $80 million in retail sales. But it was all-consuming, and the complexity of the business was beyond what one person could manage by herself. She decided to sell or to take on an operating partner.

A rising tide lifts all ships: The rapid growth stage

Searching for the right capital and operating partner, she met with scores of private equity firms and weighed two key criteria: Valuation of her company and 'fit' with her values and beliefs. This would give the greatest chance to continue growing the business consistent with the values she had instilled in it. She methodically worked her way through 97 potential partners and employed non-traditional methods such as tarot card readings and astrological analysis to determine trust and fit. She ultimately selected AEA Investors as her partner and sold 80 per cent of the business for a reported $155 million. The plan was to bring in an outside chief executive officer with Roxanne retaining responsibility for the creative vision and product development.

The transition was challenging. The growth strategy called for aggressive expansion into mainstream health and beauty care retail channels and a wider product assortment covering larger personal care categories. A secondary priority was to maintain the business in the existing natural channel and specialty retail channels. A CEO was hired who had extensive experience as a division president for large, multi-national consumer products companies. He built a leadership team of similarly experienced health and beauty care industry professionals to lead each function, but the new team, including Roxanne, failed to operate effectively. The result was an awkward sharing of power and decision making, with a cascading dysfunctional effect on the organization and culture. By default, not by design, the organization was practically split into two. The new people, with loyalties to the new CEO, working on new products and new customers, bringing conventional industry practices, commanding a disproportionate share of resources, were perceived as the future. The incumbent people, with loyalties to Roxanne, working on the existing product lines and with the existing specialty channels, were perceived as less capable holdovers from the past.

The team developed and launched several new products and successfully entered the two leading national drug store chains. However, the organization's dynamics proved unsustainable and went through an extensive restructuring. Roxanne removed herself from her operating role and limited her role to the board of directors. The CEO was replaced by John Replogle, a highly regarded strategist, operator and leader. John's source of authority was rooted in experience leading large, growing businesses combined with a strong values system that was compatible with Roxanne's. John focused on three core parts of his job:

1 Developing a long-range strategy and annual operating plan.

2 Building an effective organization and company culture.

3 Cultivating high-quality external stakeholder relationships.

Taking a more strategic approach to purpose and profit

Critical to this strategy was alignment and commitment to the company's Mission and vision. In many businesses the Mission and vision are treated as more perfunctory tasks, with the real strategy work focused on resourcing

FIGURE 17.3 'Learning from nature' connects the Brand Myth and Mission: An education wall in the store at Burt's Bees headquarters relates Burt's nature insights and experiences to the product and brand

SOURCE JP Kuehlwein (2016)

the prioritized choices. In Burt's Bees case, because of the stage of develop-ment and in the absence of the founder's daily influence, it was important to declare unambiguously a Mission and vision for the company.

Mission (why we exist): To make people's lives better every day – naturally!

Vision (what success looks like): The leading global natural personal care brand, adored by consumers, desired by customers, and working in harmony with stakeholders and the environment

The company rooted its strategy in a declaration of purpose called The Greater Good Business Model. The model identified the parts of the busi-ness that enabled health and well-being, environmental sustainability, and social impact in the context of stakeholders that would play a collaborative role. This purpose framework was integrated into the business plan and was referred to as a People, Planet, Profit strategy.

People

The goals were: (1) To ensure the integrity of a natural product to deliver on health and well-being benefits; and (2) To establish criteria for the ethical treatment of employees and suppliers.

The company created and published the Burt's Bees Natural Standard, which defined standards for a natural personal care product formula. It:

- set minimum criteria for natural raw material concentration (>95 per cent);
- set conditions for when non-natural ingredient can be used (no viable natural option, no suspected human health risk);
- listed prohibited processing methods (ie ethoxylation) that were harmful to either human health or the environment.

Given Burt's Bees' leadership in the segment and the collaborative, inclusive approach taken to its development, the standard was widely adopted by the industry, including the Natural Products Association and most leading retailers, and served as an effective moat against brands that were more naturally positioned than they were naturally formulated.

The model further specified the company's policies and principles for the ethical treatment of employees and suppliers. For employees, it set expecta-tions for individual participation in The Greater Good humanitarian and sustainability initiatives. A portion of the annual bonus programme was tied to achievement of those goals. It also standardized compensation and benefits across the organization. For suppliers, a supplier code of conduct was created and implemented complete with criteria and auditing requirements that ensured compliance with quality assurance, traceability and ethical treatment of employees. For the community, the model funded The Burt's Bees Foundation, which made grants to organizations with shared values and with whom employees would devote significant volunteer time throughout the year.

Planet

Set a '2020 vision' for sustainable operations with specific goals set for packaging, water consumption, electricity use and landfill waste. The packaging standard set ambitious goals for the development of biodegradable packaging, while specifying the use of better materials including forest stewardship certified paper, recycled and recyclable plastics, aluminium and soy-based inks in printing. The packaging standard banned certain materials outright, including PVC bags that had been used in gift sets and Styrofoam packaging material. The water and electricity goals were set to hold consumption at current levels, which effectively meant, for a business growing 25 per cent per year, a reduction in water and energy on a per-unit basis. The waste goals were designed to reduce, re-use and recycle *all* materials used in every facility and resulted in Burt's Bees becoming the first zero-waste-to-landfill company in the state of North Carolina in 2010 and eliminated 55 tons of landfilled material.

Profit

A typical long-range business plan was created to set financial expectations for revenue growth, gross profit, investments in marketing support and organization, operating profit and major capital expenses. It included a set of prioritized choices for retailer expansion, product expansion and country expansion. A major effort was made during this phase to dramatically improve the gross profitability of the business to deliver the 'fuel for growth' enabling sustained investments in marketing and the organization. Notably, none of this work involved reducing the formula and packaging costs by using cheaper raw materials. In fact, during this time the formulas became *more* natural and direct costs went up. Gross profit was achieved through pricing increases, optimizing trade investments, and capital investments that allowed the manufacturing plant to run more efficiently.

The company's financial plans were transparent within the organization and all employees participated in an annual incentive plan based on meeting or exceeding these goals. Cash bonus payments were determined by a weighted system that considered revenue growth, operating profit achievement, sustainability goals, and personal goals. The incentive targets could flex up or down, depending on the degree of over- or under-achievement of each of those four dimensions. This system created an alignment of interests between the private equity financial partners and each member of the operating company and put financial considerations alongside Mission considerations.

A culture programme was designed and implemented to reinforce desired values and behaviours and to create one unified team. The culture was

TABLE 17.1   Burt's Bees culture programme

Values	Behaviours	Reinforcing Systems
Steadfast commitment to The Greater Good	• Uncompromising on core values and principles	• Formula and package standards • Supplier code of conduct • Sustainable living credits
Harmonious tension (jazz!)	• Robust debate • Clarity of decisions	• Town hall meetings each quarter in each facility • Open door office hours (1:1) • Friday coffee with leadership team members
Embrace change	• Don't fear every change • Address legitimate concerns • Focus on what you can control • 'Take a beat'	• 'Five Whys' to surface root concerns • Prioritize concerns and create 'what needs to be true' to successfully mitigate • After action reviews to assess 'the good, the bad, and the ugly' and document lessons learned
Passionate teamwork	• Execution excellence • Engagement • Collaborative environment • Personal commitment	• Service hour requirements • 'We care' award recognition • Burt's Bees Growth Award • Burt Shavitz environmental stewardship • Roxanne Quimby humanitarian award • Culture Day events and celebrations

grounded in the four values that the team thought would be most important to success in the coming years:

1 Steadfast commitment to the Mission and The Greater Good Model.

2 Harmonious tension – healthy debate and constructive conflict so decision-makers could hear *all* voices on a topic.

3 Embrace change – become comfortable with change and harness it for good as opposed to resisting change for fear of 'selling out' or compromising principles.

4 Passionate teamwork – *one* aligned team, supporting each other, aligned on priorities, getting fun and satisfaction from the hard work.

Cultivating external relationships with values-aligned partners

A significant piece of the 'profit with purpose' success model was engagement with external stakeholders. The posture of the business was to encourage the development of the wider natural personal care category. By default, Burt's Bees as the market leader would benefit disproportionately. Raw material suppliers, agencies, community leaders, regulators – it was a big tent. But the collaboration with competitors and customers was the most significant category unlock. The realization among competitors was that they had far more in common than they did differences, that they all shared similar core values and beliefs, and that the real competition was with brands who saw the popularity of natural products and who exploited the consumer confusion to market 'pseudo natural' products. The cooperation in development of the natural standard was challenging to produce but effectively set good parameters for a product to be called natural. While the standard was not as high as the German BDIH definition, it was practically high enough to isolate the merely naturally positioned products. When major retailers generally adopted that definition and applied it to their natural category merchandising strategies, it sealed the deal. Target's comment was indicative of the market at the time:

> We know that natural and organic products are viable in the mainstream, and we feel like we are behind and need to get caught up. We are not getting proper advice from our usual category advisors because they are focused on the marketing of natural as opposed to the formulation of natural. Can Burt's Bees help us create a category?

Participating brands had access to a far bigger pool of consumers without 'selling out' or compromising their principles, and consumers could make better-informed decisions. Win–win–win.

The period from 2004–08 was brief but commercially successful:

- tripled size of the business;
- launched 15–30 new products each year;
- extended retail distribution to target both major drug store chains and many grocery stores while retaining natural channel and specialty distribution;
- entered five international countries and acquired the Canadian distributor as a wholly owned subsidiary;
- built a high-performing, highly engaged team capable of scaling the business;
- improved the margin structure of the business to allow for sustained healthy operating investment.

The commercial successes were matched by the Mission successes:

- In the absence of a Federal Trade Commission definition or Food and Drug Administration guidelines, Burt's Bees led an industry self-governing process to agree high standards for natural products. These were adopted by the company, many competitors and most retailers.
- Established 2020 goals for environmental sustainability improvement, including packaging standards, 'never use' materials, wastewater reduction, energy reduction and carbon offset, and achieved zero waste to landfill designation.
- Established the Burt's Bees Foundation, which made grants to philanthropic organizations.
- Created a culture where 100 per cent of employees participated directly in activities designed to further the company Mission and support community partners.

The financial pressures on the business during this phase were different than the cash-constrained pressure that the founder generally faced. The private equity firm had reportedly leveraged the business with debt that needed to be serviced, and it justifiably wanted to maximize its return on the investment it had made. However, it had unwavering faith in the underlying trend towards natural personal care products and a keen understanding of the value of purpose to the brand equity and the culture. Its commitment to the People, Planet, Profit strategy and The Greater Good Model never caused reconsideration of those root principles. Fortunately, after the management transition, the business performed consistently well, the category experienced accelerated consumer adoption, and there was good execution against each of the strategic priorities.

Transaction to The Clorox Company

Beginning in 2007, widespread mass retailer support and rapid mainstream consumer adoption combined to make natural products the fastest growing personal care segment, and major multinational personal care companies wanted to participate. Given the fundamental differences in creating, procuring and producing truly natural products versus synthetic personal care products, companies preferred to acquire existing companies rather than develop their own brands and products. L'Oreal had acquired Kiehl's and The Body Shop. Johnson & Johnson had established a partnership with the Greek brand Korres. All of the major global players were active in the market.

The Clorox Company acquired Burt's Bees for a reported $925 million in December 2007, which surprised many given that Clorox does not compete in the broader health and beauty care market. But, on closer inspection, Burt's Bees was a remarkably good fit for Clorox's portfolio. It specializes in managing brands that have a #1 or #2 market share ranking in smaller secondary categories. For example, it holds a leadership position in laundry additives, but doesn't compete in the larger but more competitively intense laundry detergent category. In Burt's Bees it found a leading market share brand in natural personal care, which although it is personal care, has a narrowly defined set of competitive brands and none of which was at the time prohibitively threatening. In defining NPC as a secondary category, Burt's Bees fitted nicely into the broader, eclectic portfolio strategy which ranges from laundry additives to salad dressing to cat litter. Moreover, Clorox, as part of its Centennial Strategy, was reshaping its portfolio to be relevant in this new century and adapting to evolving consumer trends. It was in the process of shedding legacy businesses like automobile care and was focused more on natural and environmentally friendly brands and products like Brita water filters and Green Works household cleaners. Burt's

Bees fitted comfortably in that emerging portfolio, which had greater strate-gic importance than its size would indicate at the time. In Burt's Bees, it also found a company with an experienced team, good operating fundamentals and a strong culture that could operate as a semi-independent business unit with a degree of freedom to continue to grow the business. Therefore, by integrating some of its team into the North Carolina-based business it could capture learning and integrate the business over an extended timeframe.

The lessons learned during the private equity period and having a culture that was better at embracing change made the transition to Clorox owner-ship rather easy with relatively simple changes to strategy and operating model.

Strategy

There was no desire to alter the Mission or vision of Burt's Bees, now a stra-tegic business unit of a publicly traded company. Clorox fully endorsed the People, Planet, Profit strategy and recognized the intrinsic value people and planet brought to the overall value proposition for consumers, employees and all stakeholders. More rigour was put into assessing the channel, prod-uct and country choices due to the new strengths and capabilities that Clorox brought and better tools to assess those options. Walmart was the major distribution gap closed after the sale, in January 2008, but launch prepara-tion had been underway for over a year so was not a new choice. International expansion was a big growth opportunity enabled by a multinational partner, and the team explored how Burt's Bees might capitalize on the significant opportunity in China without compromising its commitment to not testing on animals, a regulatory requirement of all imported cosmetics in China at the time. With no viable paths around the regulation, animal testing's risk to the equity outweighed the commercial benefit of entering so it was unanimously agreed to advocate for regulatory change, which was the stance taken as well by L'Oreal's The Body Shop brand. The decision-making process and the decision itself were reassuring to people in the company who were unsure how it would work when principles conflicted with commercial opportunity. And, in fact, the process caused The Clorox Company to amend its animal testing policy for the rest of its portfolio and it has since been an outspoken advocate against discretionary testing requirements.

With the Mission and vision intact, work was done to simplify the artic-ulation, programming, measurement and reporting in support of The Greater Good Model. *Good for You* contained all the health and wellness

FIGURE 17.4 'Formalizing the brand purpose – Burt's Bees' guiding principles of serving People, Planet, Profit are expressed through the Greater Good Model and guide execution after the acquisition by Clorox

SOURCE Reproduced with permission of Burt's Bees (2020)

aspects of the natural formulations with no change to the natural product standard, *Good for All* combined the humanitarian and environmental projects into one coherent collection of projects, and *Good for Us* explicitly recognized the financial and operating parts of a for-profit business that ultimately make it sustainable and deliver a reasonable return to financial stakeholders.

The business unit continues to report its progress against its Greater Good goals in a bi-annual, simple to digest, rigorous and transparent report that is published prominently on its website.

Financial performance

Financial goals were set, including revenue and profit targets and parameters for investing in marketing and other operating expenses. The targets were stretching but broadly in line with management estimates made during the sale process. The financial results generally met expectations over time except during the global economic recession in 2009–10 and with a concurrent delay in the pace of international expansion. According to published reports, Clorox took a $250 million write-down of the Burt's Bees asset on the balance sheet. However, the business remained a fast-growing unit in the Clorox portfolio with accretive gross profit, and there was never a significant compromise of purpose in favour of profit.

An example of the relationship between purpose and profit was the debate about whether to enter the China market. The China market was attractive given its size, the popularity of foreign natural products and consumer attraction to American brands. However, there existed at the time a regulatory requirement that all imported cosmetic products submit to safety testing on animals, which was in direct conflict with Burt's Bees practices and principles. After a complete review of the local, provincial and federal regulations and a scan to see how other companies had dealt with the issue, the decision was made to delay the entry into China until the regulation changed. The determination was made that the damage to the brand trust caused by such a compromise to principles was not worth the economic benefit. So, while some other competitors made a different decision, Burt's Bees, as a matter of principle, avoided the Chinese market for several years until the regulatory environment changed in 2016 allowing untested products to enter the country for personal use only via e-commerce.

Organization and culture

As a business unit of a publicly traded company, Burt's Bees would have different operating configuration requirements than it had as a private company in a private equity portfolio. However, the Clorox CEO was also a board member of The Kellogg Company, which had tried various integration strategies with its acquisition of Kashi, the natural foods brand, and the Burt's Bees integration was informed by that experience. The 'semi-independent' status of the Burt's Bees unit was characterized by a separate physical location in Durham, North Carolina, a single point of contact between each function and various degrees of integration by function.

Clorox initially treated Burt's Bees as it would a business in another country. Functional support was determined by an executive function owner in Clorox working out an appropriate support with their counterpart in the Burt's Bees unit. As a division of a public company, finance, legal compliance and strategy needed to be fully integrated as a matter of basic governance. However, the demand functions, sales and marketing remained broadly independent. Most other functions co-created a practical arrangement where they were able to achieve a 'best of both' relationship where the capability of Clorox met the agility of a leaner business. Over a decade, the relationships have evolved to where the business is considered fully integrated including operating on common ERP systems, but there remain certain differences from other business units due to location or to uniqueness of the Burt's Bees business. Overall it is more common than not. It is a unique configuration that has been continuously refined and improved, and it works remarkably well.

Consistent with the organization structure evolution, the business unit culture has evolved over time. The main objective with culture refinement was to embrace being part of The Clorox Company while retaining authenticity to the brand values and business unit Mission and vision. After seven years, and mostly due to its physical distance from the Oakland HQ, there was a pervasive feeling that the Burt's Bees culture was too separate from Clorox and it still behaved as an independent, private company. And nine years after defining the 'we care' culture, the most urgent issues facing the team were not embracing change and organization effectiveness anymore. The key organizational challenge was to get people to re-commit to The Greater Good, which had seen significant erosion, and to be able to more directly connect the business unit to the Clorox company values and growth culture.

This was achieved by fully adopting the four Clorox values and five desired behaviours which were not in any way inconsistent with the Burt's Bees brand values and behaviours. The Burt's Bees culture statement then went a further step to clarify its Mission (purpose), convictions (beliefs) and People, Planet, Profit operating model. It took the opportunity to further simplify the Greater Good Model by clarifying how the model drove 'what we make', 'how we operate' and 'how we give back'. Elegantly depicted through the metaphor of a flower growing in soil, it is well understood and embraced.

RECAP: BURT'S BEES

Burt's Bees is a compelling brand story. Bearded Burt is a special beauty care brand icon who combines a purpose that helps elevate people into something bigger, better and more meaningful with a personality that is quirky, eccentric, unconventional and unique. The identity is both authentic and inherently inviting, enticing people to want to learn more about the company's products, its people and its practices. It celebrates its accomplishments while continually raising its expectations for improvement, and it is comfortable admitting when it has fallen short of its goals. That is the essence of the brand equity. It is an equally compelling business story. Over the course of 35 years, the business has been highly successful *because of* its purpose. It is a modern example of how stakeholders and shareholders can be served simultaneously and extraordinary value can be created for each. It is an enduring legacy for the succession of committed owners, leaders and employees who contributed to what it is today.

- *Mission, vision and values are the compass* for the entire business and the north star for every strategy: Business, brand, product, supply chain, organization and culture, finance, sustainability and social impact.
- *Hire for will and train for skill.* People must embody the purpose at all levels of the organization and across all functions. Weed out people who don't walk the talk. Embed the purpose in the culture and the recognition systems.
- *Align incentives.* Build purpose goals into compensation schemes alongside the business goals and ensure 100 per cent participation.
- *Codify operating standards.* Be specific about how purpose will translate into products, service and operations and the conditions under which exceptions will be considered. Ensure buy-in from all relevant stakeholders.
- *Be as strategic about purpose as you are about business.* Long-range planning and annual objectives, goals, strategies and measures. Ensure all strategies are integrated and ticked-and-tied together.
- *Build a community of like-minded external stakeholders.* Suppliers, customers, consumers, investors, even competitors who share your values. Value 'fit'.
- *Be transparent.* Celebrate where you meet or exceed your goals and be honest and transparent about where you fall short. Humility and imperfection are strengths, not vulnerabilities.

Case 4: Starbucks

*The renaissance plan, or: How to leap ahead
by going back to quality and service*

An Ueber-Brand should never forget what made it big in the first place: Its iconic products and services. Starbucks in Europe is a great case to illustrate this principle. After being initially more successful than perhaps even it expected, the brand hit a slump in 2012. The competition was becoming fierce and customers' view of the brand was starting to erode, questioning its quality and not making Starbucks part of their routine as much as intended.

Samantha Yarwood as Director of Marketing in Europe and the Middle East shares her views on the ambitious 'renaissance' project that re-asserted coffee quality, barista craft and personal service – the three pillars that had made Starbucks big. And the brand took off.

In this article Samantha shares some unique insights and experiences, as well as challenges along the way, taking an iconic brand back to where it belongs – at the top.

Samantha Yarwood

For the past 15+ years, Samantha Yarwood has been working in marketing and communications with Starbucks/Nestle in the Americas and as Director of Marketing EMEA. Currently she is doing a Masters of Change at INSEAD in France. Her Mission is to give people and organizations what they need to unleash their inner master; the tools, guides and insights to boost the way they live their lives, innovate and create. Current projects include CMO at Scout Canning; Chief Marketing and Human Resources Officer at Abundance Behavioural Health; and Service Line Director, THNK.

I never thought I would work for a big brand, let alone a global coffee giant. However, what I found at Starbucks was truly unique. A company where you could bring your best self to work, be recognized for your passions and strengths, and truly make a difference in the communities you worked in. Starbucks' Mission might seem grand, 'To inspire and nurture the human spirit – one person, one cup and one neighbourhood at a time'. However, every partner (that is what employees are called at Starbucks as everyone who works for the company is a shareholder and therefore a partner in the business) is empowered to deliver on the company's Mission and vision. I believe one of the reasons Starbucks has become one of the world's most loved and recognized brands is because of the commitment each partner makes to do their best work and bring the organization's values to life. The partners are Starbucks' biggest brand differentiator. It is through their passion and expertise that the organization has been able to change the way the world drinks coffee outside of home and work, creating the third place, where people can relax, enjoy a cup of coffee and most importantly, an experience. But it isn't easy to maintain this commitment, and continuously bring the Mission and values off the paper to life, especially in international markets, and that is what I want to share with you – one of my experiences and stories of how we revived the Starbucks brand in Europe, the Middle East and Africa (EMEA).

The situation

The first Starbucks store opened in the US in 1971 in Seattle's Pike Place Market. The story goes that a few years later when Howard Schultz was on a trip to Europe, Italy inspired him and gave rise to a vision for Starbucks as a purveyor not just of coffee beans and equipment, as it was when he joined the company, but espresso beverages and a unique place to drink them while escaping the everyday. In 2001 the first store opened in Europe, and despite many naysayers the brand was well received. Stores flourished, the brand continued to expand, and by 2012 there were stores in over 36 countries across the EMEA region. Although the brand was continuing to expand, the region was underperforming against the US and other markets. What Starbucks was going through in Europe was in many ways reminiscent of what Starbucks went through in the US in 2008/2009. The economy was fractured, there was record unemployment, we were operating in the most competitive coffee market in the world, and we were also dealing with our own self-induced mistakes. The new market opening strategy was to partner with local operators who knew the market, and already had an infrastructure in place. This meant the majority of markets across the region were either joint venture partnerships or fully run by a licensee (licensed operator for that market). Starbucks was the way the brand was operated but the Mission/vision wasn't always fully lived as the businesses had competing priorities and organizational cultures of their own.

Don't get me wrong, the business was solid and our belief in the brand was strong, but we were in a part of the world that loves coffee and was the birthplace of the coffee house culture. Locals knew the Starbucks name and had top of mind awareness. They knew us to be the place they could go to for a large selection of coffee beverages, friendly and personal service, good coffee to take away, but most importantly they saw us as the place they went to treat and reward themselves. We were not seen as the 'daily ritual' or the place they wanted to go to for their regular cup of coffee; instead they went to independent coffee shops or other branded coffee shops. Frequency was an opportunity for us across the region, with the average customers across the region visiting between 1.8–2.8 times per month and our best customers visiting us 3.5 times a month. In comparison, the US had an average of 5–6 visits per month. Copycats had become the leaders, with many branded coffee shops beating us to market, and investing more significantly out of store. In digging into the data, we realized the biggest hurdle to non-customer visitation was perception of coffee quality and price. Quality was the most important factor to customers when purchasing coffee, and we were underperforming. As one customer in Spain said, they perceived us as the 'Sangria of coffee' – the coffee obviously wasn't high enough quality and didn't taste good, otherwise why would we put so much milk into the beverages and add syrup? Plus, ethical sourcing and environmental stewardship were important to our customer and non-customers and although we were doing a lot, we weren't communicating it enough. Lastly, we also discovered that locations were definitely a barrier to purchase as our customers couldn't always find a coffee house on the way, and they weren't willing to make a detour to Starbucks when there were so many other options.

The reality was that we were all chasing the same customer, and the reason customers were visiting cafes was the same across the board. For us to win we needed to earn every visit. We knew what we had to do, play to our strengths. From the very beginning, the brand grew off experiences and things that were seen as defying conventional thinking. Our

FIGURE 18.1   The Starbucks customer experience and service was what had to make the difference

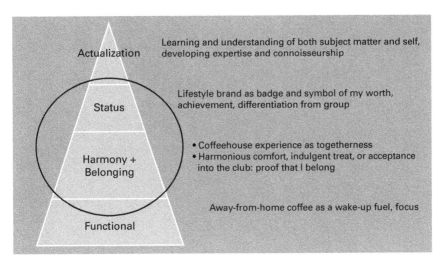

Actualization — Learning and understanding of both subject matter and self, developing expertise and connoisseurship

Status — Lifestyle brand as badge and symbol of my worth, achievement, differentiation from group

Harmony + Belonging
- Coffeehouse experience as togetherness
- Harmonious comfort, indulgent treat, or acceptance into the club: proof that I belong

Functional — Away-from-home coffee as a wake-up fuel, focus

SOURCE Sam Yarwood (2020)

customers expected more from us, excellent product was a basic expectation and our customer experience and service was what had and would make the difference.

The vision is clear

Our vision was clear. We needed to refresh the brand and become the local coffee house for the EMEA region. In other words, be the most loved brand in EMEA by partners/employees and customers. New York had a store on every corner; what did we need to do to drive the same brand awareness, engagement and penetration? As marketers, our job was to drive the funnel. That was what we were doing every day but to deliver growth in an ever more complex environment we needed to do more.

We needed to go deeper to build routine. We believed we needed a significant shift in our go-to-market approach and we needed to focus on what truly made us different. To do the things that no one else could do. We looked at ourselves closely to see if we were living up to our brand promise, and we discovered that we could do more. We needed to build on the areas that had made us famous and were continuing to make us the leading brand in the US.

FIGURE 18.2 We needed to go deeper in our consumer relations to grow our business

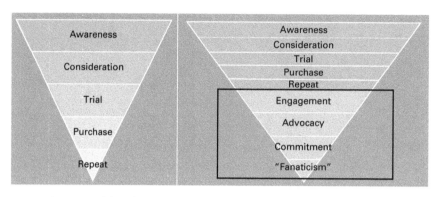

SOURCE Sam Yarwood (2020)

First, we needed to focus on the core, our partners and the barista. Partner Pride was probably the most important thing we could get right, as the company was built on the barista: it is and always will be where the Starbucks experience starts. We knew we needed to consistently deliver an excellent product, but we wanted to do more, and to be recognized for the quality of our product and specifically our espresso, and secondly for our barista craft. We had a real opportunity to build on our core, while dialling up our innovation or uniqueness which had made us famous. I will get into more details later, but we did world firsts like a second espresso bean launch and other coffee forward beverages like Flat White, and changing our beverage standards. Our product was premium, and we sourced the highest quality coffee in the world, we just needed to let the world know it. Thirdly, we wanted to exceed our customers' expectations by driving loyalty. We wanted to be known as the local coffee house. Lastly, we needed to change our go to market approach and have one plan across the region versions individual plans by market. One voice would be stronger and have more of an impact. We also wanted to shift our focus from in-store marketing to out-of-store marketing. By shifting our marketing approach to one plan for the region (versus individual country plans), we were able to drive more efficiencies. The time and money we saved gave us more resources to extend our reach and shift our focus from in-store marketing to out-of-store. We had never invested in advertising or TV spots, and knew it was time to change our approach. We recognized an opportunity to create a flywheel by connecting with our customers through all channels, owned, earned and paid. We determined the best focus would be to support our core, and to create campaigns around coffee quality and sourcing. We called this our 'always on' brand narratives. Although we did support some promotional campaigns, the majority of the heavy lifting was focused on our core narratives.

Partner pride

So, what did that really mean? The mantra was clear. In the EMA region, 14 March 2012 marked a new day. It was the day that we demonstrated to the world espresso perfection. First, it started with our Partner Pride. We needed to re-inspire our baristas to believe in the Starbucks Mission and vision. We gathered 350 of the top leaders (district managers and above) from 36 countries and various ownership models to share the plan and inspire belief to connect them to the Starbucks Mission and to the coffee. Their two days in Amsterdam included a re-education on what it meant to be a Starbucks partner and barista. They were also immersed in coffee training, including a trip to the local roasting plant. When the district managers went back to their markets, they were energized and engaged. We knew we needed to keep that momentum going and we shut all our stores across the region to re-train all our store managers and baristas on preparing the perfect espresso and latte, the core of the Starbucks experience. It was during this conference that the bar for a new level of performance was set. Probably one of the most impactful experiences of the conference was the launch of the Barista Olympics. Every day, baristas across EMEA make thousands of hand-crafted beverages. During the conference the teams were exposed to every element of the barista craft from the first 10 feet to the last 10 feet. The first 10 feet being education on how coffee is grown, harvested and roasted and the last 10 feet being the barista craft. We wanted to find a way to celebrate coffee craft and the art our baristas were doing every single day in a fun way. The Barista Olympics were developed to celebrate the best of what our baristas do and to give the baristas the opportunity to showcase their skills and share their passion for beverage quality. Over several months, in every country across the region, competitions were held for stores, districts, countries and finally the region. The barista champion from each store would compete for the district title. The district would then complete for the country title, and all the country winners would compete for the honour of the regional title. Judges evaluated the baristas on their ability to perfectly prepare and present espresso, lattes and flat whites with latte art, all while engaging the audience in an approachable and inspiring way. They also had to answer questions from the judges that demonstrated leadership in elevating beverage quality and customer experience in their stores. Each barista was challenged to create their own beverage, and the winning barista had their beverage launched across the entire region.

Craft and service

As I already mentioned, in Europe, you can get espresso on every corner and everybody was competing for the shrinking wallet. So, for us, we knew it needed to be the best, and we knew we could do better. When we re-trained our baristas on espresso quality, we also introduced the latest and greatest steaming pitchers to prepare the perfectly steamed milk for a latte or cappuccino that took hundreds of iterations to develop in order to ensure the perfect beverage. We also brought in new serve-ware since every new innovation and beverage deserved only the finest. Our mugs were old and outdated. We only had one type of mug, which varied by size. Instead we moved to the right serve-ware to showcase the uniqueness of each product. Flat White had its own cup to showcase latte art, where our other beverages were now served in a premium china simple mug with embossed logo. We also started to launch new serve-ware with unique beverages, like the Caffe Freddo, a beverage developed and inspired from Greece, that was launched in a beautiful glassware instead of a plastic cup. At the end of the store meeting and re-training, all our baristas signed and posted a Barista Promise in their stores to make every customers beverage to perfection or if not it would be re-made.

Using a local lens

We also made a few big local investments, as we knew our coffee experience had to be locally relevant to capture the everyday consumer. In the UK, where the market had defined a stronger latte, we redefined our standards. Half of our customers ordered tall size and added an extra shot, so we decided to change our standard to two shots in a tall instead of one. Feedback from customers was overwhelmingly positive, and our customers reinforced this was their preferred beverage. Making that small change enhanced the image of Starbucks for our customers in the UK. In France, the preferred beverage by locals is solo espresso, and French consumers wanted choice. So, just like the US where you had a choice in brewed coffee every day, for the first time in our company's history we introduced a second espresso roast. The blonde espresso quickly commanded over 20 per cent of the mix and grew espresso sales by 30 per cent. The launch of a second espresso bean elevated our espresso credentials, and inspired customers and partners so much so that in 2013 we decided to build on the success and continue the momentum. On 14 March 2013 Starbucks again proved its espresso leadership to the world. On that day we launched a second, premium bean for all our handcrafted espresso-based beverages across the region. For the first time our customers had a choice of bean for their favourite espresso beverage.

A people company serving coffee

We knew a great product was not enough. As Howard Behar once said, 'We are a people company serving coffee, not a coffee company serving people.' The hallmark of the Starbucks experience had always been about the personal connection. As we started our journey, we asked ourselves what more could we do? How could we improve the relationship between the customer and the partner? We started with holding round tables, small, intimate gatherings, where partners and/or customers were asked to join us so we could understand their needs first hand. It is where a lot of the ideas mentioned above were born. But we also did something else – we put our coffee on a first-name basis. In every market across EMEA we started putting names on cups. It was something no other region had done before and was eventually picked up globally. Then we took it one step further and put names on aprons so every customer would also know our baristas' names. We put our barista at the centre and made them the 'rock star' of coffee.

From marketing roulette to winning big

Changing what was happening in our stores wasn't enough. We knew we needed to get out there and tell our story. But, we had a problem. We operated in 36 countries, and in each of those countries the brand showed up differently. I like to call it marketing roulette. Depending on the country you were in you might see a different message, a slightly tweaked campaign, and if you went on to social media each country's channels had different images and messaging. It really was a case of 'spin the wheel of marketing and see where you land'. Additionally, we were a retail company, which typically operate on small budgets. By simply re-framing our approach, we identified a huge opportunity. If we focused on the core of Starbucks, coffee and barista craft, the message would be the same no matter what market we were in. We could maximize our reach by talking about our brand narrative in all channels, regardless of the market, and drive our expertise at the same time. So, we re-visited the way we did things, and developed one marketing calendar for the region that local markets adapted. Because we were working off of one plan, that also meant we could produce higher quality assets for all channels that could then be adapted into local language. It was during this time that we executed our first regional comprehensive marketing campaign supported by a large investment in out-of-store, and even did TV spots for the first time. We created over a billion media impressions, an unprecedented number for EMEA. To get a taste of the Names on Cups campaign, scan the QR code at the front of the book for a link.

Worth paying more for

We also addressed another very important issue for the European customer – value. Learning from the US, we committed to launching the Starbucks Card and Starbucks Rewards across the region to address how to be relevant from a value standpoint. In markets where we didn't yet have Starbucks Rewards we looked at what was relevant for that consumer. For example, in Germany where we knew the consumer didn't usually drink coffee in the morning out of home, we created an offer around our 10-year anniversary in Germany. A €1.50 latte offered in the morning to drive the morning day part and to invite them in. We believed if we could get them in once, we could win them over and get them back again. The promotion ran for 12 weeks and grew transactions by over 28 per cent. More than 50 incremental customers were visiting us every single day. The most exciting thing we saw was the routine and our morning day part comps continued to grow by more than 10 per cent.

All aboard – everywhere

As I mentioned earlier, one of our biggest hurdles was to drive daily rituals, becoming part of their routine and not just a treat. In order to do that, we recognized we needed to be where our customers live their lives and drink coffee; in the workplace, commuting hubs, hotels, grocery stores and universities. This was an area we had explored in the US but had left untapped in EMEA. The only way we could connect with all the customers we wanted to was by extending the brand beyond company owned or licensed stores into captive audiences, and what we called channel licensing. However, what was different for EMEA vs the US was space, so we needed to approach the market differently with alternative formats. One of the most exciting opportunities for us was trains. Everyone in Europe travels by train. Of course, we built a strategy and plan to open more stores in train stations, but in Switzerland we took it a step further. We dreamed of a world where there was a Starbucks on every train. In partnership with SBB we built a full-on Starbucks store inside the train's car. It was a first in the world. To see a video on the initiative, scan the QR code at the front of the book for a link.

We also wanted to tap into the shift from out-of-home consumption to in-office consumption and bring the Starbucks experience to offices, so we launched the first ever Starbucks branded vending machine, called On The Go. It was a state-of-the-art execution – with a touch of the screen, you can get, in under 60 seconds, a Starbucks-quality latte, mocha, Americano, espresso that truly rivals the quality of what you can get in our store. Originally the intent was to be in offices only. However, when we talked to customers, 80 per cent of them said it's a great fit with the brand and could see it playing a role in smaller locations where we couldn't get a store, like grocery stores or convenience stores. We could be anywhere you could put a vending machine. And it worked; 50 per cent of customers went more often because they knew Starbucks On The Go was available.

FIGURE 18.3 In Switzerland we built the world's first Starbuck's store inside a train

SOURCE Sam Yarwood (2020)

RECAP: STARBUCKS
The secret of experience, learn, apply (ELA)

The year 2012 was an incredible one for the region. We made some big investments and gained huge traction on the brand. It was a new day for Starbucks EMEA, and I believe the foundation set up the region for the success it continues to see today. Now in my role as a consultant and acting CMO there are many lessons I take from the EMEA transformation into the work I do:

1 *Retail isn't rocket science, it's harder. People are the centre of everything.* It is pretty simple. I am not sure why, but we often forget who our customer is. One of the most important things I learned at Starbucks is to talk to your customer, and the people who work with your customer every day. Listen and learn to find out what they truly need. A toolkit I highly recommend when doing any start-up or product development is the Guidion Toolkit. Scan the QR code at the front of the book for a link to the toolkit.

2 *Stay true to your core – live your values. Know your Why and never compromise.* Think of your brand as a person – who are they, what do they do? Are you truly measuring up? If not, why not? Every year, around New Year's Day, many people reflect on who they are and who they want to be. A brand isn't any different. I think it is important for every brand, young or old, to understand their values and make sure they are living them every day. I look at Starbucks as a person, she is clear on what she does, and how she does it or brings it to life (values). Study your brand's personality and characteristics, and know your Why. For a simple values exercise, download any free values cards and identify your top 3–5. Think about how you live these as a brand every day and give concrete examples of what this is and isn't. Those can become your guiding principles. And make sure you reflect. Like a person, a brand will change – everything grows and evolves.

3 *Challenge the status quo – do the impossible. Re-frame.* What got you to here is not going to get you to there. I think it is important when doing any work to identify what I call a creative question, then tease it out and re-frame it. A powerful question helps to catalyse insight, drive innovation and action. I learned a framework at THNK that has served me well:
How might we_____with_____given that_____?
For example: *How might we build regular routine with our customers given that they have multiple coffee options and see us as treat and reward?*

Once I have my creative question identified I like to challenge the thinking by understanding my supporting beliefs (why do I think this needs to be done, using facts and stats). From there, I look at the complete opposite beliefs whether they are true or not. Based on my new assumptions, I then re-formulate my creative question. What often happens is I look at the challenge from a new perspective, in turn opening up possibilities I hadn't even dreamed of.

Case 5: Airbnb

The importance of culture, or: How Airbnb found, launched and lives its purpose

Identifying an inspiring Mission for your brand is hard enough. But truly living that higher purpose as an organization, making it the guide for all you do, engraining it in the culture is even harder. However, Douglas Atkin says that all that hard work is worth it in the end, because a purpose lived provides practical guidance and is a forceful motivator – more so than money.

And Douglas should know – he was one of the orchestrators who helped Airbnb find its purpose, operationalize it and make it an indelible part of its culture. He reflects on this time below and extracts for us how Airbnb found, launched and now lives a Mission to create a world where anyone can 'Belong Anywhere'. You can also listen to an interview we did with Douglas on ueberbrands.com (ueberbrands.com, 2019c). Scan the QR code at the front of the book for a link.

Douglas Atkin

Douglas has spent the past 15 years being passionate about, and innovating in the fields of community, purpose, movement-making, culture and values. To whit...

He was Global Head of Community at Airbnb, on its Leadership Team and was also Architect of Purpose, Culture and Core Values. He worked there from 2012–17 during its hyper-growth years when 'the company was making up everything as it went along'.

Douglas also co-founded Peers with Airbnb CEO Brian Chesky, a movement for the peer-to-peer economy. He co-founded Purpose, a firm that enables organizations to launch and run movements for social change. It also launches its own movements. For example: 'AllOut', the world's first and largest LGBTQ rights movement for which he served on the board. He was also Partner and Chief Community Officer at community platform Meetup from 2007–08.

It comes as no surprise that he would be the author of the pioneering book on the subject, namely *The Culting of Brands: Turn your customers into true believers* (Atkin, 2005).

'You know a lot about brands. Can you help us figure out what ours is?'

I'd just arrived in San Francisco from my home in New York to do a project on community at Airbnb... at least that's what I thought I was doing until Brian Chesky, Co-Founder and CEO, said this to me. It was kind of him to say so, but I had left the world of branding six years previously and had focused on community and movement-building since my book *The Culting of Brands* had been published. I said, 'Let me think about it overnight and I'll come back to you in the morning.'

'I think that instead of figuring out the brand, we should figure out what Airbnb's purpose is,' I said the following morning. I went on that morning to explain that there was clearly a strong community of hosts, guests and employees... so let's figure out *why*. Why were they so committed to Airbnb? What role does it play in their lives? 'If we can figure out *why Airbnb exists...* what its purpose is... then figuring out its Brand will be relatively simple. And so will everything else: What products to build, what kinds of people to hire or not hire, which companies to buy and which to avoid. It's the rudder that guides the ship. It determines the direction of everything,' I said. Brian looked at me for a few seconds with one of his meaningful stares. Then he said: 'OK. Do that.'

How Airbnb found its purpose

Having a purpose is 'hot' for all the right reasons: Employees want to get up in the morning for more than just a salary. Customers are demanding more than just the utility of a product or service. And a good purpose clarifies and governs every decision you make as a leader. It's the *Why* that guides *What* you do (your products and services) and *How* you do it (the values that govern your behaviour).

But getting a good one is hard. To be good, it should have at least these five characteristics:

1 It needs to be *grounded in an experienced truth* to be believable. Not an overreach. Grounding it in a truth is also likely to make it *yours*. It will be *inherently differentiated*.

2 Yet it must *reach for the stars* to be aspirational and transformational. People should wake up in the morning inspired to make it real.

3 It needs to be about *one thing* to provide the focus for everything that your organization will do.

4 But it needs to be a *big thing* so that it has a meaningful impact on the world. And so that you'll never run out of runway for your products and initiatives to achieve it.

5 And it should be *memorable,* so that everyone can remember *Why* they're doing what they're doing, from the receptionist to the CEO, and customers.

To ensure Airbnb's purpose was grounded in an experienced truth, I wanted to spend the next three weeks especially talking to Airbnb's hosts, guests and employees about why they were so committed. There were two techniques that I and a small group of Airbnb employees used with the almost 500 people we talked to that were most useful in surfacing how transformational Airbnb had been to these employees and users. I asked them to write three words on a piece of card that described what they were like before they used or worked for Airbnb, and three after. I then asked each of them to say why they had chosen those words.

Geo, an Airbnb host in San Francisco, explained that before Airbnb he was 'introverted, shy and a follower'. Now he was 'outgoing and fun'. Hosting had given him a sense of purpose, and he was proud to introduce guests to his city and make them feel at home. David, a guest, said that he was no longer a tourist but an 'insider'. He was more curious about the places he visited and felt confident to explore as his host made him feel like a 'local' and 'at home': 'Actually, it unleashed this adventurer in me that I didn't know existed,' he said.

Next, I asked them to write a manifesto for Airbnb. They wrote such inspiring statements as 'We are a connected world where there are no countries, there is just one world', 'We put aside our fear of the unknown, and embrace our desire to connect', 'The world is not mono-cultural or sterile. It's a place of incredible diversity', 'We are advancing a vision of the world that is smaller, meaningful and more collaborative'.

We reviewed all the findings, and posted all the worksheets on the walls of the one big meeting room that Airbnb had at that point. There were many ideas. I was looking for the characteristics of a good purpose I outlined above: It had to be grounded in an experienced truth, but reach for the stars to be inspirational. It had to be about one big thing. And it had to be memorable. We walked the founders around the room... and, weirdly, Ashton Kutcher, who was an early investor and happened to be visiting the offices that day. He made some really smart observations, actually.

Later, after I was hired by Brian and had moved coasts, I came back to him and Joe with what became Airbnb's purpose: 'Creating a world where anyone can belong anywhere'. It was not anything that any of the five hundred people had said, but it seemed to reflect the truth of their experiences. It was transformational enough to inspire. It was about one big thing...belonging anywhere. And I thought it was memorable. The founders agreed, and within months it was given its first big test...

How Airbnb launched its purpose

'Make it about that.' Brian had just slapped 'Creating a world where anyone can belong anywhere' up on the wall in a meeting of designers. They had been tasked to devise a new symbol for Airbnb that would replace the cutesy blue and white logo it had had since its first days when it was run out of Joe, Brian and Nate's apartment in San Francisco. Brian, Joe and the lead designer Andrew Schapiro, had been clear from the start. They wanted a *symbol*, not just a logo. A symbol is a logo with *meaning attached*. If you think of cultural symbols such as the dove of peace, or religious symbols, and brands whose logos had become elevated to symbols, such as Nike, Apple and Harley, there is always some meaning or ideology bound up within them. The meaning that Brian wanted embodied in this new symbol for Airbnb was 'Belong Anywhere' (our shorthand for the full purpose).

That briefing led to the 'Belo' (short for Belong). Airbnb's new symbol and Belong Anywhere were launched in July 2014 in a way that was intended to *live the meaning*. Hosts and guests were invited to take the symbol and make it their own on a website that offered almost limitless ways to personalize it. Hundreds of thousands of people created their own versions and posted them on social media, T-shirts and their listing and profile pages on Airbnb.

This is the opposite of how most companies handle their logos with the public. Fiddle with their logos, and phalanxes of corporate lawyers will descend on you with fierce 'cease and desist' letters and threats of legal

FIGURE 19.1   Airbnb's founders wanted the 'Belo' to be more than a logo. It symbol-
izes the Mission of 'Belong Anywhere'. (From left to right: Joe Gebbia,
Nate Blecharczyk, Brian Chesky)

SOURCE Douglas Atkin (2020)

action. Instead, we wanted the launch to feel inclusive… just as the symbol's meaning of Belong Anywhere demanded. The Belo was also launched with a delightful short video (scan the QR at the beginning of the book for a link). It dramatizes that in this large, and largely disconnected, world people are seeking to connect, be accepted and feel safe. In other words: To belong. It continues: 'What if you could have that feeling, anywhere? Airbnb stands for something much bigger than travel. We imagine a world where you can Belong Anywhere'.

There were, of course, other adaptations of the new symbol. 'Is it balls, vagina or both? Airbnb logo sparks wave of internet parodies' was the headline in the *Guardian* newspaper (Wainwright, 2014). Our 'equal opportunity genitalia logo', as I liked to describe it at the time, was creatively parodied across social media… which we loved, and gently encouraged.

We knew, notwithstanding these parodies, that we were on the right track with both the symbol and its meaning. A few months earlier Brian, Joe and I had spent the weekend with some hosts and guests in New York to show them the new symbol and its meaning. Their response was even more than we had hoped for. For example, David, a middle-aged Brooklyn host, said with tears in his eyes that he felt Belong Anywhere finally expressed *why* he was hosting. He said it was more than just the money. And now it made him feel like he was part of something bigger.

We had also launched the purpose and the new symbol to employees a few weeks previous to the public launch in July. We had selected a hundred employees to 'live Belong Anywhere'. They were given a budget to go on a three-day trip of their choice and document what happened in a diary, with video and photos of their experiences. At the employee launch some came up on stage and described how they also had felt like a local. How their hosts had made them feel like part of the family and showed them a side of their town or locale that tourists never see.

It felt it was important to show staff that Airbnb's purpose was not the result of some predictable management offsite, but was an authentic ideal, sourced from our users and employees. The best way to drive this home, I thought, was to show our users some hosts and guests talking about their experiences. And especially to get employees to explain to their peers their personal experience of Belong Anywhere. It was a very successful launch. It's now so embedded as the driving motivator amongst employees that if they feel a leader, colleague or company decision does not live the purpose, they are extremely vocal about it.

In effect, Airbnb *launches its purpose every day* in every decision it makes, every recruit it hires, every product it launches and every company it acquires. You can never really live your purpose unless you think of it this way: As a daily launch, manifested in everything you do, as we shall now see...

How Airbnb lives its purpose

Living your purpose is the hard bit. Really hard, actually. Finding and launching your purpose is easy by comparison. It's hard because everyone has to live it every day about everything. It should lead everyone's decision-making, recruiting, reviewing and rejecting. It should lead how they behave and relate to each other. It should come before profits, growth and share-holder returns. It will make you focus on the long term, often with short-term costs of money, time and energy. It will force you to innovate because, if it's good, it will determine a path that no one else has taken.

This sounds daunting. And it is. Especially when you know that most companies, with the best of intentions, fail at some or all of the above.

The three Airbnb founders know that failing the purpose is all too easy. And so they put enormous effort, focus and energy into operationalizing it. This is, in part, because they believe it *will not* compromise growth, profits and shareholder returns over the long term. The opposite in fact: That it will be critical to delivering them. In any event, Airbnb experienced what Marc Andreesen calls 'hyper-growth' (2–3x year-on-year growth) over those first seven or eight years even though it felt that the decisions we made at the time would compromise short-term growth in favour of the long term.

But the founders also invest heavily in living the purpose primarily because they want the impact it will make. They want a legacy that's more than just shareholder returns. They want to 'Create a world where anyone can belong anywhere'.

Here's a list of the actions that we have learned are critical to living your purpose.

1. Put it first

Mission, obviously Mission-led. The simplest way to describe it is the Mission comes before everything.

It comes before personal gain of the people who work at the company. It comes before the valuation. It comes before profits. It comes before business performance. It comes before all the other values. It theoretically comes before the quality of the product.

I mean, I could keep going on, right?

This was Brian Chesky, CEO and co-founder, on a Sunday afternoon in 2016. I had just asked him and the other two founders to rank-order the most important principles by which they lived at Airbnb. It's not something you often hear from a CEO of a large, successful multinational company. In fact, I've *never* heard a CEO give so much importance to the purpose. But it takes this kind of focus from a CEO to drive the purpose through an organization. Brian acknowledged this at the annual all-staff get-together called OneAirbnb, in 2015:

Hold me accountable ultimately. If the founders are the caretakers of the vision and values, then as CEO, I'm really responsible for executing on the values and the vision. So, if our vision is to create a world where anyone can belong anywhere, whether we're on that path or not, that's on me.

Being accountable for executing the vision and values is exactly what he has become. His second use of the purpose... after briefing the designers for the new symbol... was to brief the company on how it would extend Belong Anywhere from the original product – Homes – to the whole trip. Brian personally led a small development team in 2015–16 to re-imagine travel in a way that would deliver the purpose. Internally called Magical Trips, his goal was to re-invent the trip from the moment you left home until your return. Then, he re-geared the company in terms of focus, money, people and structure to launch the series of products that would deliver the purpose to more parts of the trip.

The first of these was Airbnb Experiences, launched at the end of 2015. You could now meet locals who hosted experiences built around their passions: Like making pasta in Tuscany or getting an inside view of Sumo wrestling from an ex-wrestler in Tokyo. It was another way to feel welcome, to get to know locals and other guests, and experience an authentic aspect of the place you were visiting. Since then, Airbnb Adventures launched in 2019. Groups of fellow travellers go on adventures to exotic locations hosted by a local over an extended period. Another way to experience Belong Anywhere. Expect more... including a reinvention of the least pleasant part of the trip: Getting there and back. 'There was a time when getting on a plane was a magical trip of its own, but over the years, how you get to where you're going has become an experience we endure, not enjoy,' according to Chesky. 'We believe that needs to change' (Future Travel Experience, 2019).

Putting the purpose first is also manifested in countless other ways. For example, having that annual all-staff get-together (OneAirbnb) is a huge investment of money, energy and focus. In the short term it hurts the bottom line by millions. For a whole week thousands of staff are not working on creating growth, but creating connections with each other instead (for that is its primary purpose). Of course, fights were had with CFOs and investors about this and other initiatives the founders view as essential to executing the purpose.

Here's Brian, that same Sunday afternoon, talking about why he fought those fights:

> I think the decision of having OneAirbnb... like even this year I got pushback for doing it. The pushback I got for flying-in all the employees! It's expensive and time consuming. Some people say it's not the best use of time or money.

Well, *we do* think it's the best use of time and money. It depends on your horizon. Long term, you need these investments. If you're trying to build a company that outlives you, then people have to believe [in the purpose and Values]. There have to be believers and they have to want to go way above and beyond.

If you think about it that way, people need to feel deeply committed to something, and those commitments need huge amounts of deposits. And OneAirbnb is a huge deposit into the brand, the vision, the values and the culture. And it's hard to imagine over the arc of a company having that commitment without these seminal moments.

2. Drive the purpose from the inside out. Use culture as your 'How' to deliver your 'Why'

'Culture' is too often seen as an accidental but happy outcome of the *real* focus of leaders: Growth, product, people, profitability. It's rarely considered to be a 'must-have'. If it's thought of at all, it's when there's a 'morale problem' and some dollars are tossed half-heartedly to HR to create some 'fun in the workplace'.

As we have seen earlier, this is not how the Airbnb founders view culture. It's one of the 'sacred three' with purpose and core values that they will always have at the top of their priority lists. They will devote millions, their energy and their attention to making Airbnb's culture as powerful and healthy as they possibly can.

Why?

Because they know that culture can create a team that's single-mindedly driven to deliver the purpose. And that's what's needed when you have an insanely ambitious one such as 'Creating a world where anyone can belong anywhere'. You need a team that gets up in the morning motivated and focused to do the impossible.

You also need a cohesive team. Something else that a strong culture will deliver. One that's not distracted by infighting or territorial ambitions. You need a team that's unified by agreement on what's important, without it having to be spelt out every time. One that knows the guidelines of how to behave, relate and decide things together. 'The rules of the game', as Brian Chesky calls Airbnb's core values. There's no time wasted on negotiating how to engage with each other, for every project. They already know.

So, culture is the internal galvanizing force that will enable you to deliver your purpose externally to your users and the world at large. It provides the focus, cohesiveness and passion *internally*, to do the impossible *externally*.

I introduced this 'inside out' idea to the founders and the company with a very simple slide (Figure 19.2). It's taken from a presentation I wrote called 'Operationalizing "Belong Anywhere" from the Inside Out'. The point I was making was that we would never deliver credibly or authentically our purpose externally, or in fact at all, if we didn't deliver it *internally* first.

So, what does Airbnb do to deliver Belong Anywhere from the inside-out?

Two of the most important ingredients of any culture are the purpose and core values. The purpose is the meta-goal that everyone is focused on. The core values are the 'rules of the game' that define how everyone will behave, relate and decide things together cohesively to achieve the purpose.

These two things are reinforced almost daily at Airbnb. At the all-staff weekly 'World@' meetings run by the founders, new plans, updates and launches are presented... but in terms of how they will deliver the Mission, and how the team acted according to the core values. Every week Brian conducts a live CEO Q&A. He answers every question put to him, and uses his answers to reinforce the purpose and core values.

FIGURE 19.2 Shining from the inside out: Airbnb leads with its internal culture to radiate out and deliver on its purpose

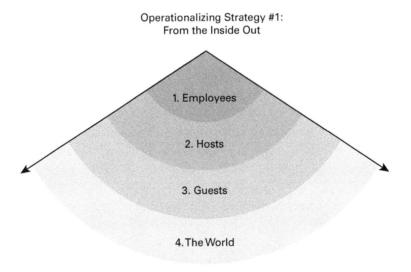

SOURCE Douglas Atkin (2020)

The annual OneAirbnb all-staff gatherings are an experiential hot house to create a feeling that everyone 'Belongs Here' so that they can deliver 'Belong Anywhere' externally, authentically. It's a huge, and very expensive exercise in creating team belonging. Yes, there's an agenda of launches and updates. But the real purpose is for people to meet each other, form friendships and have fun together. To 'get sticky', as Nate put it when asked 'Why is everyone here?' at the beginning of the 2017 OneAirbnb.

These daily, weekly and annual events are all part of a programme of experiences and rituals that an international team called Ground Control is dedicated to creating. This team's work is an essential part of the magic that makes the culture cohesive and coherent. For example, when you arrive at an office in, say, Singapore after an endless flight from San Francisco, you're instantly made to feel like you're at home. They host you ('Be a Host' is one of the most important core values) with breakfast or a stiff drink, whatever you need to feel yourself again.

And as you look around the office, it also feels like home. There is another dedicated team (this is one made up of architects) that are focused on making the environments feel uniquely Airbnb. And to reinforce the 'Belong Anywhere' purpose. Every meeting room in every office is an exact re-creation of an Airbnb host's home somewhere in the world. You might be having a budget meeting in an Airstream trailer. Or a product review in a kitchen modelled on a host's in Mumbai. You're literally immersed in the venues that our hosts use to create belonging, whatever you're doing, wherever you are, all of the time. The San Francisco office has its own Airstream. And the Founders meet in a room that's modelled on the very first Airbnb: Their own apartment in Rausch Street where it all started!

Even before you join Airbnb you are made to feel like you 'Belong Here'. The internal recruitment team appoints one person who hosts you through the entire recruitment process. They're at your side through the many visits with tea, sympathy and encouragement, and you have their personal phone number to call at any time with anything. Once you join, your first week is an induction, and starts with a day immersed in the purpose and core values. At some point that week you are likely to go through the 'Human Tunnel' (Figure 19.3)… a ritual that emerged (no-one can remember quite how) to welcome new members of the team. They have to run through a tunnel of the team members and jump onto a big Airbnb beanbag where they're handed their Airbnb backpack and T-shirt.

Culture is an investment. It should be considered in the same light as R&D or capital investment. It should get as much of leaders' attention and energy

FIGURE 19.3   Using rituals to express a unique culture and cement the feeling of 'belonging': The 'human tunnel' at Airbnb

SOURCE Douglas Atkin (2020)

as is given to growth, profit, team and all the other normal priorities. Without a high-functioning team internally that's focused and aligned on your ambitious purpose, you have very little chance of delivering it externally.

3. Use it to recruit, review and reject everybody

Sometimes even customers.

From the first moment, Airbnb used its purpose and values to recruit. The founders took a long time to hire their first employee. They interviewed over a hundred candidates searching for the right one, with all the attendant short-term costs of slower growth and fewer launches during that early make-or-break period. This is because, from the beginning, 'skills' and 'culture fit' were given equal weighting. 'Culture fit' effectively meant being a 'believer' (in Brian's words) in the Mission, and someone whose personal values matched Airbnb's. Here's Brian talking about it:

> Our first engineering hire. We desperately needed an engineer, but still waited
> four or five months, maybe six months 'til we hired Nick Randy because we

wanted to hire somebody that we felt like could represent the culture. That had a cost of growing slower because of an investment in the culture. Culture is really a short-term price you pay for long-term results, very long-term. Like you pay a short-term price to not hire your first engineer because you believe in the long term that they'll hire 10 people that will represent the culture.

In 2012, the founders realized they could no longer interview everybody. The company had grown in size and geographical spread to the point where that was impossible. Instead, they deputized this important role by enlisting and training 18 employees who they felt were the true embodiment of the purpose and values.

There are now 500 'culture' interviewers (roughly 10 per cent of the total employee population) who interview all candidates globally. And they have founder-like power. Like most companies, each candidate has six to eight interviews that assess their skills with their potential peers in, say, engineering or marketing. Then, they have two interviews with culture interviewers who have nothing to do with their discipline. If those interviewers judge that the candidate is not a 'believer' in the purpose, or that their personal values don't align with Airbnb's, then they are not hired. No matter how good the engineer or designer is, or how urgently their skills are needed, the culture interviewers have veto power.

This use of the purpose and Values to recruit has now been extended to the Acquisitions team. They have been trained to assess, and give equal rating to, a company's alignment with the purpose and Values, as well as the usual criteria. At least one potential and important strategic acquisition in the past couple of years was not made because of the organization's lack of purpose and Values-fit.

'Ah', you may be thinking, 'what happens if non-believers slip through this net?' Performance reviews no longer measure just the usual performance criteria. They measure, and give equal rating to 'how' a person did 'what' they did. If *how* they did *what* they did fell short of the purpose and Values, then they're warned and trained to get back on track… and fired if there is no improvement.

Recruiting, reviewing and rejecting according to the purpose is critically important in the case of leaders. They should especially be seen to live the purpose and Values in both their actions and decisions, given the magnitude of their influence. There was a period in 2015–16 when Airbnb's famously strong culture became wobbly. One of the causes was the perception amongst the majority of staff that two or three of the leadership team were 'mercenaries, not missionaries'. Their decisions favoured 'growth at the expense of the Mission'. Thankfully, they are no longer with Airbnb.

Recruit, review, reject customers according to the purpose too.

This obsession with the purpose extends to Airbnb's customers. Every new host and guest has to sign an agreement to live by the 'Anyone can belong anywhere' purpose before they are accepted on the platform. It reads: 'Our mission is to build a trusted community where anyone can belong anywhere...'.

And it's real. Over a million potential customers felt they could not sign the 'Community Commitment' that asks them to welcome everyone irrespective of their race, religion, national origin, ethnicity, skin colour, disability, sex, gender identity, sexual orientation or age. And many others have been removed by a team that scours the platform for any behaviour that infringes this code.

Lost customers. But saved purpose. Fortunately, many more *do* sign and live by this code. There are now over 5 million hosts globally and over half a billion cumulative guest arrivals. Belief in 'Anyone belonging anywhere' has generated a community of trust that's essential to Airbnb's functioning and success.

Airbnb has been very public about its stand on its purpose of 'Creating a world where anyone can belong anywhere'. It telegraphs what's expected of its customers even at the cost of alienating some people, including politicians. During Trump's 'travel ban' in 2016 Airbnb ran a Superbowl ad called 'We accept'.

A *New York Times* article at the time described how committed the organization was to living its purpose:

> In a memo to employees after the executive order, Airbnb's chief executive, Brian Chesky, was more explicit about his opposition. 'This is a policy I profoundly disagree with, and it is a direct obstacle to our mission at Airbnb,' Mr Chesky wrote on Jan 29. That weekend, the company began to provide free and subsidized temporary housing for people who had been affected by the immigration restrictions.
>
> (Benner, 2017)

And in 2018, just hours after the Supreme Court's decision to uphold the ban, Airbnb ran another campaign making its stand crystal clear to everyone.

These campaigns that publicly declare Airbnb's uncompromising commitment to its purpose are controversial amongst some people. For the rest of

FIGURE 19.4   Buying into something bigger: At Airbnb you join a culture, community and with a shared commitment

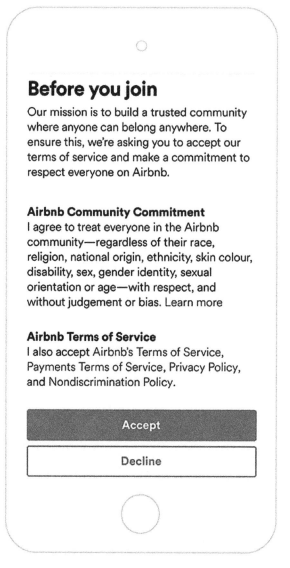

SOURCE Douglas Atkin (2020)

us, we feel that it's exactly the right thing to do. Especially when you have a brand that's dependent on over 5 million individuals to deliver the experience. It's essential that everyone, especially our hosts and guests, are aligned around the most important of things: Our 'Why' of 'Creating a world where anyone can belong anywhere'.

This obsession with purpose may seem excessive to some. But for Airbnb, it's fundamental to its operation. It's necessary to create the trust amongst strangers that allows the platform to work. It's critical to why employees and customers join and stay. And it's vital to have 'believers' who will strive to make the purpose a reality. And, vigilance is necessary because it's all too easy to acquiesce to urgent short-term demands and compromise…

4. Use it to forge your own path

If you have a good purpose… one that's based in an experienced truth and therefore differentiated and yours… then it stands to reason that if you truly live by it, you'll find yourselves forging your own path.

Airbnb has found this to be true countless times. At just the moment when some crisis has occurred and all you want to do is take the predictable and safe route, you instead opt for the one that requires you to invent and hustle in order to fulfil your unique purpose. This is Nate Blecharczyk, Airbnb co-founder: 'It's like there's a path before you and you can go down it and it's kind of safe, but you don't like it. And you say, "No, I'm not going to do that", but then it's not really clear what the alternative is and you have to forge a new path.'

Nate was with Brian and Joe that Sunday afternoon describing to me the many moments in Airbnb's short history when they had made decisions that lived its purpose. In this particular case, Nate was referring to the decision *not* to acquire Wimdu in 2011. Wimdu is the copycat business that the Samweer Brothers had built in Europe just so that Airbnb would be forced to buy it. It was the Samweers' modus operandi. They had done the same thing to Ebay and Groupon, who had acquiesced, and handed over millions to the Samweers to buy their copycat versions.

Nate, Joe and Brian had sat on a street bench in Berlin after visiting Wimdu's HQ, and decided not to do the predictable thing. The predictable thing would have delivered a large turn-key operation and customers in a critical market. Not doing it would mean creating your own European operation and building your own customer base from scratch *while facing off against the competitor you didn't buy*. But the cost was too high in terms of purpose and culture for the founders. They felt that Wimdu was so un-aligned it would even infect the original in San Francisco and destroy three years of hard work building their young purpose-led and culture-rich company.

So, they forged their own path. They 'hustled', as they call doing the impossible. They hired their own purpose-aligned staff and built their own customer marketplace of hosts and guests. By the time I arrived in 2012, they had 10 fabulous offices across Europe that looked similar to the distinctive San Francisco HQ. They were peopled by employees who gave you the same enthusiastic welcome and instantly made you feel at home. And in business terms, Europe had just pipped the US in terms of size.

5. Measure your purpose and give it equal status to business metrics

If I were forced to pick just one of these five things that would ensure that an organization's purpose would be lived, this would be it.

I realized its importance when I showed a product manager the triggers that enabled more Belonging Anywhere to be experienced by guests, and delivered by us and our hosts. He looked at me and said: 'If this is something that's important to the company, then we need to include it in our goals'. He went on to explain that his team were measured solely by conversion metrics that cascaded down from the sole key business metric that the whole company used to measure success: 'Nights booked'. He said, 'I love our Mission of Belong Anywhere. And I want to help make more of it. But I and my team are not measured on delivering that. In fact, I feel our metrics actually drive us to undermine it by focusing on growth… sometimes at the expense of belonging.'

In a nutshell, he had identified the classic dilemma of business. Purpose, or growth? It was a dilemma that created a big wobble in Airbnb's culture in 2015 when employees felt that some leaders had taken their eyes off the ball and were focusing on growth at the expense of Belong Anywhere. 'Vacation rentals' was a new category that was getting investment at Airbnb. But it's also one where there tends to be few real hosts and homes, and more purpose-built properties with property managers. Growth at the expense of purpose.

The point, of course, is that there should never be one at the expense of the other. There should be an equal and creative tension between the goals of growth and purpose. Leaders and their teams should be incentivized to juggle the two in order to deliver more 'nights booked' *and* Belong Anywhere simultaneously. No trade-offs.

When I pitched this to the founders in 2015, there was instant agreement. However, it's taken a while to execute. Defining that big Belong Anywhere metric that can sit alongside nights booked (or its equivalent for the new businesses) and cascade down to all the teams has been difficult.

But stand by. Brian did a soft launch of what he calls the 21C Company in 2018. It's an initiative to redefine the accountability of companies away from solely shareholder value to include the delivery of purpose and the satisfaction of other stakeholders' needs (in Airbnb's case, stakeholders such as cities and hosts). At the time of writing, its full launch is due by early 2021, together with the metrics that will measure these new account-abilities. I can't wait. Metrics are everything when it comes to 'walking the talk' of purpose. They will be the enforcers that should ensure Airbnb only recruits hosts that make guests feel at home. And takes actions that ensure cities welcome Airbnb and do not repel it. All the other ingredients to living a purpose here are vital. But enshrining its importance, publicly, by having metrics will truly ensure it is delivered, will be the crucial ingredi-ent to the delivery or 'Creating a world where anyone can belong anywhere'.

Conclusion

Finding and launching a good purpose, and especially *living* your purpose, is hard. Operationalizing your purpose requires putting it first in every big decision you make. It means being vigilant in recruiting, reviewing and rejecting employees, and even customers. It means you will forge your own path, which requires you to invent and hustle constantly. It means investing in culture to create a driven and cohesive team. And it demands that you measure achievement of your purpose and give it equal status to business metrics.

All of which is counter to prevailing business instincts and culture... especially the short-termism and focus on shareholder returns that's driven by Wall Street. But, as someone who's old enough to have grown up in the prevailing culture, and lucky enough to have worked within this new vision of commerce, I'm optimistic. There are enough visionary leaders such as Brian, Joe and Nate who are changing the rules... including the rules defined by the likes of Wall Street. And there are enough employees and customers that are demanding more accountability of companies than simply good products and shareholder returns.

So, if you're a business leader, you really have no choice in this new world. You need to find a good purpose and you need to make your organi-zation live it. And, frankly, life is too short not to!

RECAP: AIRBNB

- *Every organization needs a good purpose in order to be vital.* It needs one to guide all of its key decisions, to inspire and direct its members to do great things, and to ensure a legacy beyond profit-making.Getting one is hard.

- *It should be grounded in truth, but reach for the stars in its aspiration for the world.* It should be about one thing to provide the guardrails for all it does, but it should be a big thing so that you make an impact and never run out of runway. And it should be memorable so that everyone knows it, understands it and buys into it. Getting a good purpose is hard, but implementing it is even harder.

- *Implementing a purpose means putting it first in all key decisions.* Even before growth and profit, confident that they will follow if you remain true to your Why.

- *It should be manifested in who you hire and the culture you make.* And you should have values to govern how you behave, relate and decide things together to achieve your purpose.

- *It's hard. But it's worth it.* It makes decisions easier because everyone knows why they're making them and what values they should use when they do. It's the secret sauce to creating a highly motivated and cohesive team, driven to achieve one purpose. And it's worth it because, hopefully, you're making a positive impact in the world. One that's motivated by more than just making a buck.

Note: We use 'purpose', 'Mission' and 'vision' interchangeably at Airbnb. I know some people get hot under the collar about this, but we all know what we're talking about. We're talking about our Why.

Case 6: Lakrids

Growth without end, or: How to scale a dream

Your brand is on a Mission to make people discover the true delight that is liquorice and your product is so good, it's irresistible and has become iconic... but only on the small Danish island of Bornholm. How does one go about conquering the continent and then the rest of the world? How do you scale the dream of a 20-year-old cooking up delicious batches of black candy and sampling them to tourists strolling the streets of his little holiday island town?

These are the questions Peter Husted Sylvest will answer in his first-hand account of how he helped Johan Bülow spread his dream and scaling the seductive powers of Lakrids in his role as Global Director of Sales. Spoiler alert: It's a lot about those samples.

Peter Husted Sylvest

Peter joined Lakrids in 2011, right as founder Johan Bülow was trying to figure out how to seriously scale his Danish liquorice business beyond the borders. He remained the Director of Sales through 2017. And Lakrids is just one of the many Scandinavian specialty brands that Peter has helped spread their wings. He worked for 20 years with the very best of Scandinavian interior designs products from Stelton and Normann Copenhagen, products for both home use and decoration as well as for professional use within top restaurants and hotels. Building on that experience, he founded 'pH value' in 2018, a consultancy working with premium brands in the high-end food and beverage products as well as the design sector.

This is my story of why Lakrids by Bülow is an Ueber-Brand and the *how to* of scaling a 'boyfriend/girlfriend' shop to an internationally distributed and well-known brand.

Lakrids by Bülow is a gourmet liquorice company founded by entrepreneur Johan Bülow on the Danish Island of Bornholm on 7 July 2007. Bülow had the dream of making the world love the Scandinavian classic of black liquorice; 12 years later his products are found at more than 1,500 of the best gourmet retail stores around the world including 30 of its own. Johan is referred to as the Liquorice King by fans and media.

Expansion has been fuelled by equity fund investment since 2017 and they are on a Mission to paint the world black.

How to make a plan – perhaps a business plan?

If you go back to the original idea and the *what if* of Lakrids by Bülow, this can be compressed to single A4 pages of text. In professional business school terms, such paper would be far from being categorized as a 'genuine business plan'.

Had you asked Johan to make an elevator pitch or write a single page plan, during the first 12 months of developing his business, it would have included the following bold statements.

I want to:

- create a no-compromise world class liquorice;
- teach the world to eat and enjoy black liquorice;
- work outside the traditional distribution channels for confectionary products;
- make, sell and promote it in my own branded retail stores located in major capitals and hubs;
- create a brand new gifting category where liquorice can challenge both chocolate and other top gifting categories for both private people and businesses;
- control the journey and work with partners supporting the overall agenda; should they not support this, then I want the freedom to determine the relationship without long-term damage to my company;
- not to engage with single partnerships who can have a devastating negative effect on business, should they wish to enforce this opportunity.

Plenty of business professionals would have laughed at this one-pager back in 2007 and likely recommended Johan to spend his savings and focus his energy on something else. The following is a collection of approaches to execution that will hopefully inspire you to follow your own gut feelings and adjust your actions based on market feedback and engagement.

How to build your team

When you end up with a team of more than 200 people in six years, you have hired more than you have fired. We had a record low turnover of team members and the right recruitment strategy was key from day one.

Having a good product is key, but without the right people to represent it, you are simply a manufacturer – if you want to be a brand you need people to define you, communicate and stand by your product to become your story, become your brand.

How do you find a team willing to work 12–16 hours a day, six or seven days a week for three months in a row? You call people who trust you, people who love you, so friends, family and partners. They jump into deep waters without asking too many questions or having many hesitations. Nobody from the original cast had ever produced liquorice or created a brand.

The customers came to the island mainly during summer, and as the summer faded the tourists left. It left Johan and his girlfriend sitting with a stack of business cards from visitors who wanted more than a personal gourmet souvenir. Several of these cards represented a business opportunity. The question was:

1 Should they rest and re-energize during the off season and create a perfect seasonal living?

Or:

2 Should they face the challenge to execute and make decisions towards making the initial A4 business plan?

In a small community there are plenty of stories of how small, dedicated producers had based their businesses on a single large customer and scaled their set-up to match the customer's growing demand. This only to find that the customer's sudden change of habits or demand for margins killed their business overnight.

FIGURE 20.1 A product to behold: Lakrids' product is the ultimate expression of Johan Bülow's dream to make people fall in love with Scandinavian liquorice

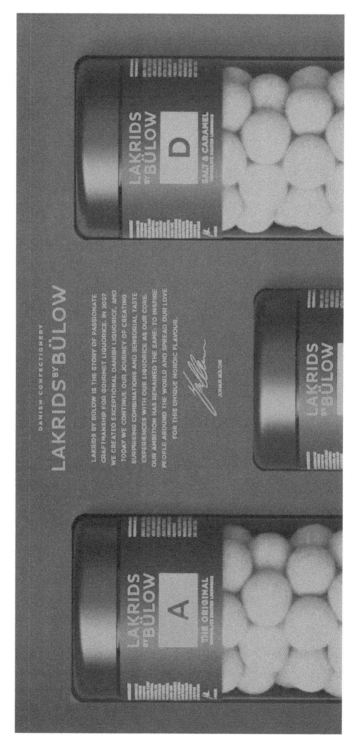

Learning from this experience, Johan initially worked solely with small, dedicated specialist stores. Stores able to communicate a quality product story face-to-face with their customers:

- who often had a store owner behind the counter;
- who likely knew their customers by name;
- who would carefully select their assortment;
- who could also replicate the serving of the important sample to engage with the consumer and make them understand the uniqueness of Lakrids.

The first call to action was reconnecting with a summer guest who owned a wine and spirits shop and had left his card with a note saying: 'When you are ready to produce more than what you can sell here, then give me a call – this is the best liquorice I have ever tasted.' He was not alone and there were more cards from passionate tradespeople from around Denmark and the rest of Scandinavia.

The role of the Black Knights

Who would say no to free candy? Who would have a problem with being the sweet person who gives away free candy? This leads us to the recruiting process of the 'Black Knights', working in our flagship stores and the most important factor in sales.

During the job interviews, when we only had a few shops, we had some five or six people attending a session with our store manager. Within the first 30 seconds he would slide a jar of liquorice across the table with a smile and say, 'Please present and try to sell this jar to my fellow colleague' (me). Many applicants froze and could not find the words, so the store manager kindly thanked them for their time and ended the interview. I was a little shocked and in between interviews asked if he was sure that he could make a call this fast. He replied that their resumes were all good, but some did not have a natural approach to selling, which, sadly, disqualified them.

The ones who survived the challenge had a very different approach to the question/challenge. A young woman took the jar, smiled at us while slowly opening it. She took one chocolate coated sweet liquorice and put it in her mouth and started chewing it, before saying. 'This is by far the best confectionary that I have ever had – would you like to try it too?' Another said, 'I eat these when I am a little sad – I call them my happy pills. [Then she smiled and continued] Do you want one?' My colleague would ask no further questions and replied with a handshake and a contract and welcomed them to the family of Black Knights.

There were a few more key elements that made the Black Knights successful: The passion for the product and the overall vision, the understanding of that superior product and being comfortable engaging while holding a bowl of samples. People are the key factor that can release the magic powers of your brand and what made our sampling strategy come to life.

The tattoo and the haircut

Setting up a team of people either not knowing about or not being held back by old habits is key. A background in outdoor advertising and selling haircare products or tattoo needles was perfect for Black Knight salespeople, battling for new grounds in new markets.

Selling outdoor advertising is all about conversion rates and cost per view – knowing the numbers quickly underlined the effect and the value of sampling in person at high-traffic locations. With this knowledge, we never just sampled, but ensured that it happened with a maximum distance of 3 metres to a cash register. Make sure your core focus to any action is to eventually *sell* your products – sampling with no selling is only marketing. But it's selling with a smile. Only the *first fix* is for free – for more, you will have to buy a jar.

The initial stores to seek Lakrids distribution were top specialist stores. News travelled fast among these types of partners and the unique sales made by such stores quickly became the benchmark for others. When we started to actively expand to the rest of the country, we could replicate the process and leverage the initial references and key learnings from our own store to prove we could replicate the sales results through others.

Entering a new export market, you do not have the same luxury. Since most countries are much bigger than little Denmark, driving round every city and ring road is not feasible. As one of our new country managers had sold haircare and tattoo equipment, he decided to visit his previous top customers and it opened a Pandora's Box of contacts and gave him valuable insights to the local peers – I call them 'cables' – to activate his mainframe network. Conversation of the hairdressers all started with 'What brings you to town?' and ended with selling a rack of jars to the hairstylist, who ended up serving it to their customers and found it gave them something engaging to talk about while they had a customer locked into the chair. And our ex-haircare sales pro was not surprised that the people in that chair could include the owner of the best fashion shop in town, the best chef with Michelin Star credentials, the best bartender listed on the top 50 list world-wide, or the editor of the local food magazine.

Do I need to say that my colleague became the best-groomed member of staff and with the most tattoos, during the early years?

How to be a turtle

We often pictured our approach to risk taking as the 'strategy of the turtle' – the company and organization being a turtle with a very uniquely long neck. A neck that could reach out, so we could nibble and test the grass on the other side. Testing far beyond the normal reach, but always with the opportunity to retract to the safety of our shield, should it be bitter. The body would move slowly but steadily forward, once we found it was worth moving.

Be agile, but do not be foolish. Build a solid home base (aka the body of the turtle) before you venture into unknown territory.

How to know your product and know it better than the customers...

We tested on humans. We created products, branding and storytelling that we believed in and we loved. We tested with our own team. If a Black Army of front women/men, working at our flagship stores loved our new products, then we knew we were on to something good and they would spread happy pills with a smile and shining eyes. Having these touchpoints will strengthen your poker face, knowing that you hold cards to win the majority of games you will play.

These 'games' could be:

- at the first professional tradeshow;
- at the first sales tour visiting existing clients;
- being interviewed for a trade magazine about the expected response of our new launch.

How to create a pull

It is tricky to create demand, when you bring a new story to both the end consumers and the distribution network. Distribution channels are not asking for products, and especially those they do not know exist. In new markets and with new contacts you need to step up the game and shift gears in every aspect of the game. You need to make it easy and relevant for them to engage and dedicate their brief focus to your cause and product.

Having been operating as a small retailer with production on the side was the perfect setting when initiating wholesale to individual specialist shops within gourmet food, wine and gifting. Us having the data to prove the ratio of samples to sales made most retailers stop and listen. Having this experience and data was particularly effective with bigger retailers that are used to operating their businesses on numbers and relying more on data, rather than being present on the sales floor. When negotiating with the biggest players within international gourmet department stores, the dialogue was initiated, due to them having seen our brand in action locally. Still, we were told that our flavour profile did not match the majority of their market and they emphasized that our data was not as relevant to them as we were outside Scandinavia.

When we disclosed that our numbers in Scandinavia were made from doing *active sales* and from running our own full concessions, the dialogue changed. Within 10 minutes we were asked, 'How soon can we sign a contract?' The rest is history. We opened as the very first full food concession in their store.

Knowing what your products can do in terms of sales, when presented right, was an amazing tool in connecting with retailers. Being a retailer ourselves meant that we could often look at the business case as colleagues from the same side of the table. A dialogue between two retailers, discussing a joint business opportunity, rather than the traditional supplier and customer set-up.

How to export from the comfort of your home

Lakrids has successfully entered a gifting market. With a clear 'Made in Denmark' profile it has been considered a local gourmet souvenir that travels well. Surely selling to a Chinese customer travelling through Copenhagen or Keflavik is not the same as standing up against the competition at a

Shanghai-based retailer, but you get to practise and perfect your story with a foreign customer at home base.

The main lesson learned from 20 years of travelling with a story and range of products is that the world can relate to 95 per cent of the original and well-documented story. But you do not win or finish, should you only run 95 per cent of the distance. To finish, you need to seek and define the magic 5 per cent that makes your product a must-have locally.

The traditional approach of companies defining themselves as producers and distributors as only distributing is long gone. With today's full market transparency, where a retailer or consumer can have access to the brand owner in fewer than three clicks, a partnership, an open exchange of data and basic knowledge, is needed.

Every single distribution partner I have ever worked with around the world has at one point presented the statement, 'You have to understand that our market is very unique.' It is from such dialogues that the insight about the 95 per cent emerged. Instead of saying they were full of XXXX, we presented how we saw them as the 5 per cent magician.

It has been remarkable to see how quickly one could change the battle-grounds, from a focus on major difference to a joint effort of defining a strategy of how to replicate our model locally. One way to quickly define and qualify a potential local partner was the concept of our mainframe computer. This mainframe is often described as a big dumb unit, holding a lot of data. To actually perform and do things you have to connect a range of different hardware or install unique software. At the first meeting with a potential distribution partner, you cannot bring five full binders of strategic plans or ask them to enrol into a six-hour tutorial, unless you want to scare people away. When we introduced the story of our success from our other markets with the metaphor of the mainframe computer we came to quick conclusions and constructive dialogues.

Adding to an already heavy workload from your home markets and tasks, it can be a real challenge, so make sure you choose to work with markets that appeal to you. You need to plan for 16-hour work days when travelling, because you will stumble on new stores, new neighbourhoods and new interesting people. You need to know about the markets you enter and the people you wish to sell to. It might seem crazy to pitch your products in the subway, sitting at a coffee shop or in the reception of your hotel, but by doing so you can open some amazing doors and help build your product story around a local twist. I have found myself with absolutely nothing from having applied this approach, but for every time I have lost, I have won 100 times.

How to partner up abroad

How do you move quickly to a detailed dialogue about how good a match you are to them and they are to you? As a start-up business that has moved at a fast pace, you are perhaps being looked at with a little scepticism. This is only natural when seen from the viewpoint of an established partner with years of experience.

In order to make the process as easy as possible, we always started with a sample of our own products. You would be surprised how many industry professionals start with talks on pricing and facts before they even try the product. 'I cannot try *all* the products I sell' is a classic, and when this was said we were the first ones to stand up and leave – but more about that later.

A piece of A3 paper and a pen were the tools in hand to define whether we had a match or not. If one point of contact was our own retail units, we could quickly ask:

- Did they know how to run their own retail?
- If the answer was no, then this imaginary cable was erased from the similar drawing representing their market, with them in the driving seat of the black Lakrids van.

We defined our home market with some 20 larger effective and productive cables. Our distribution and key retail partners should have at least 10–12 cables to engage into a more detailed dialogue. If we found a match on 15 cables or more, we had a winner.

Over time, we also found that *yes*, these relevant partners might have the same understanding of cabling, but their bandwidth could be a different width, so how do we move beyond this?

How to work with agents and distributors

Partnerships for local distribution are often partnerships based on agency or distribution contracts. As a brand owner, you are never alone, you are always part of a line-up of brands that all link to the same type of distribution channels. As a young brand you benefit from them having established contacts and track records of having worked with many of the right resellers.

But will they invest heavily into building your brand locally? The fast and honest answer is no, and why should they? They are in the situation of making sure that, if they are too *bad*, they are fired, but the same is true if they are too *good*. So how do you tackle this dilemma as a young upcoming brand with little or no stickiness in the specific market?

You enter with no accounts and no sales and hence no commission for a local partner. Their other brands already generate sales and define what the partner stands for. The local partner does not automatically get more time and focus from his audience, just because you came along; they make their business from selling products, not building brands.

So, can you work around this and can you create a setting by which you can succeed? You need to actively invest in the market, educating and supporting that distributor sales team. Countless are the hours we have been present at international tradeshows with such partners and where we presented active selling by approaching the walk-by traffic with a smile and bowl of samples – showing our partners that you do not have to be glued to your chair for 12 hours, staring at your mobile phone or laptop. Showing that you need to break old habits to create new results.

FIGURE 20.2   Passing on the passion: One of the 'Black Knights' samples the irresistible candy in a store

SOURCE   Peter Husted Sylvest (2020)

Do not blame the distributor, blame yourself, as they are never as willing to take risks as you and nor can they love your brand and products as dearly as you do. But do yourself a favour and treat these partners as you would treat your internal team – they too are front runners and your face towards your resellers and consumers.

Model for moving beyond the start-up phase

Over the years the distribution of Lakrids evolved and we moved above and beyond the classic distribution channels, making our own Mainframe model hard to replicate by a local partner. We found that we had more in common with design products and lifestyle products than traditional foods. Our branding and retail presentations were often compared to fine wine and spirits, fashion and beauty brands.

Editorial stories and coverage came from high-end business newspapers and magazines, product presentation was found in the trend section of leading design publications and magazines. We found that the leading retailers in each of these segments were brilliant storytellers and the engagement power of our products was also appealing to them, despite their usual price points being far higher.

As business expands and you find that your success is based on a complex set of distribution channels, you will naturally start to see the need to focus.

FIGURE 20.3 Peter working his audience: Internal and external education is key to executing consistently, growing everyone's appreciation and ultimately sales

SOURCE Peter Husted Sylvest (2020)

We found that we needed sales team members with very different profiles than what the industry had done previously. Knowing that it would take time, we ensured that they were not motivated by taking orders, but by making partnerships with long-term potential.

Any professional salesperson wants to sell and thrives from selling, but it was key to establish these business relationships, not 'one-night stands' with the businesses, who could have a negative effect on our brand locally. This was an expensive approach, but also the only road we could have chosen, should we want to fully control the approach and choose initial long-term partners over quick sales contacts. The trust to implement such tactics came from knowing our home market and from having made tons of mistakes in the comfort zone of our close network, where we had credit or could quickly correct a mistake.

How to map your top 10

When you have realized the effect of solid references and good case stories, you have your target locked and know what to hunt for next. You can make a list of 10–30 organizations who you would like to present your product to.

With Lakrids such a list was created early on. The team loved setting their eyes on one and brainstorming how to connect and engage. In the end, three of the top five on our list actually ended up coming to us, rather than us knocking on their doors. You cannot help but smile when someone at a trade show hands you a business card saying 'Fortnum & Mason', a UK food institution opened in London in 1707. Fortnum & Mason were on our initial list as a dream partner. When we asked her why they had chosen to come to see us, the answer was thrilling. 'At Fortnum & Mason we have sold tea, coffee, chocolate under our own brand for a very long time and we are world famous for that, but to introduce liquorice as a product under the same brand would not be true to who we are, so we have come to you, since we see you as the world's best in your category.' Walking through the doors of its amazing store on Piccadilly in London some three months later to make our first tastings was a real defining moment.

At the very same tradeshow a gentleman approached us and said that he loved the look of our presentation and would like to try a sample of our product. When he revealed that he was the owner of a New York based retail store Chelsea Market Basket, we could cross out yet another candidate on our top five global wish list. Less than two months later, the first batch was sent from Denmark to New York. Within six months, we were in New York to work with his team and present our range to many of the food tour groups coming through the market on a daily basis.

Being clear and outspoken about your dreams and dream targets will help and guide your team to actions that will lead them to strive towards these. Having been clear about which top location partners we dreamt would stock and represent our range ensured that we were mentally prepared when we finally met.

The right type of PR can set fire to your story

Foodies love TV shows, and one of the best sources for 'food porn' is the British BBC. We were fortunate enough to have them visiting Denmark and through our network we got to pitch a concept and range of stories about people in our network, which they accepted.

Seeing how the story grew on the TV host and team during the day was amazing; by the end of the day they made us great offers like: 'You should come to London and I will invite all my friends to my house, so we can cook together with the flavour of liquorice and they will see how magical a product you have created'. This outcome is amazing and just proves that investing in relationships with the right people can open doors beyond your imagination and faster than you have ever dreamed of.

How to bring your ambassadors close – real close

Lakrids is a brand that makes products from scratch, and has the advantage of telling the story from its cradle. This can bring people to the holy grail. It is not always the same with your re-sellers, with you extended team and your distribution network of agents and distributors. Just as we teach our children, you should teach your network. If you have the advantage of having your own factory, invite them inside, and do not just show them around – get them involved. We learn better and we remember things better if we learn using all of our senses, so dress them up and teach them first hand about the premises of making a quality product. The story becomes your own, having held warm liquorice in your hand and tasted it while still soft. It will make your own stories become more lively and real, when meeting with a top retailer in New York to promote your brand.

When you find and identify the right potential ambassadors, bring them real close and see the amazing effect as they return home to spread the story or simply stand by it strong enough for you to build on it. Yes, it is expensive to bring people to Copenhagen, but if you ask Lakrids if they would do it again and again the answer would be *yes*. Today some 2,500 guests (customers, partners, press and VIP) pass through the halls of Lakrids annually. We have seen the level of knowledge grow exponentially, and with it sales.

RECAP: LAKRIDS

- Ueber-Brands are not created overnight, so make sure you are on a path and quest of passion. If you do not enjoy the journey, you can easily burn out before you achieve your goals.

- To make an Ueber-Brand, you need an Ueber-Team. Hire by passion and make sure you are with kindred spirits, people you want to spend time with.

- Make sure your products have a strong appeal to the end consumers. Having a positive 'like for like' feedback will ensure the snowball rolls faster and you generate momentum over time. Invest in building a strong ambassador/fan base, who will pass on your dream and DNA, making the circles bigger and bigger.

- Seek inspiration from other types of businesses. If you want to break away, you need fresh input to push your industry standards.

- Practise at home and perfect your case before you engage with markets abroad. Build your model of 95 per cent and be very open about the key value of the final 5 per cent to succeed.

- Once you have a clear vision about where you want to go, do act on it. Execution is key.

Case 7: YouTube

Platform or brand of the future, or:
How to be one when you are many

Like any platform that has developed over the last decade, YouTube is often seen as just that, a platform, and not necessarily a brand. We believe, however, they might actually show us the way into the future – not only in terms of technology but also in the way it builds and lives 'its' brand. Much more open and agile, community-driven rather than company-controlled. A true interactive ecosystem with all stakeholders partaking, united by a core set of principles, but beyond that free to build 'their' brand together, as each sees fit.

We sat down with YouTube's Global Head of Communications and Public Affairs, Chris Dale, to talk about YouTube's Mission, its sense of identity, its culture... And apart from sensing Chris' passion for YouTube's Mission, you will gain interesting insights and a good sense of how difficult, but also how rewarding, it can be to make freedom your number one brand value. You can also listen to the full interview on ueberbrands.com. Scan the QR code at the front of the book for a link.

Chris Dale

Growing up in Davis, California, Chris expected to become a lawyer, but an uninspiring summer job at a New York law firm stamped out that desire. Instead, armed with an English literature degree from Colgate University and a Master's from Cambridge in 17th and 20th century poetry, Chris landed in San Francisco at a high-tech PR firm where he merged his two passions: Writing and technology. He arrived in 2000, just in time for the dot-com debacle. His employer went bankrupt; Chris survived by starting his own marketing firm and then joining a small but growing tech-focused PR agency. All the while, he kept hearing 'all these cool things this company called Google was doing'. In 2008 he joined Google. He's worked at Google and Alphabet's [X]. Today, he runs communications and public affairs for YouTube.

YouTube's Mission

YouTube's Mission is 'To give everyone a voice and show them the world'. YouTube's brand is a combination of myriad voices from all over the planet that are uploaded, speaking out, for and to one another. These voices form this kind of ephemeral connection that binds all of these different people together and to the platform.

What makes YouTube complex from a brand's point of view is that it isn't really what we dictate, as the employees of YouTube. It's really what the community of creators, viewers or fans and even advertisers dictate YouTube to be. This means that as a brand we are really a reflection of a common voice and the various different cultures, beliefs and points of view from all over the world. So, I think that's the simplest way to articulate our brand, but that voice changes. It changes all the time.

When we started back in 2005 our Mission Statement was just 'Broadcast yourself'. This is probably one of the best Mission Statements ever created for any company – and I had absolutely nothing to do with it. It was such a radical concept at the time. Concluding the second decade of the 21st century and looking at how entertainment has transformed our culture as a whole, it really comes back to that kind of initial concept of 'broadcasting yourself'. And so, we continue to create a platform that does exactly that. It's only that nowadays we have different sized companies use it – individuals use it, massive media companies use it, publishers use it... and YouTube is to each of them whatever they want their brand to be.

Four values

At YouTube, we don't have a value system that is based on political values. We want to be a platform for free expression, not particular to any groups or entities who are using YouTube. We tend to think about our values as freedoms. There are four freedoms that we talk about quite frequently.

FIGURE 21.1   The free and airy architecture of the company headquarters expresses and inspires the sense of freedom YouTube puts at its core

SOURCE   Chris Dale (2020)

The first freedom is 'the freedom to belong'. The idea is that you can come to YouTube, upload a video or find videos and connect with people that share similar interests. This can be as simple as finding a community of Lady Gaga fans. But it can also be something totally niche. I remember years ago we saw a tradition out of England called 'cheese rolling', where they would take giant wheels of cheese, roll them down hills and race against them. And there was a massive community who loved not only to video these moments but also to share them with everybody around the world. There is also a YouTuber, DieselDucy, who likes to take videos in elevators. He has autism, but through YouTube this guy has found a community of people who love his videos. He is now making a good amount of money month to month simply videoing his experience in different elevators. Not something that I would ever think of. But, clearly, it relates to some people. And that's the idea behind that first principle or that first value, which is 'the freedom to belong'.

Second is 'the freedom of information' and this is probably the one that's closest to Google's original and continued Mission of 'organizing the world's information and making it universally accessible and useful'. The idea here is that you can go to YouTube and be informed, find something that's useful. You can learn endlessly, and the topics can be as simple as tying a tie or as nuanced and sophisticated as learning about calculus or astrophysics. YouTube is this vast library of content that can help and inform you. I just used YouTube to fix my broken toilet. In just a few minutes, I was able to find the brand of toilet and learn how to fix it and in doing so saved myself a big bill from the plumber.

The next freedom is 'the freedom of expression'. YouTube is an open platform. Whether that's expressed as 'giving everyone a voice and showing them the world', or 'broadcast yourself', people should be able to come to YouTube and express themselves. These viewpoints are personal and can be controversial. We want to be a platform where anyone has the ability to do that, provided that they don't violate the rules we put in place for uploading content.

The fourth value, I think, is very unique to YouTube. I honestly cannot think of another platform that does this YouTube scale, which is 'the freedom of opportunity'. Anyone with an idea can come to YouTube and transform a passion into a career and begin to earn money from it. I talked about the guy who videos his experiences in elevators and how he is making an income out of those videos. The same can happen – and has happened – to a person in uploading videos from home about something they're passionate about and sharing it with the world. Things like make-up tutorials or music, or arts and crafts, in all these cases people are connecting with an audience through their creativity and earning a living from it. There is a woman in Missouri named Jenny Doan. She's an amazing quilt maker. Years ago her son suggested to her that she start a YouTube channel dedicated to quilt making. Today, that channel has created a booming business that has brought jobs to her Missouri town.

And that's just one example of many. YouTubers begin by uploading videos, then find a global audience and start to make a living. These livings create jobs and help drive economies all around the world. Another one is a woman from Germany named Sallys Welt. I met her a few months ago at an event in Cologne. She created a cooking channel that has made her the Martha Stewart of Germany. Today, she employs dozens of people and is branching into merchandise, books and more. She has the goal now of hiring 100 more people over the next 6 to 12 months. She is incredible, very down-to-earth, authentic. She speaks perfect English, but all of her videos are in German, and she clearly has found a big enough audience to not only make a living for herself, but help other people make a living as well.

The brand as balance

But not everyone who comes to YouTube and uploads a video is going to be able to earn a living from it, perhaps because the topics they're talking about are very near and dear to their heart, but they don't gain a big audience. Or, what they're discussing is controversial by nature and not finding a lot of advertisers. So, there is content that can be monetized in an ad-supported model that is inspiring and fantastic. But there is also content that many brands don't necessarily want to advertise against, but serves a great purpose for society. And we absolutely do not want to limit 'the freedom of expression' to those who only make content suitable for large brand advertisers. For example, topics like sex education, or political debates, may not be appealing to brands, but can serve a greater purpose in a free and democratic society. To this end, we offer other forms of monetization beyond ads – ticketing and merchandise sales, paid memberships and even subscription revenue.

Our brand doesn't need to be front and centre. Its strength comes from all of the people expressing themselves online all over the world through videos. The thing that motivates people who come to work here every day is that we're empowering others around us to use our platform in a way that has a positive impact on the world. Upload a video, express a point of view, find an audience. Find a community to belong to and potentially create a business or a next generation media company from that platform or experience. And so, from our perspective, we take great pride in the YouTube brand in that sense. How it has empowered millions of people around the world to connect and find places to belong or to express themselves. As a brand we are very comfortable sitting back and seeding what it means to be a YouTuber, because ultimately they are the ones who define who we are. And as long as we have strong rules of the road, or 'community guidelines' as we call them, I think that's a great place to be.

We certainly think about our brand in these terms: Are we a brand that people can relate to? Are we a brand that people feel excited about? A brand that's valued? We absolutely do. And we track it. We want to be a brand that's trusted, something that has become increasingly important over the last several years. Our community in itself is incredibly complicated because you have these different forces that make up that community, sometimes working in collaboration and in concert with one another and sometimes in opposition.

A unique ecosystem

There are really three constituents that make up the YouTube ecosystem: Viewers, advertisers and creators. And it's not always an easy match. There are times when creators are uploading content that they are super passionate about, which they think is fantastic. But advertisers, for whatever reason, don't want to appear against that content. And we have to give advertisers the control to decide what content they want their brands to appear against. Naturally, the kind of content that Harley Davidson wants to appear against is very different from the one Pampers would pick.

YouTube's Ueber-Target?

There's something on YouTube for everyone, so our demographics mirror the world, old, young, male, female, everyone can find something to relate to on YouTube and that's part of our success.

Now having said that, there are certainly audiences that come to YouTube more frequently than others. Younger generations like Gen Y or Gen Z or Millennials don't have a concept of 'time delayed' or 'windowed' entertainment. They don't have a concept of one channel, three channels, two actors, seven artists... Their 'channel' is not a channel of 10, 100, 1,000 – it's infinite channels. And yet it's also a channel of one, one person with infinite interests.

We do find that many of this younger generation come to YouTube and that's where their stars are. Their stars are not traditional Hollywood stars, they are people who are uploading YouTube videos on a frequent basis. And they connect with these stars because they feel invested in them, which in turn is why those stars invest back in their fans. They communicate with each other. There's a two-way relationship that never existed in traditional television. There is an expectation among this generation that entertainment is not a one-way medium but a two-way conversation. And this conversation can happen in the comments, in the videos or on other social platforms... but there is a sense that this group of fans, this generation, is creating and investing in the content that matters to them. It gets back to that reflective quality that YouTube has: Creator and viewer are in a dialogue, a feedback loop. And this dynamic is shifting the perception as to what entertainment is. It's making it much more bespoke, much more interactive. And much more global.

Psy, a Korean pop star who came out with a hit song 'Gangnam Style' at the beginning of the decade, took a largely regional movement of K Pop and made it a global sensation. Ten years later, you saw a Korean movie win Best Picture at the Oscars. That globalization of entertainment started on

YouTube. The song, 'Despacito' was another, more recent global phenomenon that happened on YouTube that really helped put Latin American music front and centre on the global stage in a way where everyone felt connected to it. It wasn't just one community, it was the world, and not even a single language could separate fans. And I think that's a really unique place to be. And it's very different from where we were 10 or 20 years ago when it comes to concepts of entertainment and culture.

Brand culture

The culture inside of YouTube and inside of Google is very open, very supportive. There is certainly a belief system of expressing oneself, really speaking up and talking out. And I think that's one of the things that makes Google culture fantastic. But just like with the YouTube platform, it's important that both YouTube and Google have rules of the road, principles or guidelines around respecting one another as colleagues and professionals. Some of these challenges have played out publicly, but at the end of the day I'm convinced that every single Google employee comes to work here because they're inspired by the work they do. They feel that YouTube and Google are collectively making the world a better place. Creating products that help in your everyday life, connecting you to information and providing you with services that are not only helpful, but can be transformative. And I think this idea of being helpful and useful is the single galvanizing force that binds us all together.

Naturally, as companies get bigger, reflecting more voices, it can be challenging to retain this culture at scale. One of the things that we at YouTube have done and continue to do is hold weekly town hall meetings. This helps to take a culture and a company that's really big and doing a lot of different things and narrow it down to a smaller community of people who are more focused on a specific product with a specific Mission. It makes us all feel connected. And those weekly town halls are really fantastic. Employees have the opportunity to come in and ask any question they want and hear from leadership the answers. I think this is really good and it shows accountability from the leadership team and it shows a real respect for anyone in the organization to have a point of view and deserve an answer to a tough question.

Besides these, we have other things that are important for our culture. Many people have heard about our cafes and micro-kitchens. These food spaces provide places to grab something to eat when you're hungry. But they

FIGURE 21.2 Comfortable and inspiring areas allow YouTube employees to spontaneously connect and exchange ideas

SOURCE Chris Dale (2020)

also are spaces where people congregate and have conversations. Many of these conversations are about what's happening in people's lives, or brainstorms about new products. Some of the most incredible products Google has created over the years have come out of these kinds of conversations. The workspaces, from floor plans to cafes, foster open connection. There's a real sense of coming together and collaborating

We also have employee resource groups, made up of employees who hold common interests, or share similar backgrounds. These can be political or religious, they can be around gender identity, or race. Each group provides a place for people to come together and talk about not only their own personal experiences, but also their experiences within the Google culture. And there are numerous examples where these groups have spoken out and created positive change across the organization.

While YouTube is its own distinct product area, it is deeply connected to Google. You have a Mission but that Mission and goals are complimented and connect up to Google's Mission and goals. We are all collectively rowing towards a common place.

I've been working at YouTube for the bulk of my Google career because it reflects what I'm passionate about. I love Android products, I love Chrome products, I love everything we're doing across AI. All Alphabet companies are fantastic and inspiring, but YouTube is unique in the sense that it sits at this cross-section of media and technology. And that's appealing to me right now in my career.

FIGURE 21.3 While YouTube has monitors everywhere inside to watch what's being broadcast, the park outside provides a calming and liberating antidote

SOURCE Chris Dale (2020)

At the YouTube HQ there are screens everywhere. And they're all playing YouTube videos and YouTube branding is out front and centre. So, you always know that you're at YouTube. But you also see, if you've been to a Google office, that there are similarities. There's a consistency of resources and amenities and common day-to-day practices.

The only constant is change

One of the things that you learn on the very first day that you start at Google is that the only constant at Google is change, and change happens quickly. It is the people who are the most adaptable and who can create a semblance of structure that moves within this constant change that I think end up being the most successful. YouTube and Google exist in an incredibly competitive space. It keeps us on our toes. We have to keep evolving. We have to keep iterating and we have to move at the pace that our users are moving. If they are shifting, we want to shift along with them, or even ahead of them. If we see something that we think is going to be absolutely beneficial to users and could create a better experience, we want to launch those products, very, very quickly.

It's a bit like white water rafting. You're moving very quickly and you're heading down the river. You want to see ahead, what the challenges are, where the areas of opportunity are, and you want to be able to move your raft very nimbly and the better you are doing that, the more successful you're going to be. But it doesn't mean paying attention to the others rafting left and right, or obsessing about them is probably even a better way to put it. You shouldn't obsess about the raft that's next to you or the one that's coming up fast behind you. All you should do is stay forward-thinking focused.

Looking ahead

We have over 2 billion users. We're growing fast all over the world. While we have physical studios around the world, and invest in original programming, our big investments will stay focused on our core value proposition: Creating the very best viewing experience for users, the best place for creators to earn a living and the best place for advertisers to reach global, engaged audiences.

RECAP: YOUTUBE

- A platform can be a brand – but one that 'sits back' a bit more, allowing its users to shine.

- It's less about brand identity and control and more about impact and collaboration.

- YouTube is built on four freedoms: the freedom to belong, the freedoms to inform and express yourself, and the freedom of opportunity (to turn passion into business).

- Even freedom needs rules: limits on hate speech etc, and different monetization models to balance content.

- Culture plays a key role for YouTube. It's all about initiating dialogue and discourse, including the office architecture.

- As with any brand built on freedom, YouTube's only constant is change – but driven by its own sense vs obsessively following the competition.

Epilogue

Crises – Times of Ueber-Opportunities

Just as we were wrapping up the script for this book in the spring of 2020, the world as we knew it seemed to collapse: A pandemic started spreading around the globe, infecting millions, killing tens of thousands a day at its peak, making most try to socially distance and work, shop, work-out, live… at home. Millions were furloughed or even lost their jobs and businesses went into bankruptcy or faltered as most countries issued mandatory lock-downs, shutting down schools, retail, hospitality, events. And then, as if this all wasn't enough, in May, a video appearing on social media of a black man being choked to death by a Minneapolis police officer became the match in the powder barrel that ignited sustained, sometimes violent, protests against systemic racism in the United States and around the world. Some called it the 'perfect storm' of crisis, observing its far-reaching waves of economic, social, cultural, political consequences that will impact our lives for a long time to come.

The publishing date of this book was delayed by the crisis, as were so many things. But this opened up an opportunity to observe how brands in general and Ueber-Brands in particular were affected by the crises – and how they dealt with them.

Talk is cheap, the right action is tough

After the initial shock, and the frenzy of solving organizational issues, supply chain, distribution, etc, questions that quickly emerged among brand owners and marketing professionals were how to communicate, advertise and act in the face of such severe and overlapping crises. Many felt they needed to field messages along the lines of 'We are here for you', adding images of compassionate behaviours to associate with their brand, be it automotive, fast food or financial. There was literally an inflation of emotional but ultimately inconsequential declarations of empathy, which quickly got made fun of by observers posting compilations of almost identical looking scenes and ad spoofs on YouTube (Diaz, 2020) or by cartoonists like Tom Fishburne who, in a comic strip, let a couple wonder why they got an email of empathy from a brand they hadn't heard from for years (Fishburne, 2020).

Equally, many brands developed public-service-announcement-like messages about social distancing or mask-wearing. For example, in Brazil, McDonald's 'distanced' its golden arches on a billboard and Coca-Cola spread out its lettering on Times Square in New York. In Germany, car brands VW, Audi and Mercedes-Benz played around with their logos trying to gain attention (designboom, 2020). These efforts also fizzled out rather quickly.

Other companies, however, understood early on that many people desired to see them take meaningful actions beyond their words. They ranged from US logistics company U-Haul offering students free truck rentals and storage as they had to vacate dorms, to Heinz, which realized the central role its affordable and easy-to-prepare comfort foods played in the crisis – particularly for millions of poor pupils who were suddenly cut off from free nutrition at school. Heinz committed in print ads to deliver 12 million meals to them through a collaboration with non-profit organization Magic Breakfast. Brilliant decisions, we think, to give brands that are perceived as rather utilitarian or 'passé' a more meaningful presence while sticking to what they are best at, like letting people haul stuff or eat while fitting their restricted budgets.

Unfortunately, too many brand actions turned out to be temporary, tactical moves that ceased once the budget was depleted. Or worse, they simply turned out to be disguised promo tools, like fast-food chain Popeyes' 'free' Netflix passwords which you could only get with a proof of purchase. The opposite of a meaningful contribution (Beer, 2020).

And, quite a number of brands got 'caught' for not living up to their communication. McDonald's, Uber, Amazon and others were called out – most prominently by social-democratic US Senator Bernie Sanders – for not offering the kind of healthcare benefits or safety precautions to their workers and contractors that they were advocating for in public. Adidas became ensnarled in a PR disaster as they broke their leases and stopped paying rent while other, much smaller and harder-hit businesses stuck to their commitments.

FIGURE 22.1   Heinz Beans take on new meaning when they feed 12 million school-children who would otherwise go hungry

SOURCE   Reproduced with permission of H. J. Heinz Foods UK Limited

Adidas later publicly touted using their patented shoe technology to make face masks as a 'Thank You for Healthcare Heroes', but this hardly made up for their earlier shown lack of civil responsibility and collective conscience.

Consequently, when the protests against systemic racism spread broadly across the US and the world, misalignments between brand statements and their past or current behaviours quickly became a key point of the debate. Appeals like #pulluporshutup by black entrepreneur Sharon Chuter gained significant momentum, demanding brands to not only pay lip service to Black Lives Matter but reveal and fight the barriers causing people of colour to be under-represented among company leadership or suppliers (Shacknai, 2020).

In the case of brands having previously made a higher Mission a centre-piece of their existence, actions perceived to betray that Mission naturally backfired all the more violently. Take Everlane, for example, which prides itself on 'radical transparency' and putting people first, as we reviewed in Part One, Principle 1 of the book. It, too, was called out by Senator Sanders for HR 'misbehaviour', here for quietly laying off part-time workers at the onset of the crisis, presumably in an attempt to avoid unionization. The issue was widely disseminated and discussed in the fashion media, amongst bloggers, influencers and many of the progressive Millennials on the Sanders team (Farra, 2020) – all segments from which the brand recruits its 'Ueber-Target'. A response by founder Michael Preysman explaining the severe business decline that necessitated the 'impossible decision' was widely perceived as too little too late, and not to live up to the transparency expected. The damage was done, and it is likely to leave bad feelings among many of their Ueber-Target, if not the public at large, which will take time and effort to heal.

Learning 1: Do vs declare – with humility, not hubris

So, what is an Ueber-Brand to say and do in such times of exceptional crisis, then – if anything? We think it is no different from what they should always do to be at their best and most meaningful: Focus on their core and live it truthfully inside out – serving all their key constituents in line with their Mission and in light of the situation.

For Ben & Jerry's (see Part One for its Mission), this quite naturally meant drawing the public's attention to the impact the crisis had on social inequality and the disadvantaged, for example with a headline-making campaign to protect prison populations, which are particularly prone to infections due to their close confinement (Ben & Jerry's, 2020a, 2020b). In the case of Patagonia it meant – more quietly – screening naturalist films on their website for people locked up at home, telling them how they should and could still support NGOs in their fight to protect the environment while the world's attention turned elsewhere (Preda, 2020).

But most Ueber-Brands do not have 'activist brand' written in their DNA and they should not attempt – or worse pretend – to be one. That does not mean, however, that their responses to crises have to be less meaningful. Quite the contrary.

The King Arthur Baking Company traces its origins back to Boston and the year 1790. At the same time, it has evolved to be a rather progressive, employee-owned, co-CEO and mission-led company that refuses to let us think of flour as a commodity. Instead, it wants to help 'inspire connections and community through baking, and to use [its] business as a force for good' (King Arthur Baking Company, 2020) through its premium baking flours and tools as well as online and offline schools, recipes, books, baker's hotlines – all for hobby and professional bakers, alike. It was in the COVID crisis that this brand came to the fore by drumming up its Mission and Myth from the inside out – growing exponentially in volume and stature, way ahead of most of its much lower-priced and bigger competitors. Where many floundered and failed, King Arthur shone as the 'Best Workplace' it had been rated to be for years, during the pandemic as well. And it was discovered as a great product to use and an expert friend to have – far beyond its dedicated baking community. Because King Arthur was there when thousands suddenly started seeking comfort – and often finding challenges – in baking their own bread, or things even more daunting. They served and grew a rapidly expanding community with rich content, remote classes like the 'The Isolation Baking Show', and specially developed tips and recipes like 'Baking bread when flour is scarce'. The effect: Business exploded 20- to 60-fold, retailers ran out of stock and their employee–owners answered thousands of monthly hotline calls vs the usual hundreds – 'mostly by newbies' (Collings, 2020; Freedman, 2020). After some six months, the crisis high has started to taper off, with people returning to their normal lives and routines. But, we can safely expect King Arthur to keep benefiting from the positive impressions and impact it made and to reign in what many expect to be a growing kingdom of home baking (Horsley, 2020).

FIGURE 22.2   Helping bakers in distress comes naturally to the King Arthur Baking Company. Only the recipes and producing the content needed some tweaking

SOURCE Reproduced with permission of the King Arthur Baking Company, Inc.

Punk-inspired craft beer brand BrewDog, on the other hand, did what many alcohol-related businesses started to do after the initial shortage of sanitizers became apparent: It put its tanks and technologies in crisis mode and began distilling hand sanitizers at its Aberdeen brewery. But, it did so in typical BrewDog fashion, enrolling its fan community to help pack the sanitizers in its closed bars and adding its idiosyncratic humour by labelling some of them 'BrewGel Punk Sanitizer' to lighten up an otherwise gloomy situation (The Drum Creative, 2020; BrewDog, 2020b). And this wasn't just a witty band-aid, it was its Mission radiating out what it lived inside as well: In an effort to keep as many of their workers employed and their devoted 'drinker–shareholder community' impacted as little as possible, the founders were among the first to declare foregoing their salaries for 2020 and top managers volunteered to half theirs. One of the co-founders, James Watt, provided perspective on what motivated these actions, namely to show that 'It is not the size of the dog in the fight, but the size of the fight in the dog.' And that is what BrewDog is all about, crisis or none (American Craft Beer, 2020).

Learning 2: Keep evolving and surprising – yourself as well as all of us

Premier luxury group LVMH, owner of Louis Vuitton, Moët, Hennessy, Dior and many other luxury *maisons*, also made early headlines showing its caring side by converting some of its perfume production to make and donate sanitizers, sorely needed at French hospitals at the time (BBC News, 2020). But much more interesting is how it kept its brands on their respective Missions yet adapted and evolved them along the way, growing with the challenges we were and are all facing.

LVMH's eponymous travel and fashion brand Louis Vuitton is well known for driving the Myth of 'Life as a Journey'. Consequently, its communication (in China) initially translated this into a message of hope with the campaign 'Every paused journey will eventually restart' (Wang, 2020). But with their menswear spring 2021 collection Louis Vuitton took this narrative to a whole new level: Following the words of CEO Michael Burke, 'We know people are not going to be able to travel, so let's not have people travel to the venues. Let's have the clothes travel to the venues' (Li, 2020), it turned its annual fashion show into a global roadshow, kicked off in Shanghai. Under the theme 'The Adventures of Zooom with Friends', a droll, rock 'n' roll troupe of cartoon-characters was sent on a global adventure-trip-cum-fashion-show, all captured on video, of course, surprising, delighting and entertaining not only those invited to the regional live events but all fans around the world through a big influencer and social media push. Of course, the funky characters will also be featured in the collection itself, but the important part is that the brand's Mission and Myth of 'Life as a Journey' was lived and brought to life in a whole new, meaning-ful way, expressing empathy and creating relevance in a very unique and credible manner and thus letting the brand and its narrative not buckle but grow under the challenges. Or, as the Artistic Director for LV Menswear, Virgil Abloh, said in his accompanying 'Message in a Bottle': 'I run a studio of optimism, and I have a general belief in good and beauty' (Li, 2020).

Equally interesting is how online music platform Spotify evolved and lived its mission of 'unlocking the potential of human creativity… letting artists live off their art' (see Part One, Mission Route 2) during the crises. As the mass cancellations of live events throughout 2020 had a devastating effect on many musicians, Spotify reacted by enabling them to receive tips directly from their fans on the platform without taking a cut (Lewis, 2020). A small but inventive gesture – Mission-fed and heartfelt. And another step in living its purpose in new and surprising ways that will certainly help grow the goodwill of its fans.

Last but not least, let's talk Airbnb, which you already read quite a bit about in the previous chapters. It also rose to the occasion, so to speak. Though some of that rising was also coerced by other factors rather than inspired by COVID and Black Lives Matter – like the long-negotiated data sharing agreement with EU authorities in spring 2020 that will help regulate and control short-term rentals. As the crisis unfolded – and travel halted – it quickly switched focus to long-term rentals for those fleeing cities for the country to escape infection. And for the healthcare workers moving into the cities, Airbnb donated one hundred thousand stays and activated its commu-nity to recruit volunteers and raise funds to broaden free offerings for 'frontline stays for COVID-19 responders' (Airbnb, 2020). The company also ramped up the nascent 'experiences' offerings by hosts, allowing them to provide online interactions including discussions on art and culture or local cooking classes.

Not all went down smoothly, of course. The host community complained bitterly that Airbnb was not as generous in protecting them financially as it was with its employees and the guests. But they were most upset about not being consulted with before the brand decided to allow unrestricted cancel-lations with a full refund. CEO Brian Chesky apologized and established a $250 million aid fund for the hosts affected most. The leadership team also realized that they had strayed too far from that core mission of making people 'belong anywhere' (the creation of which Douglas Atkin describes in Part Three of the book). Chesky committed to re-focus the company and fight the negative 'airbnbification' of neighbourhoods – including via the aforementioned EU partnership as well as a ban on unauthorized parties in rental properties. He initiated steps to move away from large commercial operators back to smaller, more engaged hosts and away from dominating entire buildings or city blocks to making Airbnb destinations unique and intimate experiences again.

All these actions and evolutions are certainly also motivated by the company's imminent IPO, which has been in the works for years and has finally been filed for (Griffith, 2020). But they are at the same time truly moving the brand forward, adapting and evolving in bringing its Mission to life and making true on its philosophy of 'stakeholder capitalism'. A 'moment of truth', as founder Brian Chesky called the COVID crisis (Griffith, 2020), put to good use.

In sum: Keep writing your Myth while living your Mission

In our last book (Schaefer and Kuehlwein, 2015) we talked about CEO Angela Ahrens and Creative Director Christopher Bailey successfully writing the next chapter in the venerable history of Burberry. Unfortunately, that success has not held up consistently over the past years, not the least during COVID (Reuters, 2020), despite the highly lauded hiring of Riccardo Tisci as Chief Creative Officer and the well-received collections he created.

The problem: Reinventing product, recalibrating distribution and many other wonderful things brands do to live their Mission are only as good as they are in feeding and furthering their Myth. And Burberry is a perfect example. It did many of the right things, and they worked for a while, but it has as of yet failed to sustainably capture the heads and hearts of today's younger audiences. Because despite its initial intentions it has not yet written the next chapter in the brand's Myth. It may have acted it out in quite a number of ways, but it has not successfully coalesced all of it into a compelling narrative, a memorable and captivating red threat that is easily understood by their audiences and can weave its way into today's collective conscience and culture. Re-ignite the Zeitgeist again and again.

Because for that you must connect the dots, link your actions with your story, write the past during the present into the future. Carve out a plot with surprising and twisting turns, but one that people can follow and relate to, one that continues an innate logic and narrative. Else you have more hopscotching and tactical reacting than believable, visionary, past-forward measures.

Many brands unfortunately proved this again during COVID. Their 'messages of empathy' came spur-of-the-moment and not part of a credible Mission and Myth – and they were rightly often met with cynicism. Others, like Heinz for example, did good and their actions were meaningful and in line with their competencies. The question is whether the brand will make them become part of a bigger picture and story or let them become a past campaign that is soon forgotten.

As we have emphasized, repeatedly: Building an Ueber-Brand is not a destination, it is a journey. A journey to fulfil one's Mission and further one's Myth that never ends. Overcoming crises on that journey are great opportunities to prove yourself and feed the legend. And such opportunities Ueber-Brands will not want to miss.

REFERENCES AND FURTHER READING

2nd Vote (2018) [Accessed 14 January 2020] Ben & Jerry's just reminded everyone how much they hate conservative values. 2ndVote.com, 1 November [Online] https://www.2ndvote.com/ben-jerrys-just-reminded-everyone-much-hate-conservative-values/ (archived at https://perma.cc/A2N5-4R76)

Abad-Santos, A (2018) [Accessed 14 January 2020] Nike's Colin Kaepernick ad sparked a boycott – and earned $6 billion for Nike. Vox.com, 24 September [Online] https://www.vox.com/2018/9/24/17895704/nike-colin-kaepernick-boycott-6-billion (archived at https://perma.cc/VKL4-DBS3)

Abbott, M (2018) The radical rise of vegan menswear, *Financial Times*, December, pp 18–19

Aiello, C (2018) Social change is part of business, Ben & Jerry's CEO says. 17 August [Online] https://www.cnbc.com/2018/08/17/ben--jerrys-ceo--social-changeis-part-of-business.html (archived at https://perma.cc/KS8J-YB3T)

Airbnb (2020) [Accessed 9 September 2020] Frontline stays for COVID-19 responders. Airbnb [Online] https://www.airbnb.com/d/covid19relief (archived at https://perma.cc/2F6J-CG5B)

Alnuweiri, T (2019) [Accessed 15 January 2020] We can't stop wondering: Why are Birkenstocks so popular right now? Well + Good, 1 February [Online] https://www.wellandgood.com/good-looks/why-are-birkenstocks-so-popular/ (archived at https://perma.cc/B5AK-4HHP)

Alsever, J (2019) [Accessed 15 January 2020] Attention startups: Big corporations want to work with you. Inc, 5 November [Online] https://www.inc.com/magazine/201304/jennifer-alsever/attention-startups-big-corporations-want-to-work-with-you.html (archived at https://perma.cc/P9KL-MZE9)

Amed, I (2019) [Accessed 2 April 2020] Mastering the McQueen challenge. Business of Fashion, 4 March [Online] https://www.businessoffashion.com/articles/professional/mastering-the-mcqueen-challenge-how-to-grow-a-young-luxury-business (archived at https://perma.cc/NYH3-ERQH)

American Craft Beer (2020) [Accessed 9 September 2020] BrewDog founders forgo their salaries amid global pandemic. American Craft Beer, 2 April [Online] https://www.americancraftbeer.com/brewdog-founders-forgo-their-salaries-amid-global-pandemic/ (archived at https://perma.cc/KN3W-6MSP)

Andersen, R (2014) [Accessed 20 January 2020] Exodus. Aeon, 30 September [Online] https://aeon.co/essays/elon-musk-puts-his-case-for-a-multi-planet-civilisation (archived at https://perma.cc/YE5X-FF74)

Andrews, TC (2017) *Building Brands in Asia: From the inside out*, Routledge, London

Arendt, H (1958) *The Human Condition*, University of Chicago Press, Chicago

Arnold, A (2019) [Accessed 16 January 2020] Damn, people really hate that Peloton ad. The Cut, 6 December [Online] https://www.thecut.com/2019/12/peloton-stock-drops-9-percent-following-widely-criticized-ad.html (archived at https://perma.cc/5ETX-HLEQ)

Atkin, D (2005) *The Culting of Brands: Turn your customers into believers*, 4th edn, Portfolio, New York

Atwal, G, Bryson, D and Kuehlwein, J (2020, forthcoming) Luxury in emerging markets: Towards understanding new prestige brands in India, in *Oxford Handbook of Luxury Business*, Oxford University Press: Oxford

Barthes, R (1957) *Mythologies*, Editions du Seuil, Paris

BBC News (2020) [Accessed 9 September 2020] Coronavirus: Louis Vuitton owner to start making hand sanitiser. BBC News, 16 March [Online] https://www.bbc.com/news/business-51868756 (archived at https://perma.cc/34GS-54QV)

Beer, J (2019) [Accessed 14 January 2020] One year later, what did we learn from Nike's blockbuster Colin Kaepernick ad? Fast Company, 5 September [Online] https://www.fastcompany.com/90399316/one-year-later-what-did-we-learn-from-nikes-blockbuster-colin-kaepernick-ad (archived at https://perma.cc/4ZJ6-E3N5)

Beer, J (2020) [Accessed 8 September 2020] Popeyes gives away Netflix passwords in tone-deaf campaign during Coronavirus crisis. FastCompany online, 24 March. [Online] https://www.fastcompany.com/90481469/popeyes-gives-away-netflix-passwords-in-tone-deaf-campaign-during-coronavirus-crisis (archived at https://perma.cc/5YF7-CKTK)

Belk, R (1988) [Accessed 14 January 2020] Possessions and the extended self, *Journal of Consumer Research*, 15(2), pp 139–68 [Online] https://doi.org/10.1086/209154 (archived at https://perma.cc/MU3C-RARA)

Ben & Jerry's (2020a) [Accessed 9 September 2020] Mass incarceration in the time of COVID-19: Racist, risky, and reversible. Ben & Jerry's, 27 March [Online] https://www.benjerry.com/whats-new/2020/03/incarceration-covid-19 (archived at https://perma.cc/78UR-VYH3)

Ben & Jerry's (2020b) [Accessed 16 September 2020] Ben & Jerry's wants incarcerated people #FreeAndSafe from COVID-19. Ben & Jerry's, 14 April [Online] https://www.benjerry.com/about-us/media-center/incarcerated-people-freeandsafe (archived at https://perma.cc/94NC-EFET)

Benner, L (2017) [Accessed 6 April 2020] In Airbnb's Super Bowl Ad, Implied Criticism of Trump's Travel Ban. The New York Times, 5 February [Online] https://www.nytimes.com/2017/02/05/technology/airbnb-super-bowl-ad-trump-travel-ban.html (archived at https://perma.cc/66PL-5BRV)

Booker, C (2004) *The Seven Basic Plots*, Continuum International Publishing Group, London/New York

Brave Gentleman (2020) [Accessed 27 March 2020] Accessories [Online] https://www.bravegentleman.com/accessories (archived at https://perma.cc/5JY7-2BB6)

BrewDog (2020a) [Accessed 27 March 2020] About [Online] https://www.brewdog.com/uk/about (archived at https://perma.cc/C6XF-AAF3)

BrewDog (2020b) [Accessed 9 September 2020] BrewDog hand sanitiser, BrewDog, September [Online] https://www.brewdog.com/uk/hand-sanitiser (archived at https://perma.cc/3TKA-AZ7X)

Brown, M (2019) [Accessed 27 January 2020] Tesla Roadster 2020: Price and specs for the plaid-powered supercar. inverse, 12 September [Online] https://www.inverse.com/article/50995-tesla-roadster-price-release-date-and-autopilot-for-next-gen-supercar (archived at https://perma.cc/RPA2-USM9)

Buchanan, L (2014) [Accessed 16 January 2020] How to grow without losing what makes you great. Inc, March [Online] https://www.inc.com/magazine/201403/leigh-buchanan/how-to-scale-your-company.html (archived at https://perma.cc/723Q-9BTZ)

Buly1803 (2020) [Accessed 1 January 2020] L'histoire du siècle [Online] https://www.buly1803.com/fr/content/27-histoire (archived at https://perma.cc/YWG7-VEPH)

Burlingham, B (2016) [Accessed 6 April 2020] The coolest little start-up in America. Inc, 1 July [Online] https://www.inc.com/magazine/20060701/coolest-startup.html (archived at https://perma.cc/H38N-ENGB)

Burning Man (2019a) [Accessed 14 January 2020] The ten principles of Burning Man. BurningMan.org [Online] https://burningman.org/culture/philosophical-center/10-principles/ (archived at https://perma.cc/VHX8-TZQW)

Burning Man (2019b) [Accessed 8 December 2019] Tickets, https://tickets.burningman.org/ (archived at https://perma.cc/2GXG-9ZGA)

Business Roundtable (2019) [Accessed 9 January 2020] Business Roundtable redefines the purpose of a corporation to promote 'An economy that serves all Americans'. Business Roundtable, 19 August [Online] https://www.businessroundtable.org/business-roundtable-redefines-the-purpose-of-a-corporation-to-promote-an-economy-that-serves-all-americans (archived at https://perma.cc/WS7B-ZKUV)

Bybee, JL (1997) The fantasy, ideal, and ought selves: Content, relationships to mental health, and functions, *Social Cognition*, **15**(1), pp 37–53

Campbell, J (1978) *Der Heros in tausend Gestalten*, Suhrkamp, Frankfurt

Campbell, J (1988) *The Power of Myth*, Doubleday, New York

Camper (2020) [Accessed 27 March 2020] Camper [Online] https://www.camper.com/en_US/ (archived at https://perma.cc/KCW3-UZPT)

Care/of (2020) [Accessed 26 January 2020] Home page [Online] https://takecareof.com/ (archived at https://perma.cc/T6YN-7HTN)

Chan, J (2019) [Accessed 15 January 2020] The ultimate guide to creating the perfect founding team. Foundr Magazine, 16 March [Online] https://foundr.com/founding-team (archived at https://perma.cc/YP2L-S3AX)

Cheng, M (2018) [Accessed 14 January 2020] How this 244-year-old company made 'ugly' shoes popular and stylish. Inc, 27 July [Online] https://www.inc.com/michelle-cheng/innovate-summer-products-birkenstock-244-year-brand.html (archived at https://perma.cc/5AL9-WK66)

Chesky, B (2014) [Accessed 27 March 2020] Don't fuck up the culture. Medium, 20 April [Online] https://medium.com/@bchesky/dont-fuck-up-the-culture-597cde9ee9d4 (archived at https://perma.cc/8U56-44MM)

Chobani (2020) [Accessed 27 March 2020] Chobani [Online] https://www.chobani.com/ (archived at https://perma.cc/DBD2-DLNE)

Christensen, C (2016) *The Innovator's Dilemma: When new technologies cause great firms to fail* (reprint ed.), Harvard Business Review Press, Boston

Collings, R (2020) [Accessed 9 September 2020] King Arthur's flour sales rise more than 2000% in March. AdWeek, 21 April. [Online] https://www.adweek.com/brand-marketing/king-arthur-flour-sales-up-over-2000-percent-march-coronavirus-baking/ (archived at https://perma.cc/6QFV-BZQ9)

Cracken, G (1990) *Culture and Consumption*, Indiana University Publishing, Bloomington

Danziger, P (2019) *Meet the Henrys*, Self-published

De Botton, A (2012) *Religion for Atheists*, Penguin Group, London

designboom (2020) [Accessed 8 September 2020] Social distancing brand logos for Audi, Volkswagen and Coca-Cola. designboom, 2 April [Online] https://www.designboom.com/design/social-distancing-brand-logos-audi-volkswagen-coca-cola-coronavirus-04-02-2020/ (archived at https://perma.cc/B3SP-U9CT)

Diaz, A-C (2020) [Accessed 7 September 2020] See all the COVID-19 cliches in one big fat supercut. AdAge, 23 April [Online] https://adage.com/creativity/work/microsoft-sam-every-covid-19-commercial-exactly-same/2251551 (archived at https://perma.cc/QU28-AGM6)

Dolce & Gabbana (2018) [Accessed 24 January 2020] Dolce & Gabbana founders apologise for controversial China campaign. YouTube, 23 November [Online] https://www.youtube.com/watch?v=bTl16mQsU9U (archived at https://perma.cc/AU7J-GMDC)

Doucet, J (2019) Personal interview

Dreher, R (2018) [Accessed 14 January 2020] Seven-dollar social justice ice cream. The Conservative, 30 October [Online] https://www.theamericanconservative.com/dreher/ben-and-jerry-social-justice-ice-cream-pecan-resist/ (archived at https://perma.cc/BN28-AVK4)

Eco, U (1986) *Travels in Hyperreality*, Harcourt Brace Jovanovich, San Diego

Eisenstein, PA (2017) [Accessed 14 January 2020] Legendary Cadillac brand now more popular in China than in the US. NBC News online, 16 February [Online] https://www.nbcnews.com/business/autos/cadillac-counting-china-overcome-home-market-stumbles-n719246 (archived at https://perma.cc/SY22-HLXW)

Eliot, TS (1952) *The Complete Poems and Plays*, Harcourt, Brace and Company, New York

Equity.de (2020) [Accessed 2 April 2020] Ueber uns. Equity [Online] https://equity.de/ueber-uns/ (archived at https://perma.cc/3F7X-3V3R)

Etsy (nd) [Accessed 14 January 2020] Keep commerce human, Etsy [Online] https://www.etsy.com/about (archived at https://perma.cc/V9QX-4KTK)

Everlane (2020) [Accessed 9 January 2020] About us [Online] https://www.everlane.com/about (archived at https://perma.cc/C6C7-YCSH)

Fahrun, J (2019) Lebenslanges Lernen 2.0, *Berliner Morgenpost*, 18 November, p 10

Farra, E (2020) [Accessed 8 September 2020] Everlane is losing the optics game in the age of Coronavirus. Vogue, 31 March [Online] https://www.vogue.com/article/everlane-union-dispute-coronavirus-response (archived at https://perma.cc/JM2F-RFZM)

Ferry, D (2017) *The Aeneid*, University of Chicago Press, Chicago/London

Fishburne, T (2020) [Accessed 3 September 2020] How not to communicate right now. Marketoonist, 22 March [Online] https://marketoonist.com/2020/03/communicate.html (archived at https://perma.cc/K3YT-J4VT)

Flatt, M (2012) Silence really is golden, *Admap*, April, p 5

Frankl, V (1962) *Man's Search for Meaning: An introduction to logotherapy*, Beacon Press, Boston

Freedman, D (2020) [Accessed 9 September 2020] Inside the flour company supplying America's sudden baking obsession. Medium Marker, 20 May. [Online] https://marker.medium.com/inside-the-flour-company-supplying-americas-sudden-baking-obsession-623034583579 (archived at https://perma.cc/8QMT-ZYUX)

Freitag (2019) [Accessed 1 December 2019] Holacracy [Online] https://www.freitag.ch/de/holacracy (archived at https://perma.cc/9Z8P-NS5G)

Friedman, V and Testa, J (2019) [Accessed 7 August 2020] The Metaphysics of Kylie Cosmetics Being Sold to Coty. *The New York Times*, 19 November [Online] https://www.nytimes.com/2019/11/19/style/kylie-jenner-coty-cosmetics.html (archived at https://perma.cc/Q5WP-B9K6)

Frieswick, K (2016) [Accessed 12 January 2020] This startup will keep you from ever going to the gym again. Inc, May [Online] https://www.inc.com/magazine/201605/kris-frieswick/peloton-studio-cycling-home-fitness.html (archived at https://perma.cc/B7G7-EXA3)

Fryer, B (2003) [Accessed 27 March 2020] Storytelling that moves people, Harvard Business Review. June [Online] https://hbr.org/2003/06/storytelling-that-moves-people (archived at https://perma.cc/G2WB-X9BX)

Future Travel Experience (2019) [Accessed 6 April 2020] Airbnb sets out to create an 'end-to-end travel platform' with appointment of Global Head of Transportation. Future Travel Experience, February [Online] https://www.futuretravelexperience.com/2019/02/airbnb-sets-out-to-create-end-to-end-travel-platform/ (archived at https://perma.cc/EAR5-F2D9)

Giese, F (2019) Mach mal Tempo!, *Lufthansa Magazine*, November, p 56

Globescan (2019) [Accessed 1 October 2019] Aspirational consumers are rising. Are brands ready to meet them? [Online] https://globescan.com/aspirational-consumers-are-rising-are-brands-ready-to-meet-them/ (archived at https://perma.cc/Y4V6-8GB8)

Gough, C (2019) [Accessed 7 February 2020] Distribution of players of Fortnite in the United States as of April 2018, by age group. Statistica, 20 November [Online] https://www.statista.com/statistics/865616/fortnite-players-age/ (archived at https://perma.cc/W6ZY-YA7E)

Green, P (2019) Luxury living that includes more than a home, *The New York Times International Edition*, 8–9 June

Greimel, H (2017) [Accessed 14 January 2020] Chinese buy into Cadillac. Automotive News China, 1 May [Online] https://www.autonews.com/article/20170501/GLOBAL03/305019960/chinese-buy-into-cadillac (archived at https://perma.cc/LW4L-UGQK)

Griese, I (2019) Wir stellen uns gegen die Mode-Terroristen, *Welt am Sonntag*, 21 July, p 58

Griffith, E (2020) Airbnb, 'sharing economy' pioneer, moves toward public offering, *The New York Times*, 20 August

Gross, EL (2019) [Accessed 25 January 2020] Glossier raises $100m and now has a billion-dollar valuation. Forbes, 19 March [Online] https://www.forbes.com/sites/elanagross/2019/03/19/glossier-raises-100m-and-now-has-a-billion-dollar-valuation/#7606b059720d (archived at https://perma.cc/A6X7-QDNU)

Haas, RM (2019) [Accessed 14 January 2020] Paris theatre. cinematreasures.org [Online] http://cinematreasures.org/theaters/307 (archived at https://perma.cc/XNZ2-MDNS)

Habermas, J (2011) *Theorie des kommunikativen Handelns*, Suhrkamp Verlag, Frankfurt am Main

Halo (2019) [Accessed 10 January 2020] Our story. Halo, 18 July [Online] https://halo.coffee/blogs/blog/our-story (archived at https://perma.cc/PSM6-ABEC)

Hass, N (2019) The Defiant Ones, *T – The New York Times Style Magazine*, 15 February, p 75

Hermès (2019) [Accessed 1 December 2019] Silk: Inspirations [Online] https://www.hermes.com/fr/fr/story/177666-inspirations-soie/ (archived at https://perma.cc/279B-D63R)

Hitchens, A (2018) [Accessed 16 January 2020] Hey, where's my oat milk? *The New Yorker*, 30 July [Online] https://www.newyorker.com/magazine/2018/08/06/hey-wheres-my-oat-milk (archived at https://perma.cc/6J3L-XQQL)

Hoggines, T (2019) [Accessed 9 February 2020] Fortnite earned record $2.4bn in 2018, the 'most annual revenue of any game in history'. *Telegraph*, 17 January [Online] https://www.telegraph.co.uk/gaming/news/fortnite-earned-annual-revenue-game-history-2018/ (archived at https://perma.cc/795Y-ZVWX)

Holt, D and Cameron, D (2012) *Cultural Strategy*, Oxford University Press, Oxford

Horsley, S (2020) [Accessed 9 September 2020] The great pandemic bake-off may be over. NPR, 16 June [Online] https://www.npr.org/2020/06/16/877479936/the-great-pandemic-bake-off-may-be-over (archived at https://perma.cc/JDS5-2YWX)

Howarth, D (2019a) [Accessed 14 January 2020] Dezeen's guide to Hudson Yards phase one in New York. Dezeen, 14 March [Online] https://www.dezeen.com/2019/03/14/hudson-yards-phase-one-guide/ (archived at https://perma.cc/KRJ8-REW9)

Howarth, D (2019b) [Accessed 14 January 2020] Snark Park provides Snarkitecture with permanent exhibition space at Hudson Yards. Dezeen, 15 March [Online] https://www.dezeen.com/2019/03/15/snark-park-snarkitecture-exhibition-space-hudson-yards/ (archived at https://perma.cc/5D59-WQHU)

Huddleston, T (2019) [Accessed 12 January 2020] How Peloton exercise bikes became a $4 billion fitness start-up with a cult following. CNBC make it. CNBC Online, 19 February [Online] https://www.cnbc.com/2019/02/12/how-peloton-exercise-bikes-and-streaming-gained-a-cult-following.html (archived at https://perma.cc/8KYT-ZY4P)

Idle, T (2019) [Accessed 6 April 2020] SB'19 Paris, day 2: Virtuous value chains, next-gen CSR and redesigning the #GoodLife. Sustainable Brands, 24 April [Online] https://sustainablebrands.com/read/collaboration-cocreation/sb-19-paris-day-2-virtuous-value-chains-next-gen-csr-and-redesigning-the-goodlife (archived at https://perma.cc/7TQG-QCWD)

Intothegloss (2020) [Accessed 2 April 2020] Intothegloss [Online] https://intothegloss.com (archived at https://perma.cc/ZG6F-FGUW)

Johnson, RE-Y (2010) Acting superior but actually inferior? Correlates and consequences of workplace arrogance, *Human Performance*, **23**, pp 403–27

Jung, CG (1936) Der Begriff des kollektiven Unterbewussten, Lecture at the Abernethian Society at St Bartholomew's Hospital, in *CG Jung Gesammelte Werke in elf Bänden*, 2001, dtv, Munich

Kahneman, D (2011) *Thinking, Fast and Slow*, Penguin Group, London

Kane, J (2018) [Accessed 10 January 2020] Burning Man sells out 26,000 tickets in a half hour. Reno Gazette Journal. USA Today online, 28 March [Online] https://www.usatoday.com/story/travel/nation-now/2018/03/28/burning-man-sold-out/467730002/ (archived at https://perma.cc/K56D-PVYR)

Kelner, M (2018) [Accessed 27 March 2020] Nike's controversial Colin Kaepernick ad campaign its most divisive yet. Guardian, 4 September [Online] https://www.theguardian.com/sport/2018/sep/04/nike-controversial-colin-kaepernick-campaign-divisive (archived at https://perma.cc/JC9F-FU27)

King Arthur Baking Company (2020) [Accessed 9 September 2020] About us. King Arthur Baking Company [Online] https://www.kingarthurbaking.com/about (archived at https://perma.cc/95X5-YB23)

Koch, KD (2020) Werte statt Mode, *Werben und Verkaufen* No1, 8 January, p 28

Lam, T (2018) [Accessed 27 March 2020] Glossier is opening its two-story flagship store in NYC this week. Hypebae, 5 November [Online] https://hypebae.com/2018/11/glossier-flagship-store-new-york-manhattan-makeup-skincare-beauty-emily-weiss (archived at https://perma.cc/F3JL-MGPU)

Lambert, F (2017) [Accessed 14 January 2020] Tesla Model X door gets torn off by truck as it automatically opens, owner and Tesla argue over what happened. electrek.co, 26 September [Online] https://electrek.co/2017/09/26/tesla-model-x-door-gets-torn-off-by-truck/ (archived at https://perma.cc/E4LL-GUF3)

Lego Education (2019) [Accessed 14 January 2020] Professional development and training. lego.com [Online] https://education.lego.com/en-us/training (archived at https://perma.cc/VLJ5-PFW3)

Legoland Discovery Center (2019) [Accessed 14 January 2020] Lego education workshops. Legoland Discovery Center [Online] https://philadelphia.legolanddiscoverycenter.com/lego-education-workshops/ (archived at https://perma.cc/MNG6-HGRE)

Lewis, I (2020) [Accessed 9 September 2020] Spotify allows fans to directly pay musicians with new in-app fundraising feature. Independent, 22 April [Online] https://www.independent.co.uk/arts-entertainment/music/news/spotify-pay-artist-fundraising-pick-donate-a9478496.html (archived at https://perma.cc/MWA7-NGXR)

Li, E (2020) [Accessed 8 September 2020] Louis Vuitton and GQ China reimagine fashion show marketing in Shanghai. Jiing Daily, 9 August [Online] https://jingdaily.com/louis-vuitton-and-gq-china-partner-to-promote-a-physical-fashion-show-amid-covid-19/ (archived at https://perma.cc/ME7X-SUYV)

Limbachia, D (2017) [Accessed 22 January 2020] Mark Zuckerberg unveils Facebook's new mission statement. Variety, 22 June [Online] https://variety.com/2017/digital/news/mark-zuckerberg-changes-facebook-mission-1202476176/ (archived at https://perma.cc/2SDT-CMVT)

Louis Vuitton (2020) [Accessed 1 January 2020] Asnières, the heart of Louis Vuitton [Online] https://eu.louisvuitton.com/eng-e1/la-maison/asnieres # (archived at https://perma.cc/5UTY-D3RR)

Lund, E (2017) [Accessed 27 March 2020] What small business owners can learn from Apple's former and current mission statement. Businessing, 27 July [Online] https://businessingmag.com/5252/strategy/learn-from-apples-mission-statement/ (archived at https://perma.cc/HJD4-U5VC)

LVMH Luxury Ventures (2019) [Accessed 14 January 2020] Portfolio. lvmhluxuryventures.com [Online] https://www.lvmhluxuryventures.com/project/where-to-get-4/ (archived at https://perma.cc/BW7R-GVGX)

MacGregor, N (2018) Living with the Gods, Alfred A Knopf, New York

Mainwaring, S (2015) [Accessed 10 January 2020] Starbucks finds itself in hot water for talking about race. Forbes, 23 March [Online] https://www.forbes.com/sites/simonmainwaring/2015/03/23/starbucks-finds-itself-in-hot-water-for-talking-about-race/#2cf742ab1b59 (archived at https://perma.cc/U6BS-H46K)

Mangold, J (Director) (2019) Ford vs Ferrari [motion picture], USA

Mark, M and Pearson, C (2001) The Hero and the Outlaw, McGraw-Hill, New York

Markert, B (2019) Jedem Druck gewachsen, Lufthansa Journal, 11(19), p 59

Martin, R (2019) The high price of efficiency, *Harvard Business Review*, January/February, p 43

Mautz, S (2019) [Accessed 27 March 2020] A Peloton ad sparked huge controversy over its sexism. Inc, 6 December [Online] https://www.inc.com/scott-mautz/a-peloton-ad-sparked-huge-controversy-over-its-sexism-its-also-just-a-terrible-commercial.html (archived at https://perma.cc/9T5S-SDTF)

McCann, C (2003) *Dancer*, Phoenix/Orion Books, London

McCracken, G (1988) *Culture and Consumption*, Indiana University Press, Bloomington and Indianapolis

McEwan, I (2019) *Machines like Me*, Doubleday, New York

Meltzer, M (2017) [Accessed 27 March 2020] Patagonia and The North Face. Guardian, 7 March [Online] https://www.theguardian.com/business/2017/mar/07/the-north-face-patagonia-saving-world-one-puffer-jacket-at-a-time (archived at https://perma.cc/K7XT-W25D)

Montague, T (2013) *True Story*, Harvard Business Review Press, Boston

Mosher, D (2018) [Accessed 14 January 2020] Elon Musk explains why he launched a car toward Mars – and the reasons are much bigger than his ego. Business Insider, 13 March [Online] https://www.businessinsider.com/why-elon-musk-launched-tesla-mars-falcon-heavy-2018-3 (archived at https://perma.cc/3BN5-PRA8)

Motavalli, J (2018) [Accessed 14 January 2020] Cadillac: In China, it's a bestselling luxury brand with youth appeal. Mediavillage Knowledge Exchange, 26 November [Online] https://www.mediavillage.com/article/cadillac-in-china-its-a-bestselling-luxury-brand-with-youth-appeal/ (archived at https://perma.cc/6DF5-BDQ3)

Moyers, JC (1991) *The Power of Myth*, Anchor Books, New York

Mueller-Oerlinghausen, J (2019) Undconsorten, Berlin. Interview, 19 December

Neate, R (2017) [Accessed 16 January 2020] British cycling brand Rapha sold to Walmart heirs for £200m. *Guardian*, 7 August [Online] https://www.theguardian.com/lifeandstyle/2017/aug/07/british-cycling-brand-rapha-sold-to-walmart-heirs-for-200m (archived at https://perma.cc/ZP9N-ERN2)

Netflix (2009) [Accessed 27 March 2020] Netflix culture: Freedom and responsibility. Slideshare, 1 August [Online] https://www.slideshare.net/reed2001/culture-1798664 (archived at https://perma.cc/8YVQ-87VD)

Nike (2019) [Accessed 27 March 2020] About [Online] https://about.nike.com (archived at https://perma.cc/3HL7-CUDX)

Novy-Williams, E (2019) [Accessed 27 March 2020] Nike pulling its product from Amazon in e-commerce pivot. Bloomberg, 13 November [Online] https://www.bloomberg.com/news/articles/2019-11-13/nike-will-end-its-pilot-project-selling-products-on-amazon-site (archived at https://perma.cc/8NCY-7XJV)

Numero (2019) [Accessed 14 January 2020] Dior presents a collaboration with the artist Marc Quinn in limited edition. Numero, 10 June [Online] https://www.numero.com/en/accessories/dior-home-collaboration-artist-marc-quinn-limited-edition-lady-dior-london#_ (archived at https://perma.cc/KX8Q-GGUX)

Oatly (nd) [Accessed 10 January 2020] The Oatly way. Oatly [Online] https://us. oatly.com/pages/the-oatly-way (archived at https://perma.cc/69ZA-BHTC)

Ovide, S (2019) [Accessed 27 January 2020] As bad as WeWork is, it could get even worse. *The Washington Post*, 23 October [Online] https://www.washingtonpost.com/ business/as-bad-as-wework-is-it-could-get-even-worse/2019/10/22/e8bf28c4-f4e4-11e9-b2d2-1f37c9d82dbb_story.html (archived at https://perma.cc/CRA8-ADWX)

Patagonia (2019a) [Accessed 8 January 2020] Hey, how's that lawsuit against the President going? The cleanest line. Patagonia, 9 April [Online] https://www. patagonia.com/blog/2019/04/hey-hows-that-lawsuit-against-the-president-going/ (archived at https://perma.cc/CL6G-K28H)

Patagonia (2019b) [Accessed 8 January 2020] Patagonia's mission statement. Patagonia [Online] https://eu.patagonia.com/gb/en/company-info.html (archived at https://perma.cc/VFM4-RZTW)

Patagonia (2020) [Accessed 27 March 2020] Traceable down standard [Online] https://www.patagonia.com/traceable-down.html (archived at https://perma.cc/ C5NF-V2Z4)

Paton, E (2019) Roger Federer has a sneaker for you, *The New York Times Sunday Styles*, 24 November, p 1

Paton, E and Maheshwari, S (2019) H&M makes its pitch for transparency, *The New York Times*, 28–29 December, p 1

Pätzmann, J and Hartwig, J (2018) *Markenführung mit Archetypen*, Springer-Gabler, Wiesbaden

Peck, E (2017) [Accessed 10 January 2020] Sure, the Audi ad was sweet, but very few women actually work there. Huffpost.com, 2 February [Online] https://www. huffpost.com/entry/audi-ad-women-employees_n_5898d5cae4b0c1284f2778fa (archived at https://perma.cc/T2KB-JZM5)

Peters, JW (2010) [Accessed 14 January 2020] *The Economist* tends its sophisticated garden. *The New York Times*, 8 August [Online] https://www. nytimes.com/2010/08/09/business/media/09economist.html (archived at https:// perma.cc/D6NJ-T2RV)

Peterson, R (2016) Enduring human needs, *Admap*, March, p 23

Pierce, CS (1983) *Phänomen und Logik der Zeichen*, Suhrkamp Verlag, Frankfurt am Main

Pierce, D (2017) [Accessed 14 January 2020] The year the home button died. Wired, 27 December [Online] https://www.wired.com/story/death-of-the-home-button/ (archived at https://perma.cc/ZV2U-MGDP)

Pierce, L (2017) [Accessed 6 April 2020] Is there a market for recycled-content in flexible packaging? Packaging Digest, 28 March [Online] https://www. packagingdigest.com/flexible-packaging/is-there-a-market-for-recycled-content-materials-in-flexible-packaging-2017-03-28 (archived at https://perma.cc/ FKJ2-YGV4)

Pine II, B and Gilmore, J (1999) *The Experience Economy*, Harvard Business School Press, Boston

Preda, M (2020) [Accessed 9 September 2020] What you can do from home. Patagonia [Online] https://www.patagonia.com/stories/what-you-can-do-from-home/story-85919.html (archived at https://perma.cc/3ZFF-CUKB)

Prose (2020) [Accessed 15 January 2020] Shop. Refinery29, https://www.refinery29.com/en-us/shop/product/custom-shampoo-174924 (archived at https://perma.cc/RBJ5-AVXY)

Rachel Strugatz, KC (2019) [Accessed 14 January 2020] Fenty Beauty vs. Kylie Cosmetics: The race to a billion dollar brand. Business of Fashion, 5 February [Online] https://www.businessoffashion.com/articles/beauty/fenty-beauty-vs-kylie-cosmetics-the-race-to-a-billion-dollar-brand (archived at https://perma.cc/Q6XF-F4SC)

Rapaille, C (2006) *The Culture Code*, Broadway Books, New York

Rapha (2017) [Accessed 14 January 2020] The Rapha Why [Motion Picture]. YouTube, 1 January [Online] https://www.youtube.com/watch?v=9xhdxRSm-MU (archived at https://perma.cc/52UP-N9GW)

Rapha (2020) [Accessed 16 January 2020] Work at Rapha. Rapha [Online] https://www.rapha.cc/eu/en/careers (archived at https://perma.cc/5WLC-8UG4)

Reformation (nd) [Accessed 10 January 2020] Our stuff. The Reformation [Online] https://www.thereformation.com/pages/our-stuff (archived at https://perma.cc/USC9-ECTN)

Reinik, T (2018) National Heritage Academies, Grand Rapids. Interview 20 November

Reuters (2020) [Accessed 13 September 2020] Burberry's sales plunge 80% as coronavirus halts luxury shopping. Reuters, 19 March [Online] https://de.reuters.com/article/uk-burberry-outlook/burberrys-sales-plunge-80-as-coronavirus-halts-luxury-shopping-idUKKBN2160X4 (archived at https://perma.cc/NUP6-EYG7)

Rial, J-F (2019) [Accessed 16 January 2020] Faire un bon voyage (et a quel prix)? Voyageurs du monde [Online] from https://www.voyageursdumonde.fr/voyage-sur-mesure/esprit-voyageurs/qui-sommes-nous/jean-francois-rial (archived at https://perma.cc/CH7P-WDUS)

Richardson, B (2017) [Accessed 12 January 2020] Why Rapha is the new Harley-Davidson. Medium. People & Company, 12 October [Online] https://research.people-and.com/why-rapha-is-the-new-harley-davidson-3981832d83b8 (archived at https://perma.cc/PJ4H-HXUD)

Ritson, M (2019) [Accessed 27 March 2020] Peloton ad is bad, but will ultimately benefit the brand. Marketing Week, 10 December [Online] https://www.marketingweek.com/ritson-peloton-ad-benefit-brand/ (archived at https://perma.cc/ELF3-DXDK)

Ritz-Carlton (2020) [Accessed 16 January 2020] Gold standards [Online] https://www.ritzcarlton.com/en/about/gold-standards (archived at https://perma.cc/3WP2-WPSQ)

Robinson, M (2018) [Accessed 14 January 2020] This apparel startup fixed the worst part of shopping for clothes in stores – and it could defy retail's curse. Business Insider, 18 January [Online] https://www.businessinsider.sg/how-reformation-clothing-stores-beat-online-shopping-2018-1/ (archived at https://perma.cc/97EB-9P8C)

Rosa, H (2019) *Resonanz*, Suhrkamp Verlag, Berlin

Rose, L (2018) [Accessed 27 March 2020] Ben & Jerry's new flavor gets political. The Daily Meal, 31 October [Online] https://www.thedailymeal.com/eat/ben-jerrys-new-flavor-gets-political/103118 (archived at https://perma.cc/E7HK-WZUC)

Rose, L (2019) [Accessed 8 January 2020] One year for the blue heart of Europe: The cleanest line. Patagonia, 20 June [Online] https://www.patagonia.com/blog/2019/06/one-year-for-the-blue-heart-of-europe/ (archived at https://perma.cc/FYA2-CU88)

Rosso, C (2019) [Accessed 15 January 2020] How Elon Musk's neuralink plans to unify the brain with AI. *Psychology Today*, 17 July [Online] https://www.psychologytoday.com/us/blog/the-future-brain/201907/how-elon-musks-neuralink-plans-unify-the-brain-ai (archived at https://perma.cc/3FFB-K6Z7)

Salden, S (2017) [Accessed 2 April 2020] Warum Birkenstock nichts mehr mit Amazon zu tun haben moechte. Der Spiegel, 23 December [Online] https://www.spiegel.de/spiegel/birkenstock-gegen-amazon-oliver-reichert-erklaert-die-hintergruende-a-1184691.html (archived at https://perma.cc/C6WD-7W9J)

Schaefer, W and Kuehlwein, JP (2015) *Rethinking Prestige Branding: Secrets of the Ueber-Brands*, Kogan Page, London

Schaefer, W and Kuehlwein, JP (2018) [Accessed 14 January 2020] High Line Park, NY: Ueber-Brand of a different kind. YouTube [Online] https://www.youtube.com/watch?v=x-rPQFkbEmg (archived at https://perma.cc/2M2Z-39D7)

Schaffer, A (2015) [Accessed 14 January 2020] Tech's enduring great-man myth, *MIT Technology Review*, 4 August [Online] https://www.technologyreview.com/s/539861/techs-enduring-great-man-myth/ (archived at https://perma.cc/AGL5-VQFF)

Scharrer, J (2019) Oops, he did it again, *Horizon*, 16, 18 April, p 4

Schott, S (2014) [Accessed 12 January 2020] Leave no gentleman behind: Rapha gent's race. Munich: 8Bar Bikes [Online] https://8bar-bikes.com/blog/leave-no-gentleman-behind-rahpa-gentlemens-race-bavaria/ (archived at https://perma.cc/NR6M-QYRM)

Schulze, G (1993) *Die Erlebnisgesellschaft*, Campus, New York

Searle, JR (1980) Minds, brains, and programs, BBS target article, Cambridge University Press

Seedlip (2020) Seedlip Drinks [Online] https://seedlipdrinks.com (archived at https://perma.cc/46GG-PKKW)

Segran, E (2018) [Accessed 16 January 2020] How Everlane is building the next-gen clothing brand. Fast Company, 22 February [Online] https://www.fastcompany.com/40525607/how-everlane-is-building-the-next-gen-clothing-brand (archived at https://perma.cc/AVX6-59R6)

Shacknai, G (2020) [Accessed 9 September 2020] UOMA Beauty's Sharon Chuter is holding brands accountable with 'Pull Up Or Shut Up'. Forbes, 8 June [Online] https://www.forbes.com/sites/gabbyshacknai/2020/06/08/uoma-beautys-sharon-chuter-is-holding-brands-accountable-with-pull-up-or-shut-up/#31ffb51170de (archived at https://perma.cc/MLL5-6KW6)

Shapiro, J (Director) (2013) *Burt's Buzz* [motion picture], Canada

Sharp, B (2010) *How Brands Grow: What marketers don't know*, Oxford University Press, South Melbourne

Sherman, L (2019) [Accessed 27 March 2020] At Kering and LVMH, corporate branding goes beyond the logo. BoF, 4 June [Online] https://www.businessoffashion.com/articles/professional/at-kering-and-lvmh-corporate-branding-goes-beyond-the-logo (archived at https://perma.cc/3AGA-4V5R)

Shiller, RJ (2019) *Narrative Economics: How stories go viral and drive major economic events*, Princeton University Press, Princeton

Shoot (2019) [Accessed 27 March 2020] P&G unveils partnerships at Cannes Lions Fest. Shoot Online, 24 June [Online] https://www.shootonline.com/news/pg-unveils-partnerships-cannes-lions-fest (archived at https://perma.cc/G7YU-CEF3)

Sinek, S (2009) *Start with Why*, Portfolio/Penguin, New York

SoulCycle (nd) [Accessed 27 March 2020] Our story. SoulCycle [Online] https://www.soul-cycle.com/our-story/ (archived at https://perma.cc/88YC-NM7F)

Spence, R (2009) *It's Not What You Sell, It's What You Stand For*, Portfolio/Penguin, New York

Spotify (2020) [Accessed 27 January 2020] Company info. For The Record [Online] https://newsroom.spotify.com/company-info/ (archived at https://perma.cc/RCN8-6TUZ)

Sproule (2019) Personal interview

Square (2020) [Accessed 27 March 2020] Dreams. Square Up [Online] https://squareup.com/us/en/dreams/flint (archived at https://perma.cc/4UC3-DMF8)

Staab, W (2016) [Accessed 27 January 2020] HOG's sweet sound. HearingHealthMatters, 25 October [Online] https://hearinghealthmatters.org/waynesworld/2016/hogs-sweet-sound/ (archived at https://perma.cc/4JGM-UJFN)

Stevens, CR (1973) *Person to Person: The problem of being human; a new trend in psychology*, Souvenir Press, London

Stevens, M (2017) [Accessed 10 January 2020] Firm behind 'Fearless Girl' statue underpaid women, US says. *The New York Times*, 6 October [Online] https://www.nytimes.com/2017/10/06/business/fearless-girl-settlement.html (archived at https://perma.cc/9EG2-B8WX)

Strasser, D (2020) Benetton kommt zurueck, werben und verkaufen, January, p 19

Strugatz, R (2019) [Accessed 27 March 2020] How Ulta is winning over America's youth. BoF Professional, 10 May [Online] https://www.businessoffashion.com/articles/professional/why-ulta-is-winning-the-war-for-americas-youth (archived at https://perma.cc/R2BP-E3MC)

Taschjian, R (2019) [Accessed 12 January 2020] Is Supreme about to create a whole new generation of porcelain freaks? *GQ (Gentlemen's Quarterly)*,15 March [Online] https://www.gq.com/story/supreme-meissen (archived at https://perma.cc/NW46-X4A6)

T3N (2017) [Accessed 1 October 2019] Birkenstock verlaesst Amazon jetzt auch in Deutschland wegen Produktfaelschungen. Damit beliefert Birkenstock weltweit keinen Onlineshop des US-Konzerns mehr. T3N News [Online] https://t3n.de/news/amazon-birkenstock-884847/ (archived at https://perma.cc/5WMK-VJQ3)

TFL (2019) [Accessed 16 January 2020] How Custom Footwear Co. Shoes of Prey went from retail success story to bankruptcy. The Fashion Law, 4 October [Online] http://www.thefashionlaw.com/home/how-custom-footwear-co-shoes-of-prey-went-from-retail-success-story-to-bankruptcy (archived at https://perma.cc/EP5E-X57X)

The Drum Creative (2020) [Accessed 9 September 2020] BrewGel Punk Sanitizer. The Drum, March. [Online] https://www.thedrum.com/creative-works/project/brewdog-brewgel-punk-sanitizer (archived at https://perma.cc/N4S2-F98N)

The Economist (2013) [Accessed 16 January 2020] Why are the *The Economist*'s writers anonymous? *The Economist*, 5 September [Online] https://www.economist.com/the-economist-explains/2013/09/04/why-are-the-economists-writers-anonymous (archived at https://perma.cc/F93Q-HXYF)

Turnherr, V (2015) [Accessed 16 January 2020] Voyageurs du Monde. Awwway, 4 August [Online] https://www.awwway.ch/voyageurs-du-monde/ (archived at https://perma.cc/CH63-KV9Y)

TV Ad Music (2018) [Accessed 1 January 2020] Square-the-thing-ummy-bob. TV Ad Music [Online] https://www.tvadmusic.co.uk/2018/05/square-the-thing-ummy-bob/ (archived at https://perma.cc/QQ8T-2FJL)

Uber (2020) [Accessed 22 January 2020] About us. Uber [Online] https://www.uber.com/us/en/about/ (archived at https://perma.cc/3K3Q-Z8Q6)

ueberbrands.com (2016a) [Accessed 15 January 2020] A Freitag visit: Manufacturing as manifestation of mission. Ueber-Brands, 26 October [Online] https://ueberbrands.com/2016/10/26/a-freitag-visit-manufacturing-as-manifestation-of-mission/ (archived at https://perma.cc/88S9-FU2M)

ueberbrands.com (2016b) [Accessed 26 January 2020] Audemars Piguet: Adversity and complications make a brand – interview with Tim Sayler, CMO. Ueber-Brands, 9 October [Online] https://ueberbrands.com/2016/10/09/audemars-piguet-adversity-and-complications-make-a-brand-interview-with-tim-sayler-cmo/ (archived at https://perma.cc/YV9F-3HPF)

ueberbrands.com (2016c) [Accessed 18 February 2020] Johnnie Walker: Appeal at $1 and $1,000 a sip, alike – interview with Matteo Fantacchiotti, Diageo. Ueber-Brands, 18 February [Online] https://ueberbrands.com/2016/02/18/johnnie-walker-appeal-at-1-and-1000-dollars-a-sip-alike-interview-with-global-vp-diageo-preserve-brands-podcast-episode-06/ (archived at https://perma.cc/5YK9-KXKB)

ueberbrands.com (2016d) [Accessed 20 January 2020] Renova: Toilet paper to live, love and style with, also. Ueber-Brands, 19 April [Online] https://ueberbrands. com/2016/04/19/renova-toilet-paper-to-live-love-and-style-with-also-podcast-with-paulo-pereira-da-silva-ceo-07/ (archived at https://perma.cc/382H-NXZS)

ueberbrands.com (2016e) [Accessed 20 January 2020] Seedlip: Beyond Making Teetotaling Totally Trendy – Interview with Ben Branson, Founder. Ueber-Brands, 22 June [Online] https://ueberbrands.com/2016/06/22/ seedlip-beyond-making-teetotaling-totally-trendy-interview-with-ben-branson-founder/ (archived at https://perma.cc/78TH-U7L5)

ueberbrands.com (2017) [Accessed 14 January 2020] Burt's Bees: Mission, myth and a buzzing business. Ueber-Brands, 5 January [Online] https://ueberbrands. com/2017/01/05/burts-bees-mission-myth-and-a-buzzing-business-interview-with-jim-geikie-general-manager-vp/ (archived at https://perma.cc/NH9V-CYSE)

ueberbrands.com (2018a) [Accessed 26 January 2020] B2B beyond the material: Interview with Mohawk Fine Papers' Creative Director Christopher Harrold. Ueber-Brands, 4 April [Online] https://ueberbrands.com/2018/04/24/ b2b-beyond-the-material-interview-with-mohawk-fine-papers-creative-director-christopher-harrold/ (archived at https://perma.cc/C2A4-ZS2X)

ueberbrands.com (2018b) [Accessed 14 January 2020] Master myth maker: Ramdane Touhami, mind behind Buly and other exquisite brands. Ueber-Brands, 25 September [Online] https://ueberbrands.com/2018/09/25/ master-myth-maker-interview-with-ramdane-touhami-mind-behind-buly-and-other-exquisite-brand-re-creations/ (archived at https://perma.cc/ RG3P-7Y3E)

ueberbrands.com (2019a) [Accessed 27 January 2020] FRoSTA: Putting your money where your mission is – Felix Ahlers, CEO. Ueber-Brands, 22 August [Online] https://ueberbrands.com/2019/08/22/putting-money-where-your-mission-is-ceo-frosta-tells-food-brand-make-over-story/ (archived at https:// perma.cc/2SRN-UAL5)

ueberbrands.com (2019b) [Accessed 22 January 2020] Purpose and promotion don't mix well. Ueber-Brands, 25 March [Online] https://ueberbrands. com/2019/03/25/purpose-and-promotion-dont-mix-well-ben-jerrys-global-social-mission-officer-dave-rappaport-explains/ (archived at https://perma. cc/25M6-PY6U)

ueberbrands.com (2019c) [Accessed 14 January 2020] TerraCycle: How to brand waste – Tom Szaky, CEO and Co-Founder explains. Ueber-Brands, 3 June [Online] https://ueberbrands.com/2019/06/03/terra-cycle-how-brand-waste-tom-szaky-ceo-founder-interview/ (archived at https://perma.cc/Y7AY-22GX)

ueberbrands.com (2019d) [Accessed 14 January 2020] Trust and a shared truth are key to Airbnb's Success. Ueber-Brands, 29 May [Online] https://ueberbrands. com/2019/05/11/purpose-truth-and-trust-keys-to-airbnb-success-douglas-atkin-head-of-community-explains/ (archived at https://perma.cc/8V9X-A3QK)

ueberbrands.com (2019e) [Accessed 14 January 2020] Haven's Kitchen: About sharing life skills and sauces – Alison Cayne, Founder. Ueber-Brands, 19 November [Online] https://ueberbrands.com/2019/11/19/havens-kitchen-about-sharing-life-skills-and-sauces-alison-cayne-founder/ (archived at https://perma.cc/ADA2-R4ZV)

ueberbrands.com (2020) [Accessed 28 January 2020] Evolving the Aston Martin legend: Interview with Simon Sproule, Chief Marketing Officer, Aston Martin. Ueber-Brands, 8 January [Online] https://ueberbrands.com/2020/10/30/evolving-the-aston-martin-legend-simon-sproule/ (archived at https://perma.cc/6543-ADBR)

Van Rensburg, D (2014) [Accessed 27 March 2020] In-sourcing disruptive brands as a corporate entrepreneurship strategy. Springer Science and Business Media, 4 April [Online] https://www.academia.edu/28079784/In-sourcing_disruptive_brands_as_a_corporate_entrepreneurship_strategy (archived at https://perma.cc/99N4-38MU)

Van Rensburg, DJ (2015) In-sourcing disruptive brands as a corporate entrepreneurship strategy, *International Entrepreneurship and Management Journal*, 11(4), November, pp 769–92

Vice (2019) [Accessed 27 March 2020] About [Online] https://company.vice.com (archived at https://perma.cc/Y2FV-C4GS)

Vincent, L (2017) [Accessed 27 March 2020] The case for creating rituals around your brand experiences. Medium, 10 April [Online] https://medium.com/@larryvince/the-case-for-creating-rituals-around-your-brand-experience-89671dbafd90 (archived at https://perma.cc/J2UT-5DB7)

Vizard, S (2019) [Accessed 27 March 2020] Gillette brand takes a hit as '#metoo' ad backfires. Marketing Week, 18 January [Online] https://www.marketingweek.com/gillette-brand-takes-hit-as-metoo-ad-backfires/ (archived at https://perma.cc/88UM-FJ2D)

Vizard, S (2019) [Accessed 27 March 2020] Adidas: We overinvested in digital advertising. Marketing Week, 17 October [Online] https://www.marketingweek.com/adidas-marketing-effectiveness/ (archived at https://perma.cc/WL23-46RE)

Wahba, P (2015) [Accessed 27 January 2020] Nordstrom Tech shopping spree continues with stake in custom shoe retailer. Fortune, 7 December [Online] https://fortune.com/2015/12/07/nordstrom-shoes-of-prey-tech-investment/ (archived at https://perma.cc/7G7K-GDDK)

Wainwright, O (2014) [Accessed 27 March 2020] Is it balls, vagina or both? Airbnb logo sparks wave of internet parodies. Guardian, 18 July [Online] https://www.theguardian.com/artanddesign/architecture-design-blog/2014/jul/18/balls-vagina-both-airbnb-logo-internet-parodies (archived at https://perma.cc/5CCN-BT84)

Walshe, P (2016) 10 traits of megabrands, *Admap* 2, February, pp 40–41

Wang, X (2020) [Accessed 9 September 2020] Luxury brands' three best practices in coping with COVID-19. WARC, 17 March [Online] https://www.warc.com/newsandopinion/opinion/luxury-brands-three-best-practices-in-coping-with-covid-19/3469 (archived at https://perma.cc/97RY-6FVQ)

Waters, A (2019) [Accessed 27 March 2020] Supreme x Meissen: Why artists are recapturing the 'exquisite transgressiveness' of porcelain. Sleek Magazine, 14 March [Online] https://www.sleek-mag.com/article/supreme-x-meissen/ (archived at https://perma.cc/K92Q-HNZW)

Wertheim, B (2018) [Accessed 27 March 2020] The humble ascent of oat milk. The New York Times, Sunday Styles, 21 January [Online] https://www.nytimes.com/2018/01/19/style/oat-milk-coffee-oatly.html (archived at https://perma.cc/Z43A-C4KU)

White, J (2018) LVMH transformation is a 20 bn Euro success, Wired. 12 November [Online] https://www.wired.co.uk/article/lvmh-brands-group-digital-technology (archived at https://perma.cc/XD38-ALWM)

Whitten, S (2017) [Accessed 24 January 2020] George Clooney just sold his tequila business for up to $1 billion. CNBC, 21 June [Online] https://www.cnbc.com/2017/06/21/george-clooney-just-sold-his-tequila-business-for-1-billion.html (archived at https://perma.cc/8ZZN-VVCU)

Wikipedia (nd) [Accessed 16 January 2020] Frosta. Wikipedia [Online] https://de.wikipedia.org/wiki/Frosta (archived at https://perma.cc/H239-AA4T)

Wikipedia (2020) [Accessed 12 December 2019] Swarovski Kristallwelten. Wikipedia [Online] https://en.wikipedia.org/wiki/Swarovski_Kristallwelten_(Crystal_Worlds) (archived at https://perma.cc/6AKJ-WN2K)

Williams, F (2015) Green Giants, Amacom, New York

Wilson, B (2004) [Accessed 14 January 2020] The Hive: The story of the honeybee and us, St Martin's Griffin, New York

Wortham, J (2015) [Accessed 2 April 2020] Netromancy. The New York Times Magazine, 20 September [Online] https://www.nytimes.com/2015/09/20/magazine/netromancy.html (archived at https://perma.cc/8848-5ADF)

Wu, J (2019) [Accessed 10 January 2020] Here's how Abercrombie & Fitch ditched its past to try to bring back customers. CNBC online, 16 October [Online] https://www.cnbc.com/2019/10/16/how-abercrombie-fitch-ditched-its-past-to-try-to-bring-shoppers-back.html (archived at https://perma.cc/2EZG-5SEW)

YouTube (2020) [Accessed 1 January 2020] BrewDog: This punk's for you. YouTube [Online] https://www.youtube.com/watch?v=43qsGFydbWk (archived at https://perma.cc/XHW2-KUA3)

YouTube (2020) [Accessed 1 January 2020] Decade of Dog [Online] https://www.youtube.com/watch?v=Wmq7KlCbdYM (archived at https://perma.cc/LSP3-9XZF)

INDEX

CPSIA information can be obtained
at www.ICGtesting.com
Printed in the USA
LVHW051404161220
674185LV00002B/4